THE
BOXER
REBELLION
& OTHER TALES

THE BOXER REBELLION & OTHER TALES

BY
JOEL GOLDMAN, D.V.M.

DONALD I. FINE, INC.
New York

Library of Congress Cataloging-in-Publication Data
Goldman, Joel.
The Boxer Rebellion & other tales.
1. Goldman, Joel. 2. Veterinarians—Texas—Biography.
I. Title. II. Title: Boxer Rebellion and other tales.
SF613.G63A3   1988   636.089′092′4 [B]   88-45423
ISBN 1-55611-105-3

Manufactured in the United States of America
10 9 8 7 6 5 4 3 2 1

To the memory of my father,
Joseph Goldman

CONTENTS

INTRODUCTION

Quite a few years ago, actually more than I care to enumerate, I attended a party at the venerable Monteleone Hotel in New Orleans. As I mingled among the guests, word got round that I was a veterinarian, a fact that prompted a lady to engage me in conversation. She said she admired anyone who was attracted to animals and that she, herself, was a "cat person" and wanted to know what kind of "person" I was. I answered the lady's question by saying I could be a dog, cat, or horse person, or whatever person I needed to be, depending upon what I was called upon to treat. But now, after years of practice and months of reflection during the writing of this book, I would answer her differently and say, I'm a people and animal person and I'm interested in the welfare of both. People who are interested in the welfare of others are called caregivers. My mother would say I'm a mensch.*

Being a mensch as a child meant taking care of the less fortunate, and I, being a nature lover, gravitated toward the least able to help themselves – the animals. I determined to save every lost or injured creature I came upon, yet no matter how earnestly I tried, some always fell victim to their wounds or my inexperience. If I became discouraged my mother would say, life wasn't always fair, but – as God was her witness – the heartless of this world would face certain ruin, while the compassionate would in time triumph.

And to ensure I would be among the vindicated, her message for me was, "So, Joel, dear, take a lesson. Whatever you do, BE A MENSCH!" And so I decided to become a veterinarian.

My training as a veterinarian taught me to be a good listener and a keen observer. I listened to what the owners had to say and how they said it – but after they finished describing their pet's problems, they expanded their complaints to include personal ones, too. And on those occasions, like a pediatrician, I took the pet's history and then, like a social worker, I took the owner's history and then, like a mensch, I naively set forth to do the impossible – cure both parties. The problem was, being a mensch got me into trouble.

First of all, I labored under the impression that everyone wanted to be a mensch and unfortunately, not everyone was interested. Secondly, I thought everyone would appreciate my efforts, but regrettably, that wasn't always the case. And finally, I believed if you were a mensch, events would eventually lead to a happy conclusion, however, that didn't happen either.

The animal diseases had remedies grounded in scientific thought, while the human ailments were stubbornly unresponsive and quite unpredictable. Regardless, I struggled to bring some sense of healing to all parties concerned, myself included, and on occasion I succeeded beyond all expectations. At other times I was a miserable flop and I began to speculate if anyone was in control. Looking back now, I think perhaps the animals were. As for the owners – maybe not.

Still, I count myself lucky. The veterinarian is privy to two separate worlds, one animal and one human, yet, on occasion I have seen them overlap, perhaps more often than not. And that's the story I have to tell. For when I recall the events behind some of these tales I can't help but wonder . . . maybe my mother was right. As God is my witness.

Joel Goldman, D.V.M.
San Marcos, Texas
May 1, 1988

*A mensch is a person who, after paying scalper's prices for Superbowl tickets comes home, only to have his wife inform him that her cousin Lottie's funeral is on the same day and that he as a relative is expected to go, and he goes. (My mother's reasoning behind this is flawless. Of Superbowls there'll be plenty. A relative can only die once.)

THE
BOXER
REBELLION
& OTHER TALES

THE
BOXER
REBELLION

Bill and Evelyn Miller were a middle-aged couple with grown children. She ran an art gallery in town specializing in Texana and western art while Bill managed the local Rodeway Inn. He was bald except for a circular band of red hair that arced around the back and sides of his head; a big man, Bill seemed to fill up any room in which he stood. Affable, somewhat loud, his first comments were usually, "Say, Doc, have you heard this one?" Then he'd tell a dirty joke. I wondered if he told his doctor a dirty joke every time he saw him. If it wasn't a racy story, he'd fill me in on the latest gossip in town. Bill had ready access to news since all the service clubs had luncheon meetings at his motel. He knew who was sleeping with whom and who was available. Bill always said the biggest traffic jam in town was from midnight to six from all the people hopping from house to house and bed to bed.

Evelyn was Bill's opposite. She was quiet, soft spoken and methodical, asking me about my family and always leaving an invitation for me and the wife to come down to the shop, if only to visit and have a cup of coffee. She had satiny black hair that she wore piled on her head, was always immaculately groomed with long painted nails and she spoke in a husky tone like William F. Buckley. With a cigarette in one hand and a lighter in the other she would glide through the rooms in the gallery, pointing at her prize pieces saying, "And that's a Remington sculpture in the corner and over here is a wonderful collection of barbed wire that goes with this signed copy of J. Frank Dobie's *The Longhorns* – and isn't this a lovely gas lamp from a home in Corsicana? You do know Corsicana had the first gas company in Texas." Evelyn always knew the history behind each piece and made sure that you did, too.

Both Evelyn and Bill had been married before. She said her first husband had suffered financial reverses and became an alcoholic and they divorced after three years. Bill rarely mentioned his first wife. There were no children living at home, but filling that void was the pride of the Miller household, their two grown Boxers, Krystal and Sue Ellen.

The dogs would stay at the gallery, usually back in a small kitchen that was next to the office. When the doorbell rang they would race to the entrance, barking constantly at whoever was behind the beveled glass doors. But once a customer crossed the threshold, the commotion abated, as if the two realized the special status visitors were given, and they assumed a position behind Evelyn, like auxiliary salespersons ready to answer any questions, and serving to break the ice with strangers. The Millers treated their two pets like children, giving them presents of Neiman-Marcus rhinestone collars and preparing homemade ice cream as snacks. The dogs lived like princesses, but in return they lavished great affection on their owners, which seemed to cement the family into a happy unit.

Sue Ellen and Krystal were just nine weeks old when Bill brought the dogs in for a checkup. He carried a pup under each arm and Evelyn followed behind with the papers from the breeder. I'd only bought a veterinary practice in the small south-central Texas town of San Marcos six months before, and this was my first meeting with the Millers. Bill placed both pups on the table, told Evelyn to watch them to be sure they didn't fall and turned and shook my hand as if it were a pump handle.

"Hiya, Doc! I don't know the first thing about dogs. The only dog I had was my ex-wife and she was a rea-a-al dog!"

Since he was being so candid I decided to play along and asked, "Did she look more like a Doberman or a German Shepherd?"

He started to laugh, then a thought crossed his mind and he began to laugh harder. "Neither one, Doc," he managed to say between laughs. "She was a plain mutt," and he'd barely said that when his laughter became hysterical.

"Bill, that's not true," Evelyn scolded. "Lorraine was a very nice lady. You two just had irreconcilable differences. After all, you lived with her fifteen years. Besides, Dr. Goldman's not interested in hearing about your past. Do these pups look healthy to you, Doctor?" and she motioned to me with arms that encircled the two squirming figures.

Actually I was always interested in my clients' private lives. I had practiced for six years in New Orleans, where characters abounded, and I was discovering that the people who brought their animals to the clinic I had so recently bought, via one of life's coincidences on the south edge of the Texas hill country, could have their peculiarities, too. They ranged from college kids at the nearby Southwest Texas State University to wealthy ranchers and "cedar whackers," as many of the first-comers were called, due to their cottage industry of making fence poles from the cedar that grew on the area's limestone hills. Even when clients seemed to be normal, pleasant people like the Millers, I tried to share my personal thoughts with theirs, and they somehow sensed that if I was genuinely sympathetic with their daily concerns I would be even more concerned with their pet's needs, which were their needs as well.

"Heck, you two can discuss anything you want in here," I told the Millers. "It's all right with me. But in the meantime, let's take a look at these pups," and I proceeded to examine the dogs. I took their temperatures, examined their gums for the paleness which is an indicator of anemia, tested their stools for worms, listened to their hearts and checked for hernias and other congenital defects.

"Are they all right, Doctor?" asked Evelyn as she searched in her purse for a cigarette.

"They'd better be," chimed in Bill. "We paid over two hundred dollars apiece for these two. We'll take them back if they're not."

"Oh, no, we won't," said Evelyn. "This one is licking my hand and her sister has gone to sleep right here in my arms. Oh, Bill, have you ever seen such loveable babies? I bet Dr. Goldman hasn't either, have you?" And with that she snuggled her face next to their warm brown bodies and kissed them on their fuzzy heads.

"Except for having roundworms they're just fine," I said.

"Gawd! Can people catch those from dogs?" asked Evelyn.

She quickly wiped her mouth with her handkerchief.

"Only if you handle the dog's feces and then put your fingers in your mouth."

"Oh, well," she said. "There's no chance of that!"

"Yeah. Who in their right mind would want to eat a dog turd?" quipped Bill. "But is it serious, Doc?" Bill was now acting more like a concerned father than a man recently relieved of four hundred dollars.

"Don't worry," I said. "Most puppies have intestinal parasites of one sort or another. We can medicate for the worms and start the pups on their vaccines."

"Great," said Bill. "Let's do it."

"I can't stand needles, Doctor," Evelyn confessed. "I have to leave the room. Bill, be sure he doesn't hurt them." I wormed and vaccinated both dogs, gave the new parents a schedule of future visits and advised them not to handle the dogs too much as they would be sore from their injections.

The remainder of Krystal's and Sue Ellen's puppy visits were uneventful except for the usual growing up complaints. Krystal had a three-day stomach ache from eating an aluminum foil wrapper from a T.V. dinner and Sue Ellen suffered a nose bleed from running into a glass sliding door at the gallery.

But with each visit, Bill and Evelyn would share more of their personal affairs with me and I became very familiar with their business. The gallery had been very profitable during the inflationary years of the seventies but current high interest rates had discouraged buyers of collectibles and Evelyn was apprehensive about the future. Besides managing the motel, Bill hoped to supplement their income by working part time as a real estate salesman, but prospects for that venture were also looking poor, again a victim of high mortgage rates.

Patient visits to the clinic were down, too. Pets were getting sick just as often, but their owners didn't have the money to bring them in. However with the onset of warm weather in the spring of 1981 there came a new virulent disease of dogs that swept across the country, infecting kennels and pounds and finally household pets. It was called parvovirus.

The first indication that a new disease was occurring in our dog population was the increased incidence of protracted vomiting and diarrhea. While the symptoms were not unusual, the severity was, and dogs that would ordinarily have recovered from common intestinal diseases due to worms, other viruses or from ingesting foreign material, frequently did not survive parvovirus, or if they did, it was only after intensive therapy of two weeks or more. Young dogs were the most susceptible and reports of entire litters dying were common. The dogs died in spite of rigorous treatment with intravenous fluids, antibiotics, bowel coatings and stomach sedatives. Immediate and concentrated therapy for dehydration caused by the diarrhea and vomiting would give transient improvement at best and the next day most dogs had regressed back to the original condition in which they were admitted. As we later discovered, the virus destroyed the lining of the digestive tract, leaving the gut with severe erosions that bled profusely and allowed secondary bacterial infection.

A second aspect of the disease was the ability of the virus to destroy a dog's immune system. It did this by attacking lymphatic structures – you would call them lymph nodes – which are important in the production of antibodies. Before the immune system could recover to make antibodies, the dogs died of shock or secondary infection. Parvovirus packed a double whammy and it was deadly.

In the beginning of the outbreak a vaccine was not available and I advised all my clients to avoid exposing their dogs to any strays on the street or to dogs that might seem ill. But in spite of precautions, Sue Ellen Miller was one of the early victims.

The dogs had celebrated their second birthday just a few months before. Sue Ellen had grown to fifty pounds, all fawn color with a white blaze on her face. She was constantly moving and wriggling as Boxers are prone to do when they get excited. Her nub of a tail would constantly wag, and her tongue was always hanging out one side of her mouth. Evelyn would tell Sue Ellen to sit, which she dutifully would, then tell her, "Give mommy a kiss," which the dog gratefully obliged. Boxer kisses are sort of an external

French kiss with a huge wet tongue smearing canine saliva over your face. My greatest fear was that Evelyn would make me the recipient of one of Sue Ellen's liquid facials. Not that I minded getting wet, but among the three of us only I was aware that this same tongue had minutes ago wiped her own doggie anus after defecating on the clinic floor, a feat most dogs seem to accomplish with relish when they go to the vet's.

Today Sue Ellen wasn't giving any kisses. She lay sprawled and motionless on the exam table, her head flush with the surface. Evelyn was standing next to Sue Ellen and with all the solemnity appropriate for a trial, she glanced at her husband and then began her incriminating testimony.

"Bill fed her some Mexican food he brought home from the motel, and she's been vomiting ever since. Up 'til last night she's never been sick a day in her life."

Aiming for a speedy acquittal Bill countered, "She eats damn near anything you give her. Pizza, hot dogs. Hell, she even likes vegetables. So what could be wrong with a few enchiladas? I even left off the picante sauce. Anyway, it's up to Doc to decide – that's why we brought her. Whatta ya think, Doc?"

I thought they'd brought Sue Ellen so I could help her get well, but while they had her welfare as a primary concern they also were intent on proving themselves correct.

Sue Ellen tensed as I felt her abdomen. She groaned when I pressed in her middle. Patty, my irreplaceable assistant, took her temperature while I listened to her heart and her lungs.

"Her chest is okay. What's her temp, Patty?"

She withdrew the thermometer, wiped what appeared to be fresh blood from the surface and calmly said, "One hundred and six."

"Oh, Jesus God," gasped Evelyn. "My baby's got one

hundred and six. Bill! Did you hear that? She's got a hundred-and-six-degree fever."

"Don't get bent out of shape," said Bill. "Say, Doc, what's a dog's normal temperature?"

"One hundred one and three-quarters," I said.

"You don't think she's got distemper, do you?"

"Hell, I know what it was," Evelyn shot back. "It was that damn Mexican food. Bill, I've told you a million times not to feed that crap to the dogs. Just ask Dr. Goldman if I'm right. Go on. Ask him."

Intrafamily squabbles made me uncomfortable. I had a dog seriously ill with parvo and the owners were after each other's throats. They needed a family counselor more than a veterinarian.

Ignoring the question, I drew a syringe full of blood from the vein in Sue Ellen's right front leg and handed the specimen to Patty, who placed it in the centrifuge. Then with the needle still in the vein I connected it to a bottle of lactated Ringer's solution and began infusing the fluid. "This will help to combat the dehydration from the vomiting," I said. I had Patty add a needle full of promazine and one-quarter cc of atropine directly to the drip through the rubber tubing. "And that's for the nausea. It works like dramamine, the medicine you'd take for air sickness. It keeps you from vomiting but it can make you drowsy." Sue Ellen relaxed as the drugs began to take effect.

Bill recovered from his wife's accusing tone, and placed his arm around his dog. He began whispering in her ear. "Dr. Goldman's going to make you all better and then you can chase the squirrels in the front yard with your sister." He looked at the air bubbles rising and popping in the I.V. bottle and then turned to me and asked, "Was it really the food?"

By now the blood had quit spinning in the centrifuge and after I examined the tube I replied, "You're off the hook,

Bill. Her blood serum is clear. Severe gastrointestinal disease due to eating rich food causes the serum to be discolored and hers is normal. And her white count is down. I think she has this new disease of dogs, parvovirus. It's highly fatal and very contagious. You'd better watch Krystal for any signs of illness. Also, any place in the house where Sue Ellen may have vomited or had diarrhea needs to be disinfected. Use Clorox. It's the only chemical we know that'll kill the germ."

That was the stark, clinical truth and I felt bad about putting it that way. But it was better for them to understand the tenuous position Sue Ellen's life was in. If she got well I was a hero; if she died they would be able to rationalize her death as the inevitable end to a terminal disease. I was covering my ass."

Bill was sober now, his face was grim, his voice earnest. "Don't spare any expense, Doc. You know we care about our dogs like parents do about their children. I've never told you but I have two boys. Their mother got custody after our divorce so the dogs are the only kids I've got. You've got to get Sue Ellen well."

Evelyn nodded her head as if to second Bill's comments, then kissed Sue Ellen on her forehead and left. I could hear her crying in the hallway.

"I'll do what I can. You know I will. But it's a very iffy situation."

"Doc. If anything happens to Sue Ellen you'll have to bury Evelyn and me with her." And with that he left the room. I watched them drive away.

"Boy, are they involved with their pets," said Patty. "What are you going to do if Sue Ellen dies?"

At that moment Sue Ellen began to heave spasmodically, drawing our attention to her immediate needs and away from the sad end which Patty had forecast.

"Look, the dog's not dead yet," I said. "Let's give the full

I.V., slowly, start her on 150 milligrams Kantrim twice a day and if she doesn't spit up, two Darbazines every eight hours." Patty noted my instructions on the record. "And let's put her in the bathroom. She'll make a mess in a cage. It'll be easier to keep her clean."

We had diagnosed the disease early and I thought we had an excellent chance of pulling the dog through, but Sue Ellen's temperature hovered from 104 to 105 over the next four days, and she continued to vomit in spite of everything we tried. She passed gelatinous bloody diarrhea that stank up the clinic and overwhelmed our air fresheners. We were constantly cleaning after her.

The Millers visited daily, bringing Sue Ellen's favorite foods, broiled round steak or ice cream. Of course she was too sick to eat and even if she did it was bound to come back up. The couple sat quietly on the floor alongside Sue Ellen, murmuring endearments, stroking her velvet ears and cleaning her face after bouts of retching. It was a death-bed vigil.

Five days after she was admitted, Sue Ellen reached a crisis. Her fever hadn't broken and she was continuing to vomit. The dog's eyes were sunk in her sockets and that firm, muscular body now looked gaunt and drawn. Saliva constantly drooled from her mouth while waves of cramping resulted in her passing small amounts of fetid stool. She didn't even have the strength to get out of her own excrement. She was dying.

"Get the Millers on the phone and tell them to get over here," I said to Patty. "They need to make a decision about their dog."

I had a last-ditch scheme to get their dog well, and they both listened hopefully as I explained, "Parvo kills many of the dogs it infects, but there are some that will survive the infection. These dogs should have high levels of antibodies in their blood that protects them from the disease.

I want to take blood from a recovered donor dog, draw off the serum fraction containing the antibodies and give it to Sue Ellen. I must stress that this is not an approved treatment, but our backs are to the wall and we're going to lose her if she doesn't improve quickly."

The news stunned the Millers. It was a few minutes before anyone spoke. I listened to Bill.

"What chance does she have otherwise, Doc? I mean, if she's going to die anyway, what do we have to lose? I'm willing to try." Bill turned to Evelyn, "Don't you think it's for the best, hon? After all, what other chance has she got?"

Evelyn had knelt on the floor next to Sue Ellen. She rocked the dog's head in her lap and stroked the almost lifeless face. "She's suffering so bad now...maybe we ought to put her to sleep. She's been through so much. I can't stand to see her this way, with all those needles and tubes."

"Give me one more day," I implored. "If she's no better by morning, then we can put her to sleep."

"Yeah, go ahead, Doc. Evelyn and I will call you in the morning." He gave me a pat on the back, the kind of pat the fans give the losing team as they head to the dressing room.

As they walked to the exit, Bill stopped and turned to face me. "You know, Doc, our dogs have never been separated. In fact, Krystal's going crazy searching all over the gallery for Sue Ellen. I've always felt those dogs could sense when something was wrong. They're just as smart as humans, aren't they?"

"Yes, they are, Bill. And some are even smarter."

As soon as the door closed, I hollered for Patty. "Call Kelly Grant and ask if we can take blood from her black Lab, Sheba."

Kelly's dog had been sick with parvo six weeks ago and by some combination of luck and nursing the dog had recovered. I figured she would have a high titer (level) of antibodies against parvo.

Patty dialed Kelly's number and after a short conversation reported, "Kelly will bring Sheba as soon as she can."

Kelly lived only a few blocks away, so she arrived quickly with a lively Sheba tugging her along at the end of the leash. Sheba greeted us by crouching and barking like she wanted to play, but once Kelly commanded her to sit, she sensed the seriousness of her mission and stood patiently while I shaved hair from her neck so I could see her jugular vein.

"Disinfect the area well, Patty. We have to have thirty ccs of blood to get fifteen ccs of serum. Hold her steady. Good. Now pull her head back and over to the side and press along her throat to make the vein stand out."

The jugular vein bulged from her neck. It was easy to slip the needle into the lumen of the vessel. The syringe filled rapidly with blood.

I transferred the blood to two large sterile blood tubes and centrifuged them for fifteen minutes. Now all of the red and white cells were packed down in the bottom, leaving a champagne colored overlay of serum. I aspirated the amber fluid into a syringe and took it into the bathroom where Sue Ellen lay. Her eyes followed me as I crouched down beside her.

"Be sure the drip is going and have adrenalin handy while I give her this shot. It could cause a severe allergic reaction."

Sue Ellen trembled as I grasped her leg and slowly injected the serum into the large muscle at the back of her thigh. She whined softly and then turned her eyes back toward the wall, indifferent to our concern. Patty was pessimistic.

"I think we need to call a priest," she said as she adjusted the flow through the I.V.

"We're not quitting," I said. "Look. It's eleven now. We'll recheck her temp after lunch."

I was gambling, but I felt my procedure was theoretically and practically sound. I even had had a personal experience with a similar situation. My doctors had all but given up on me seven years ago when I was ill with fever due to an obscure virus. They injected twenty-five ccs of gamma globulin in my butt and my temperature began to drop almost immediately. It was my hope our canine globulins would work a similar cure.

"Call the Millers," I said. "Tell them we've given the serum and to check back around five. If we lose the dog before then, I'll call them first."

I sent Patty to buy hamburgers while I climbed onto the surgery table. We didn't have a couch in the clinic but I had learned to sleep on the narrow stainless steel tilt-table in the operating room. Mentally fatigued, I fell asleep and was peacefully dozing when I felt the table sway.

"DR. GOLDMAN! DR. GOLDMAN! WAKE UP!"

Patty was standing beside me with a thermometer in her hand.

"It's a hundred and two point five"

"What's a hundred and two point five?"

"Sue Ellen's temperature's a hundred and two point five."

I rolled on my side to get off the table but in my hurry I misjudged the edge and fell to the floor. Patty laughed and helped me to me feet and we hurried into the bathroom. There was Sue Ellen, sitting up, alert and feebly wagging her tail.

"Would you look at that! Damn, would you look at that. Sonafabitch. It's a miracle. She's passed the crisis. She's going to get well!"

Sue Ellen remained in the hospital for ten more days. At first she'd only retain a bland gruel of strained baby food and pablum, but she gradually improved until finally her stomach would accept regular dog food. Then it was time to send her home.

On the day she was discharged, Sue Ellen raced around the waiting room as if it were the Indianapolis Speedway, alternately jumping on Bill, then Evelyn, offering kisses to both. Evelyn took the dog to the car while her husband paid the bill.

"You know, Doc," he said, "we just can't say enough for what you did for Sue Ellen. Even Krystal thanks you. She worried over Sue Ellen just as much as we did. Oh, by the way. I thought you'd like to know – I'm changing jobs. I'll be managing a motel in Flatonia, a brand new Ramada Inn. The place is booked solid for weeks. Every lease hound working the Austin Chalk stays there."

The Austin Chalk was a major oil play centered east of San Marcos.

"The town's booming," he said. "If you're in the area, stop by. I'll treat you to coffee."

"I know you'll do well," I said, "but what about Evelyn?"

"She'll have to stay here to run the gallery, but she and I will alternate weekends driving back and forth."

I walked Bill to his car. Evelyn was sitting on the passenger side while Sue Ellen stretched her head through the rear window, actively sampling the air.

I leaned against the car door, talking to Evelyn. "I understand that you and the dogs are going to become commuters."

"That's right," she replied. Evelyn glanced at Bill, then took her husband's hand. "Bill has a wonderful opportunity in Flatonia. It'll be hard at first – I'll have to keep the gallery open – but it'll be worth it. So, don't be a stranger. Stop by and visit. The dogs enjoy seeing you, too."

I promised I'd stop to visit whenever I had the chance,

but six months passed before I saw them again.

Patty had given me the message that Evelyn was holding a sale and for me to come over and see if there was anything I might want before it began. It was dark when I closed the office, but I went there anyway.

When I arrived all the lights in the gallery were off, but after I rang the bell, a light came on in the rear and the backlit figure of a woman began making its way to the front. It was Evelyn, followed by her two Boxers, who tonight were unusually quiet. She opened the door and invited me to the kitchen.

"Sit down at the table, Joel. Can I get you a cup of coffee?"

As she spoke the dogs looked up at her and then at me, and as if on cue, lay down on either side of their mistress's chair, their heads on their paws.

"I guess you've heard the news," she said. "Bill and I have filed for divorce. Everything's marked down. I want you to have first choice before the ad goes in the paper."

Evelyn poured coffee from a pot on the stove. The dogs, acting like shadows, padded over to the range, waited for her to finish and then resumed their posts after Evelyn sat down. She pushed sugar and cream in front of me but I declined, preferring my coffee black. I noticed she seemed thinner and more subdued since I last saw her.

"No, Evelyn, I didn't know. I'm very sorry. Is there anything I can do?"

"Not a thing," she said. "Everything's arranged. Bill's coming next week to see the lawyer – to have the papers drawn. Then we decide who gets what – I get Sue Ellen and Krystal. That's already been decided. Hasn't it, girls?"

With the sound of their names the dogs raised their heads and Evelyn reassured them. "If it wasn't for these two I couldn't have survived. I know it's silly," she said, "but I had no one else to talk to. Bill kept making excuses, saying

he had to work and couldn't get home. I was driving to
Flatonia every week. Bless their hearts. It's a two hour
drive and they never had an accident. And they were
always so glad to see Bill." She bit her lip and hesitated.
I looked away so she wouldn't feel embarrassed. "You
don't have to say anymore, Evelyn. It must be upsetting."
"No, no, I want you to hear it from me, before you hear
it second hand." She took a sip from her cup. "Bill was
doing real well in Flatonia. The motel stayed full. Business
was good. The trouble was he got in with the wrong crowd
– hot shot promoters from Houston. They drove fancy cars,
dated loose women and flashed big bucks. Being around all
that money must have driven him crazy. He went in on a
drilling deal on a well near Giddings. It was a dry hole. We
lost everything."

She chose a cigarette from her cigarette case, lit it and
placed it still smoking in an ashtray. "I might have forgiven
him for that," she said, "but then he took up with some
local hussy." The end of her cigarette glowed red. "He
couldn't afford those high-priced Houston broads." Then,
slowly and deliberately, she blew a steady stream of smoke
as if to comment on Bill's errant behavior.

"I can understand about the money, but how did you
know he was seeing someone else?"

"I never caught them together, if that's what you mean,
but I was suspicious when he quit coming home. And his
attitude changed. He wasn't interested at all in the gallery.
All he could talk about were those new friends he'd made.
He didn't even miss the dogs, and they used to be all he
ever cared about."

Evelyn's eyes misted over. I sat there quietly, unsure of
what to say.

"I should've listened to Barbara," she said.

"Barbara?"

"Barbara Cox," she said. "Her husband divorced her –

after sixteen years. She says somewhere along the way you men get dissatisfied – with everything – work, marriage, family – everything. You have to screw some broad who's twenty years younger, quit your job, run a marathon. What in the world are you trying to prove?"

I could only speculate. "Maybe Bill thought this would be his last chance to make it big."

"Could be," she said. "I just feel sorry for him. He doesn't have the money to keep up with those high rollers and as soon as that gal discovers he's broke, she'll drop him." She took another drag on her cigarette and then abruptly put it out. Your coffee's cold," she said. "Let me warm it up."

Evelyn, escorted again by her two bodyguards, brought the coffee pot to the table.

"About half a cup is fine," I said. I watched her fill my cup halfway, then asked, "How did he tell you he wanted a divorce?"

Evelyn looked affectionately at her two adoring pets, who watched her every move. Her eyes never left the dogs as she continued speaking. "I had gone down to Flatonia to spend the weekend with Bill and I brought the dogs. Bill and I were having breakfast in the coffee shop, and as usual, we left the door to Bill's room open so the dogs could go in and out. There's a pasture next to the motel. They go there, to run around and do their business."

"Well, the waitress had just finished taking our order, when out of the blue, Bill said he wanted to start fresh. He said he had a chance to make a lot of money and didn't want to mess with fancy arts and crafts. He just wanted out. He wanted a divorce."

"What did you do then?"

"I tried to stay calm and I asked him if there was any way we could work it out, but he said he knew what he wanted and his mind was made up. After that, I was so upset I left and went back to the room. And that's where my babies come in."

"How's that, Evelyn?"

"Sue Ellen and Krystal were waiting at the doorway. My little angels had been in the pasture and had rolled in a pile of manure. It got on their stomachs, their paws, their chests, their backsides. They were just covered in cow shit."

Evelyn's voice became stronger and both dogs rose to their feet, as if to receive an upcoming accolade.

"They had gone into Bill's suite and wiped that crap all over his room. They smeared it on the carpet, the drapes, on his clean towels in the bathroom, on his bed and bedspread, on his sofa and chairs. There was so much shit spread everywhere the place smelled like a pigsty. It didn't make a damn to me, so I sent them on to the car and closed the door.

"You know, Joel, these dogs have a sixth sense about them. They knew Bill did something wrong and they were letting him know how they felt. They're just as smart as humans, aren't they?"

"Yes, they are, Evelyn. And some are even smarter."

Sue Ellen's and Krystal's response had been typical. They responded rationally while their owners went crazy – a situation I commonly encountered, but for which I was poorly prepared.

Early in my career, I divorced the emotional aberrations of the owners from the medical needs of my patients, concentrating all my energies on what I knew best, getting animals well. But eventually I realized that people needed attention, too, and I adjusted my treatments accordingly. Occasionally I performed tasks that were only remotely connected to the veterinary disciplines I studied. Sometimes I had to compromise my ideals. The reconciling of my formal training with the realities of my profession began many years ago with the story of Sarge.

SARGE

Unlike most of my classmates in veterinary school, I shied away from practice and entered academia where I spent my days in a research laboratory. While they pursued careers as animal doctors I grew disease-causing bacteria and dreamed of becoming another Louis Pasteur. I performed well – even isolated new organisms adding to the university's collection – but advancement was slow, the pay was inadequate and gradually I became disillusioned. I remembered how once I enjoyed treating sick dogs and cats and the pleasure it gave me when a sick one was cured – but that was six years ago and I wondered if I would ever have the opportunity to do that again. My experience was limited and my training was dated – as a practitioner my credentials were suspect. Nevertheless, after long months of soul searching, I left the ivory tower and looked for a new position as a small animal veterinarian.

I sifted through a half dozen possibilities, inquiring about jobs in Texas and Louisiana, and finally accepted a position at the Orleans-Jefferson Veterinary Hospital. I felt I was lucky. For one thing, I was raised in Louisiana, and New Orleans was close to home. For another, the clinic was a big, bustling place – the "Cook County General Hospital for Animals," as one client put it – known for its ability to diagnose and cure difficult cases. And the staff appeared

21

friendly and were anxious to have me join them.

There were four doctors on the staff at that time: Bob and Gene Burrus, the owners, men in their fifties and wise in practice matters; Leon Williams, a six-year veteran on track to become a full partner; and Harry Everson, a brand new graduate. Harry was still a baby, barely twenty-three, while I was pushing thirty, but since he and I were rookies by experience, the doctors grouped us together and treated us accordingly, although they were a little schizophrenic about me.

Most days the senior vets seemed to think they were fortunate to have me. On occasion they would even remember I had taught microbiology and would even consult me on tough diagnoses. It was, "Thanks, Dr. Goldman," when I identified an unusual organism like Cryptococcus from a cat suffering from painful nasal abscess, or when I demonstrated under the microscope an elusive Giardia from a dog with chronic diarrhea. The rest of the time it was, "Do this, Joel," and, "Do that, Joel," and, "Hurry up, Joel." This was typical treatment for new doctors and I didn't let it worry me. Truthfully, in those early months I was also a little schizophrenic about myself. Alone with a patient I was flawless, but when the owner was present I made errors like a greenhorn, which aggravated the Burruses to no end.

Considering my erratic beginning, I was more than surprised when Colonel Hampton asked that I see his black and silver German Shepherd named Sarge. During my first weeks on the job the colonel brought Sarge for a routine vaccination and I was randomly chosen to give the big dog his shots, but today the colonel specifically requested to see me, an act that labeled me competent, regardless whether the Burruses believed it or not.

Arthur, my assistant, hoisted Sarge, a large dog of ninety-five pounds, onto the examining table. Sarge positioned his feet in a show stance, radiating confidence and pride. His eyes were alert but never menacing. The dog was as gentle as a baby.

"He has a swelling on his hind leg," said the colonel.

"It's a lymph node," I said as I felt the suspect enlargement.

It was the popliteal node of the right hind leg, normally about the size of a grape, but today it was the size of a hen's egg.

"He's been acting well and eating okay?"

"Hasn't missed a meal, Doc. Fit as a fiddle."

"Any coughing or diarrhea?"

"No. He's had normal stools. Occasionally he sneezes."

"Do you remember him cutting his foot or having any punctures or abrasions?"

"Well, he did cut his pad, but that's been more than six weeks ago. How could that affect a node halfway up his leg?"

"Lymph nodes swell in reaction to an infection," I said. "They have cells that destroy germs. The nodes are enlarged while they fight the infection and go down when it's resolved. This one should have regressed by now."

"Let me feel that," a voice said. It was Dr. Williams. He always appeared when a case presented more than simple cough or diarrhea. Grudgingly, I introduced him.

"Colonel Hampton, this is Dr. Williams."

Leon was an excellent veterinarian. He was always abreast of the latest advances, practiced precise surgical technique and abounded with endless energy. I admired his skills and coveted his stamina but I considered his personality abrasive.

Nudging me aside, Leon felt the node and then compared it with others scattered around Sarge's body. By the look on his face I knew we had arrived at the same conclusion. He turned to me and said, "We'll need blood for a CBC and let's get a biopsy."

"Why a biopsy?" asked the colonel.

"Sarge could have cancer," said Leon. "A biopsy is the only way to be sure."

"It's a minor procedure," I said, hastening to cushion Leon's bluntness.

"A very minor procedure," stressed Leon. "It'll only take minutes. I'll be happy to assist."

The colonel was apprehensive but agreed to the biopsy and I, with Leon's supervision, sedated Sarge and removed the node. The specimen was sent on Tuesday and I expected an answer by Friday. Friday came and went and still no results. I made a note to call the lab first thing Monday.

Surprisingly, the colonel and Sarge were waiting at the hospital when I arrived for work. I walked over to where they were sitting, greeted the colonel with a handshake and patted Sarge on the head. Then I offered an apology.

"I still haven't heard from the lab," I said. "I can't understand why they're taking so long. They're usually very prompt."

"But we know already," said the colonel. "Dr. Williams gave us the news. He wants to start Sarge on chemotherapy. What do you think?"

I wasn't qualified to voice an opinion when I didn't have the facts. I felt stupid. "What kind of tumor was it?"

The colonel dug in his pocket and handed me a crumpled sheet of paper. "You read it," he said.

"A lymphosarcoma," I said. Lymphosarcomas are usually fatal, but with chemotherapy the disease could be held in remission, though even with early diagnosis and therapy, the average lifespan of a treated animal is only seven to nine months. Without treatment, an affected dog might only survive a month. In the face of that prognosis many clients opt to do nothing or go for immediate euthanasia. I felt sick. "We're in for a battle," I said.

The colonel seemed alarmed but he gradually heartened as I added, "But Dr. Williams has a lot of experience with this kind of tumor. He's very competent."

Suddenly, Sarge's ears pricked up and he turned his head sideways.

"Pardon me," I said. "Someone's banging on the door." As soon as I opened it, a gentleman, struggling with a cardboard box, almost bowled me over. June, our receptionist, recognized him at once and paged for Arthur to come and assist. Sarge bared his teeth and lunged forward, keeping his body between us and the perceived danger.

"Keep that dog away," warned the man. "If this cat ever gets out, there'll be hell to pay."

RRRIIPP! A black paw shot through the top of the box, tearing the seams that had been sealed with tape. ERROWLLL! wailed the cat. "He's gonna escape," said the man. "Tell Arthur to hurry."

"Here I am, Mr. Raburn," said Arthur, appearing out of nowhere. "Let me have him."

Just as Arthur took hold of the box the cat's head burst through the crack. Frantically it tried to wiggle through the narrow opening, but Arthur, armed with a magazine, smartly whacked it over the frenzied feline's head. Unhurt, the cat retreated.

"Whew," said the man. "One more second and he'd been gone."

Arthur took the box to the kennel and I followed. Once there I unlatched a cage door as Arthur jammed the box against the opening. Snarling, howling and spitting, the cat jumped into the cage but leaped back at the bars just as Arthur slammed the door shut.

"Who is that creature?" I asked as I counted my fingers.

"Manny Raburn," said Arthur. "The kennel boys call him Maneater. He's boarding. Try not to mess with him."

Making note of Arthur's warning I returned to the waiting room.

"That was certainly exciting," said the colonel.

"We've handled worse than that," I said.

Then June said that Dr. Williams was ready to see Sarge, so I led them to Leon's examing room. Leon was his usual bubbly self.

"Hiyadoin', Colonel? How's the dog? Say, Joel. I know you're wondering why the colonel is here. The lab phoned the results on the Reynold's specimen so I asked if Sarge's results were complete. The secretary gave them to me over the phone. I hope you don't mind."

"Of course not," I said. "The sooner we start treating the better."

"I knew you'd say that," he said. "I'll start Sarge on prednisone, cyclophosphamide and vincristine. You can take blood samples and follow the case along. How's that sound?"

It sounded awful. Of course his treatment was correct – it was the very same treatment that I would have prescribed – but here was Leon, taking control without even giving me a chance. I realized I was one up from the bottom in a five-man practice and I expected some servility as part of the job, but wasn't it time I had a case of my own? Still, I suppressed my injured pride and decided to do anything to help Sarge get well.

Sarge was an excellent patient. He learned to sit on the scale while I weighed him, wait motionless while I examined his lymph nodes and stick his leg out so I could draw blood. He tolerated daily intravenous infusions and never got sick, in spite of the fact that the drugs we used had the potential for serious side effects. Williams would come in, read Sarge's chart and exchange small talk with the colonel, who spent more time at the hospital with Sarge than he did at home. After four weeks of therapy, Sarge's nodes regressed to normal and since his overall condition was good I transferred him to out-patient status.

Even though Sarge was one of my special concerns the overall hospital routine overshadowed everything. Hospital hours lasted from nine until twelve in the mornings and from three until six in the afternoons. Between twelve and three we closed for surgery. Emergencies were seen anytime, night or day. When I wasn't seeing clients I spent my time examining animals that had been dropped off and whose problems were usually minor. Occasionally I assisted in surgery, but not often. On some days the hospital was so full of cases I had trouble keeping track. It was one big blur of animals of all shapes, sizes, breeds and names. There were names of owners and names of animals and names of cases, surgical or medical – not to mention services, which included boarding, bathing and dipping. It was all very confusing. I thought I would never get the hang of it.

Occasionally, however, the pace would slacken, affording us some respite, and the doctors would lounge in the office, eating lunch or watching T.V., except for Leon, that is, who spent that time on the telephone, inquiring about his patients. One afternoon, after surgery was over, I asked Leon about his telephone follow ups.

"It's just something you need to do," said Leon. "First it lets the owners know you care, and second you find out how well your patients are doing. And if they're not improving, you tell them to bring the animal back. Some owners get discouraged when a treatment fails and you never see them again. What's worse, they go someplace else. Then the new vet asks them what they've tried, he changes the treatment, the animal gets well and you look like a jackass!"

I couldn't imagine calling a client. I always thought no news was good news. Besides, whenever a client paged me on the phone I could only imagine he or she had called to tell me the worst. I related my fears to Leon.

"I guess I lack self-confidence," I said.

"It just takes time," said Leon. "You've only been with us, for what – a few months? And let me give you another tip. You don't mind, do you?"

"No, indeed," I said. "I need all the help I can get."

"Then develop some personal skills," he said. "Especially with the opposite sex."

"C'mon, Leon," I said. "What's being a veterinarian got to do with women?"

"Plenty," he said. "They're the ones that wind up taking the animals to the vet. By the time they get here with a car full of screaming kids and barking dogs they're frazzled. So tell 'em they look nice, ask if they've lost weight and play with the kids. Women appreciate that. Besides," he smirked, "they'll come back to see you again and again and again. It's good repeat business."

"I guess it is," I said, "but . . . aren't you . . . flirting?" I was sort of shy. And I was married.

"Maybe," he said. "But when a woman tells you her husband cares more about the dog than her, well, you've got to tell her what she wants to hear. Just watch how I handle Arlene Francona."

"You mean the nice looking lady with the Standard Poodles?"

"You got it," he said.

I remembered her, even though I had seen her only from a distance. She always looked stunning and she always saw Leon. He fawned over her like a moose in rut. I often wondered what she saw in him.

"Arlene has a show in the Quarter," said Leon. "She's Alphonse Bergeron's girl."

My face went blank.

"Alphonse works for the mob," he said soberly. "He pays Arlene's vet bills."

My mind reeled with these startling revelations. "And one last thing," he said. "Remember you're treating the owners, too, so be sure to keep them happy." "So they'll bring back their pets?" "No. So they'll pay their pets' bills. Have you ever seen a dog sign a check? Animals don't pay the bills. Don't ever forget it."

Leon's statement rang true and I left the room to eat my lunch alone. Leon was in on everything. He had a relationship with a kept woman who even had ties to organized crime. And he was so perceptive. When I examined a patient all I saw was a sick dog or cat, while Leon saw housewives whose egos needed boosting. And I thought the keys to success lay in anatomy and physiology. I just needed to be more forceful, more outgoing, more energetic ... more like Leon? No way. I wanted to be just as successful as Leon without becoming Leon. I had the talent and the training. All I needed was the right opportunity to show what I could do.

Saturday hours were over by noon, so we crammed a whole day's work in half the time. In between seeing patients we discharged as many cases as possible so the weekend vet would have few in-hospital cases to treat and could concentrate on emergencies. It was a constant scramble, keeping up with who was coming in and who was going out, but the Burruses had a system to keep it all straight.

On admission each patient had a band placed around its neck, listing the owner, date of admission and the hospital's phone number and address. In addition each animal had a record card. It had the pertinent medical data and the ward number where the patient was kenneled. We doctors instructed the lay help to bring us a patient from the appropriate ward and we'd give a short description of the particular animal. The scheme worked well in spite of the apparent chaos that the hospital always seemed to be in.

"Do me a favor, will you, Joel?" asked Leon one busy Saturday. "I'm stacked up with clients wanting to see me, so will you discharge Tammy, the Bertucci cat? I spayed it yesterday and Mrs. Bertucci's here to pick up. Tell her everything is fine and to bring the cat back to take the stitches out a week from today."

"I'll get right on it," I said. "Vincent!" I yelled. "Go into ward four and get the Bertucci black cat. It was spayed yesterday and it's going home."

Vincent was one of the kennel boys. He had been recently hired so I didn't know much about him but he was certainly enthusiastic. I was glad to have him with me, especially today.

"Just take me a second," he said, and he disappeared into the kennel.

"Hey, Joel, will you do me a favor?" It was Dr. Bob. He poked his head out of his room. "I've got a dog sedated on the table and I promised the Arnauds that I'd put some tapeworm medicine up for them. Their dog weighs fifteen pounds. Fix it and take it to the front, willya?"

"Sure, Dr. Bob," I said. "I'll get right on it."

DR. JOEL. DR. JOEL. PLEASE CHECK AT THE FRONT DESK. DR. JOEL. PLEASE CHECK AT THE DESK.

June was broadcasting over the intercom from her post at the front desk. She was always requesting doctors, animals, prescriptions, telephone calls or advice. I felt harassed by its clarion calls, but it saved time and could be heard over the din of growls, barks and meows. I went to the front to see what she wanted.

"This cat carrier belongs to the Bertuccis," said June as she handed me a sturdy wooden box. "Give this to your helper and have'm put her cat in the carrier. Mrs. Bertucci's in a hurry. She's waiting at the exit."

"Yes, ma'am," I said, turning halfway round.

"Watch out, Dr. Joel!"

I tripped over a leash and fell on the floor. It was Vincent. He was waiting with a Corgi. "What the hell are you doing?" I said. "I told you to get Mrs. Bertucci's cat."

"Dr. Gene's helper was holding an I.V., so he told me to stop what I was doing and help him."

"Oh, all right. Listen. As soon as Dr. Gene finishes with you, get the Bertucci cat and put it in this carrier. I'll be in the pharmacy putting up medicine. Got it?"

"Got it," he said. "Meet you back in your room."

I zipped into the pharmacy, counted out the tapeworm pills, ran to the front where the Arnauds were waiting and rushed back to my room. On the table was the cat, safely esconced in the carrier with Vincent beside it. Now all I needed was...

"Hey, Joel," It was June. "You don't have time to sit around. Mrs. Bertucci's waiting at the exit. Would you hurry up?"

"I was just about to go," I said. I grabbed the carrier with its vital cargo and headed for the exit and the waiting Mrs. Bertucci.

"It's about time," she said. "Dr. Leon would never keep me waiting. Ooh. How's my baby Tammy?" Tammy was staring through the wire mesh window. Mrs. Bertucci poked her finger in the box, wiggling it like a worm on a hook. "Just wait till we get home. I'll peel you some shrimp."

Eager to say something helpful, I spoke up. "Dr. Leon wants to see you in a week to – "

"To take out the stitches," she said. "Young man," she went on, eyeing me critically, "I've been coming here for thirty years and you're not telling me anything new." And out the door she went.

When office hours were over Leon came by to talk.

"You handled yourself well," he said, "and you never got

flustered."

"All I did was discharge some animals and dispense a few pills. Anybody could've handled it."

"Maybe," he said. "But this practice can be a killer. You're the eighth doctor we've hired in six years. Go on home," he said. "I've got the weekend duty. See ya on Monday."

Leon's praise did wonders for my self-confidence, though his statement about the hospital's employment record gave me some concern. Nevertheless, I filed my misgivings away and looked forward to Monday, as the colonel was due to bring Sarge in for his physical. I could hardly wait.

"Hi, Sarge. Hi there, Colonel," I said. "Any problems?" Sarge wagged his tail at the sound of his name.

"None that I can tell," said the colonel. "He might be drinking more water than normal."

"That's possibly a side effect of the prednisone," I said. "We'll check that when I send in the blood."

We had just lifted Sarge onto the exam table when the intercom blared, DR. LEON. DR. LEON. MRS. BERTUCCI'S ON LINE ONE DR. LEON. MRS. BERTUCCI'S ON LINE ONE.

"That's the Dr. Leon who looks after Sarge, isn't it?" said the colonel.

"That's him," I said.

"He called me last night, just to see how Sarge was doing. Not even *my* doctor does that."

I pretended I didn't hear and took a sample of Sarge's blood, which I sent to the lab. Meanwhile the colonel was being chatty.

"Have you been here long, Joel?"

"A little over four months," I said.

"Are you a native New Orleanian?"

"No. I've been teaching at Texas A&M. I got tired of university life and thought I'd try practice."

"Well you sure chose a busy place," said the colonel.

"Are you from New Awlins?" I drawled.

"No. but my wife is. She's a Charbonnet. Her family's been here since the 1800s. Her grandfather was Rex during the '27 Mardi Gras."

"I don't know much about Mardi Gras."

"It's just one big party," said the colonel.

Just then Leon poked his head in the door. "Dr. Goldman," he said. "May I speak to you in private?"

We stepped just outside. Leon was formal as usual.

"You wouldn't know why Mrs. Bertucci would be having a problem with her cat, would you?"

"No," I said. "Is something wrong?"

"She said she let the cat go as soon as she got home, but it ran under the refrigerator and wouldn't come out. Yesterday she had a chance to grab it and almost lost her hand. And it's still under the refrigerator. Now she's on the phone wanting to know what I did to her cat. She's really pissed."

"The cat was perfectly fine when it left here," I said. "Why don't you go ask somebody else?"

Leon was taken aback at my forcefulness, but he still had the gall to lean into my room and say, "Nice to see you and Sarge, Colonel. If there's any problem, be sure to call."

Relieved that Leon didn't tarry but pleased that I stood my ground, I apologized to the colonel for the interruption and resumed my conversation.

"Are you Army or Air Force?"

"Retired Air Force," said the colonel. "Been retired twenty years now. Went to work for G.E. after I left the service. Opened up the G.E. warehouse over on Bienville Street."

"Did you fly while you were in the service?"

"Been flying since I was a kid," he said. "Both my brother and my cousin learned to fly before they turned twenty.

They bought a biplane and we barnstormed all over North Carolina. We'd fly into a town and offer rides for five bucks. I sold the tickets. Just wanted to make enough to buy gas to fly to the next stop. We were crazy."

The lab report indicated all was normal, so the colonel prepared to go. After I helped him lift Sarge down from the table, Sarge took up his post alongside his owner. I sensed the trust and loyalty these two shared as the colonel patted Sarge on his head and the dog responded with a subdued whine.

"Great dog you've got there, Colonel. Any time you want to give him away I'll take him."

"No deal, Doc. Say, before I forget, the wife and I want to invite you and your wife over for dinner. You've been so nice to Sarge. We wanted to do something extra. How about it?"

"We'd love to," I said. "I'll speak to Kay and have her call Mrs. Hampton."

Putting Leon in his place had put me in a spunky mood and I carried that over into the surgery where I castrated two cats, pulled three rotten teeth on an overweight Poodle and curetted an abscess on a kitten's tail. Granted, they were minor operations, but with each procedure I gained new confidence and I was sure the owners had noticed, which they had, for by the end of the day Dr. Bob sent word he wanted to see me. So did Gene, Leon and Harry. Everyone gathered in Bob's room. Leon was leaning against the wall, cleaning his fingernails. Harry was alert and I thought overly attentive. Gene was reading a newspaper.

"Joel," commenced Bob, "we want to review our procedure for discharging patients. When you discharge an animal, be sure to check the neckband, and if the band is missing check the sex, and if there's a question about it being the right patient ask me or Leon or Gene. You and Harry are new and we expect some confusion, but if you would just pay attention to what's going on we can avoid these embarrassing screwups."

"What screwup?" I said.

"You," roared Bob, "and I give you credit for more intelligence than you showed Saturday – you sent home the wrong patient!"

"Oh." I started to laugh, but as no one else thought it was funny I quickly disguised it as a gagging choke. Meanwhile, Bob thundered on. "Don't you know the difference between a female with an abdominal incision and an unneutered tomcat with a full blown set of balls?"

"Yessir," I said, all humor aside.

"Well you didn't on Saturday," he said. "And you're a college professor."

I was completely dumbfounded.

"Don't just stand there," said Bob. "Don't you want to know how this episode ended?"

"Yessir," I said even more meekly. "Was any harm done?"

"Harm? HARM? Mrs. Bertucci's damn near had her arm amputated. She swears she'll never set foot in this hospital again." Now he was shouting. "WE CAN'T AFFORD TO LOSE CLIENTS!"

"And think what this does to our reputation," said Leon. She'll have this story spread all over town."

"We just have to be more careful," said Gene, "but it's going to take some effort on your part. That's all I've got to say," and he walked out.

Harry just looked at me sympathetically and tried to disappear into the wall.

"Any furthur questions?" asked Bob. "Okay. Meeting dismissed."

My pride was hurt by this dressing down, but I was at fault and had deserved it. Shaking with indignation, I walked into the kennel where Arthur was washing down the runs.

"OOOEEE," he said. "The old man told me you didn't have the brains of a mosquito."

"Was Mrs. Bertucci hurt bad?" I asked.

"Naw," said Arthur. "But her house sure stunk. The cat spent the weekend under her refrigerator and crapped in the sink. He sprayed everywhere. She'll never get that odor out."

"Serves her right," I said. "Didn't like that woman anyway." I slammed my hand against an empty cage.

"What cat did I send her?"

"Maneater Raburn," said Arthur.

"Oh, no! I guess I'm lucky to have a job."

"Don't let it bother ya, Doc. I've known Mrs. Bertucci ever since I started here and she and Maneater make a nice couple."

"That's no excuse, Arthur. Somebody could've gotten hurt. Just wait till I get a hold of Vincent."

Arthur laughed. "Forget Vincent," he said. "He doesn't know how to read."

The Hamptons lived on Magazine Street in a turn of the century restored shotgun house. Graced with shutters, tall ceilings and immense French doors that slid out of walls, the home was full of furniture and antiques from all over the world.

Kay and Mrs. Hampton – she said to call her Missy – sat inside, discussing cut glass and silver, while the colonel and I sat outside drinking martinis. Sarge stretched on the grass, nursing a Shirley Temple filled with ice and maraschino juice.

"The wife and I always enjoy a cocktail at night," explained the colonel, "and Sarge licks our empty glasses, so we got in the habit of pouring a drink for him. He's really part of the family."

"Of course he is," I said.

The colonel took a sip of his drink. "I can tell Sarge is slowing down," he said. "How long do you think he's got?"

"It's difficult to predict," I said. "Five or six months, maybe longer, but as long as he has an appetite and gets around, enjoy his company. There's not much else you can do."

"Well, Missy and I appreciate everything you and Dr. Williams are doing," he said. "We invited him and his wife to join us tonight, but they had a previous engagement. Do you know he still calls me once a week to check on Sarge?"

"He keeps tabs on everything," I said. I ruthlessly speared my olive with a toothpick.

"Don't you two get along?" asked the colonel.

"We haven't exactly hit it off," I said.

"That's too bad," said the colonel. "He's just doing his job."

He poured himself another drink and leaned back in his chair. "Back in the fifties I commanded an F-84 fighter group," he said. "We flew escort for 29s coming out of Okinawa. Most of the crews were reservists. They didn't give a damn about regulations. I was on their butts every day." He added cubes to Sarge's glass. "Someone had to mind the store," he chuckled. "And, man, they hated my guts."

The colonel thought Leon with his boiler room calls was just doing his job. I thought he was chasing ambulances. Who was right? We sat there, alone with our thoughts, listening to the cicadas and the tinkling of ice as Sarge lolled his tongue in his glass. Finally, Missy called us to dinner. As we left our seats to go into the house Sarge got up and trotted on ahead.

"Wants to get a good seat," said the colonel.

Missy had prepared a Cajun feast – oyster gumbo and

crawfish étoufée served with a bottle of chilled Chablis. A bread pudding coated with whiskey sauce waited in the wings.

Sarge sat on his haunches next to the colonel and looked up each time his owner passed a plate, hoping to mooch a morsel.

"Can I give him some of this crawfish, Doc?" asked the colonel. "He's used to eating it. Missy always gives him the leftovers."

I normally didn't advise owners to feed their pets scraps, but it was such a simple request, and the pleasure it would give the Hamptons would certainly outweigh any harm it could possibly cause, so I told him he could. Sarge gobbled down the juicy crustaceans with unabashed joy and sat there, pretending as if he had eaten none at all, until finally, all of us were coerced into making a contribution from our plates. Not until we demonstrated that the dishes were empty did Sarge pad off into the living room to lie down.

Kay and I stayed for dessert and then left. It had been a lovely evening and a welcome change of pace. I would need it. This weekend I was on duty.

My weekend began with words of assurance.

"Call me if you run into anything you can't handle," said Dr. Bob. "I just live down the street."

I thanked him and said I would.

"My number's on the wall," said Leon. "If you have questions about any case just pick up the phone."

"Sure thing, Leon. Thanks."

I went to the back of the hospital, where Dr. Gene was giving instructions to the kennel help. "Make sure you mop the floors and empty the waste baskets," he told them. "This place should be spotless. And Joel, don't be bashful about asking for help if you think you need it."

"I won't," I said. He nodded, took one last look around and left.

Harry was going across the lake to Covington to see a girl friend. "Good luck," he hollered as he blew through the door. "See ya Monday."

Saturday afternoon dragged by – only two emergencies, a wormy pup with diarrhea and a cat with a respiratory infection, both simple cases. Sunday was just as slow, and I was about to believe that the weekend would be a snap, when Mrs. Fournier, one of Bob's clients, called the hospital.

According to her, Tartan, her six-month-old Collie female was having difficulty breathing and she wanted to know what she could do until she could find Bob. I had to convince her not to wait and to bring her dog to the hospital. It was fortunate that she did.

Tartan, a thirty-pound sable-and-white Collie arrived in respiratory distress. Her lips were pulled back and her gums were gray. The dog was breathing twice as fast as normal. She was in desperate straits. Immediately, I rolled the oxygen tank over and directed a stream of the life-sustaining gas toward the dog's nose. Tartan began to breathe easier, though still not normally.

"How'd this happen?" I asked sharply.

"Tartan just finished eating when..."

"What did you feed her?"

"Her regular dog food – dry kibble mixed with canned."

"Anything else?" I said.

"That's all," she said. "After she ate, she drank her water, like always, then she did a lot of running – I was teaching her to catch a frisbee – when suddenly she sat down and wouldn't get up. I thought she was dying! I tried to get Dr. Bob. Do you know when he'll be back?"

I put on my stethoscope and listened to the animal's chest, but muffled rubbing was the only sound I heard.

"What is it?" she said.

"I'm not sure yet," I said.

"Dr. Bob would know," she said. "Don't you know where he is?"

"If you'd rather see someone else," I said, "I'll be happy to go home."

"Oh, no," she said. "I didn't mean it that way."

Realizing I had the upper hand, Mrs. Fournier ceased voicing her desire for Bob's opinion as I proceeded to find the reason for her dog's symptoms. I stretched the dog on the x-ray table and took two pictures. The films were still wet as I placed them on the viewer, but it was evident that the diaphragm, a muscle which separates the chest from the abdomen wasn't at all visible, and to complicate matters a mass was in the thorax.

"Here's the problem," I said, pointing to the large gray area on the film. "This glob is in her chest along with her lungs and heart. It's restricting her breathing. I think it's her stomach."

"That's impossible," she said.

"No, it's not," I said. "Tartan ate a big meal and drank a lot of water which the kibble soaked up. Then, when she started running, her stomach, filled with this heavy load, began swinging and pressing on her diaphragm. The diaphragm tore and half her insides slid into her chest. That's why she can't breathe."

"But how could it just tear like that?" she said.

"Must've had a weak spot. A congenital defect. You know, born with it."

"That's ridiculous," she said. "Dr. Bob examines all my dogs and he says they're perfect."

"Regardless," I said. "Tartan needs an operation. This won't get well by itself."

Repairing a diaphragmatic tear is a three- or four-man job requiring a surgeon, an anesthesiologist and one or two assistants. I didn't want to bother the bosses so I had

Duane, the nightman, call Leon to come down and assist. "I called everyone," said Duane. "Dr. Leon, Dr. Gene, Dr. Bob – everybody's out. I left messages everywhere."

I stalled as long as I could hoping someone would return my calls, but Tartan's stomach, squeezed into an unnatural position, began to bloat with gas from the now fermenting dog food. And as her stomach swelled, the veins returning blood to the heart were collapsing. She was going into shock and would die without immediate intervention.

I persuaded Mrs. Fournier to allow us to operate, but even then she complained, that I, a mere underling, was going to be the surgeon, a situation she equated with a death sentence. And after I placed Tartan under anesthesia I had to wonder if she wasn't right, because the dog's color changed from pale pink to morbid blue. Frantically I jammed a tube down the dog's trachea while Duane administered oxygen. Gradually the dog's color stabilized at something less than normal and we proceeded with opening the dog's belly.

I cut through the skin and muscles until I was in the abdomen. My hand searched forward toward the diaphragm, groping for a rent. There it was. A large tear in the middle. I inserted my finger through it. It was just as I thought. The stomach had herniated through the opening and was sitting in the chest. Nervously, I tugged at the duodenum, a thickened area at the beginning of the intestine that directly connects to the stomach. I pulled cautiously. The stomach loomed up next to the opening and slipped through, making a sucking sound as it plopped into position. Immediately, Tartan's color improved to normal. I rested for a minute, basking in my success, but Duane brought me back to reality.

"Ya did good, Doc, but how about sewing her up?"

"I'm sorry Duane. I was just wondering what Mrs. Fournier's going to say when I tell her the good news. Hand me some number three catgut."

First, I closed the tear in the diaphragm and then I sutured the stomach to its normal position. I had just begun the abdominal closure when suddenly the surgery door burst open.

"Hiya, Joel. I got your message and came right over. What's going on?"

It was Leon. He slipped into a surgery gown, gloved up and positioned himself on the opposite side of the table. He looked over the surgical field.

"Nice job," he said. "How'd it happen? Hit by a car?"

"No," I said. "It was a freak accident." And I explained everything that had happened. "But do me a favor," I said. "I'll finish here. Will you speak with Mrs. Fournier? She's waiting outside. I know she must be a nervous wreck."

I finished closing the incision and Duane and I put Tartan in a cage. A few minutes later Leon returned and said that Mrs. Fournier would be back in the morning. I went home pleased with a job well done.

The next day Mrs. Fournier was already there visiting. So was Leon. He was explaining Tartan's condition. "Your baby's doing fine," he told her. "I'll see that she gets her medicine personally, and if you have any questions, call me."

I felt like Cinderella after the ball.

While Tartan was my first major success Sarge was developing problems. He had a cough and ran a low grade fever. The nodes that had previously shrunken had ballooned with a vengeance, and the blood chemistries were indicating kidney and liver complications. Even Sarge's eyes had lost their glitter, and his coat no longer shined. I altered the medication, and the fever left, but the nodes still grew, and by now Sarge had lost ten pounds. I suggested to the colonel we try I.V.'s to correct the dog's blood chemistries but I was running out of options and I could sense the colonel

knew it. Then, for the first time, I discussed with the colonel the possibility of putting Sarge to sleep.

I had certain guidelines I followed to help owners come
to that decision. I advised euthanasia when an animal was
unable to eat or keep down food, when it was nonambula-
tory and couldn't eliminate without soiling itself or when
it lost bowel or bladder control. Spinal injuries, irreversible
liver or kidney damage, massive, crushing injuries or cancer were all valid reasons for euthanasia. Since Leon was
still in charge of the case I told him about my suggestion.

Leon toyed with his stethoscope as he considered my
comments. Surprisingly, he didn't object, but he did have
a word of caution. "Don't push it too hard," he said, "or
else the colonel will think you talked him into it – before
it was time."

"I wouldn't do that," I said.

"I know you wouldn't," he said, "but clients are funny.
They try to second guess. The colonel might think . . .
maybe I should've given Sarge a little longer . . . and if he
thinks that, he'll never forgive you or me – and we lose
another client. So keep your mouth shut until the colonel
tells you to put the dog to sleep. He'll thank you for it in
the end."

That was typical advice coming from Leon. I was concerned about the animal's suffering, while Leon was concerned that I didn't do anything that would get me or the
hospital in trouble. One thing was for sure. During the
months I treated Sarge, I had forged a bond with the dog
and his owner and it hurt me to watch this magnificent animal deteriorate. Over the next few days I treated Sarge with
I.V.'s and changed his diet to help his kidneys. He
responded well and I sent him home to an uncertain future.
Weeks went by before I saw him again.

"Sarge and the colonel are here," said Arthur, poking his
head through the door.

"Thanks, Arthur," I said. "You'll need to give the colonel a hand. The dog's probably pretty weak."

"It's gonna be tough putting that dog down," he said. "The colonel's sure gonna take it hard."

Sadly I filled a hypodermic with an anesthetic and then drew up a solution of T-61, a special drug that would stop the heart. I always gave the anesthetic first, which instantly and humanely rendered the animal unconscious, and then I followed it with the lethal drug. There would be no struggling, no involuntary spasms – just a painless and dignified end for the patient, and hopefully, a new beginning for the owner. I placed the loaded syringe on the counter as Arthur, followed by a somber Colonel Hampton, carried Sarge in.

Poor Sarge. He was just a skeleton of his former self. His eyes were glazed and his coat was dull. Even his back look bowed. He was having problems breathing and ended each breath with a heart rending grunt.

"I guess it's time," said the colonel. "I know we waited longer than we should." Tears streamed down his face. "But we wanted to keep him with us as long as we could." I handed him some Kleenex. "Do you think he's suffering?"

There was no doubt in my mind that Sarge was hurting, but admitting this to the colonel would only compound the pain.

"He doesn't feel a thing," I said. "If anything, I think the dog is happy just being here with you." I picked up the syringe. "If you'll hold onto Sarge, Colonel, you'll reassure him and keep him from being frightened."

"I'd like that," he said, "if you don't think I'll be in your way."

"No, sir, you won't," I said.

The colonel lifted Sarge's head from the table and held him against his chest. He sobbed as I made the injections. Sarge tensed slightly, then relaxed, slumping in his master's arms, while the colonel, feeling the dog go limp, kissed the silver muzzle and laid Sarge's head back down on the table. I closed the big dog's eyes. "He's gone," I said haltingly. It only took seconds.

The colonel wiped his eyes and cleared his throat. "I'm sorry I was such a baby," he said. "I'll go pay the bill and then I'll come back for the body. We're going to bury him in the backyard. He really loved that backyard."

Arthur and I placed Sarge in a box and waited for the colonel to return. Then our funeral cortege made its way to the exit. I stood by the door as the colonel shook my hand, thanking me profusely.

"I know you did everything humanly possible," he said, "and thanks for letting us keep him as long as we did. You were so understanding." He stopped to reflect on his thoughts, while I recalled Leon's comments. "I'd better get going," he said. "I've got to finish digging a grave. Missy wanted to help, but she broke down and started crying."

His face wrinkled in a spasm of grief and I thought he would break down, too, but he controlled his emotions like the tough soldier he was. It was a poignant moment and I have never forgotten it. When he and Arthur passed through the doorway I felt as if I had passed through a doorway, too. I had discovered what veterinary medicine was all about.

I walked into the office emotionally drained. Leon was on the phone as usual, so I slid in a chair and closed my eyes, just as I heard him say, "Mrs. Hampton? This is Dr. Williams. Hiyadoin. I'm calling to check on Sarge."

PINCH HIT

I was in the hallway, consulting with a client, when I heard Arthur warn, "Watch out! This dog is bad!" Arthur was taking the dog in to board when suddenly it went berserk. Snapping at its leash, it squirmed, bit, defecated and urinated all the way to the kennel. It was Fritz Benoit, a wiry red Dachshund that lived with its owners on Audubon Place.

"Whenever he boards he goes crazy," lamented Arthur, once Fritz was safely kenneled.

"You'd go nuts too if you knew you had to spend two weeks here," I said. "This dog lives like a king. Sleeps in his own bed, eats out of china bowls and has a private chauffeur."

The Benoits owned a fleet of tugboats that operated on the Mississippi. They contracted to haul barges upriver as far as Cincinnati. They were rich. I rarely saw Mr. or Mrs. Benoit, as they usually sent Fritz with their driver, but today, there was Mr. Benoit, at the front desk, talking to June.

"It's a struggle every time I send him. God, he hates like hell to come. The dog's a mind reader. The day he's supposed to board, he goes and hides. I had to drag him from under the couch." He turned to me. "What do you guys do, torture 'em?"

"Of course not," I said. "They're inside where it's air conditioned and we walk them three times a day."

"And we have chicken or roast beef for picky eaters," said June. I could recommend the chicken. Arthur always brought me a sample before he fed it to the dogs.

"Well, Fritz can't wait to get home," said Mr. Benoit. "Takes him a week to get back to normal."

I assured him we would do everything possible to make Fritz's stay pleasant. He took my word and left, saying he'd have the chauffeur return for Fritz in two weeks.

Besides our routine medical and kenneling services we offered reproductive counseling. Repro services had a low priority, so this job was passed down to the bottom staff – either Harry or me.

My first experience as a sex therapist involved Mrs. Mouton, a widow who lived uptown near Tulane University. Mrs. Mouton had twenty registered dogs, all Dachshunds. They came in all colors: reds, blacks, black and tans, and silver dapples. A silver dapple is a splotchy mix of black and gray. They were her favorites. That day she had brought in two silver dapples, Anton von Hesse, an eleven-year-old male and Ella von Burg, an eighteen-month-old female. Ella was in heat and Mrs. Mouton had put the two together, but without any success.

"Anton seems interested, but once he climbs on, he quits," she said.

"She certainly acts ready," I said, as Ella stood frozen with her tail to the side.

"Oh, she's a little witch," she replied. "She drives all the other males crazy. But I want to breed her to Anton. He's such a gentleman."

She lifted the male and smothered him in a hug. "I've got his pups already promised. If only he'd do his stuff. Is there anything you can do?"

"Why don't you leave them with me?" I said. "I'll give the male a good checkup and I can do a vaginal exam on Ella."

"Wonderful," she said. "Call me when you're through."

Since this would be a two-man job, I had Harry assist. We met in the rear exam room, where it would be more private. I shut the door and allowed the male to run free while Harry held the female on the table. Using a small vaginal speculum, I could see all the way to Ella's cervix. There were no obstructions or growths. All appeared normal. I swabbed the vagina with a sterile cotton tipped applicator, smeared the collected mucus on a slide and examined it under the microscope. The field was full of cornified cells with a smattering of leukocytes (white cells). Ella was in full blown heat. I put her on the floor and picked up the male.

Anton was smaller and thinner than his bride. His testicles seemed soft and his prostate was enlarged – all signs of an aging male. I put my stethoscope to his chest. Damn. He even had a heart murmur. You had to wonder about Anton's ability to perform.

"Harry," I said, "listen to this."

Harry listened to Anton's heart, then said, "No wonder the dog's exhausted. I bet he has back problems, too. Now what are we gonna do?"

"Go talk to Gene," I said, "and see if he has any suggestions."

Within minutes, Harry returned.

"What'd he say?" I asked.

"He said masturbate the male and artificially inseminate the female."

"Have you ever masturbated a dog before?"

"No," said Harry. "Have you?"

"Me, neither," I said. "Go back and ask if he'll be more explicit."

"It's your turn," he said.

"All right," I said, and off I went to receive instructions. It didn't take long.

"Now what'd he say?" asked Harry.

"He said to massage the male behind the bulb of the penis and squeeze gently. The stimulation and the hand pressure should help him get an erection."

The four of us, Harry and I and the two dogs, got on the floor. Harry positioned Ella's vulva up to Anton's nose and I stretched out prone alongside. I grasped the base of Anton's penis between the thumb and forefinger of one hand while I held a collecting tube in the other. I worked my hand slowly as Anton eyed me lovingly.

"I think you've made a friend for life," said Harry.

"Just pay attention to what you're doing," I said. I was starting to sweat, while Anton was barely responding.

"Try blowing in his ear," said Harry.

"I can do without the wisecracks," I answered.

Without warning, the door popped open and in strolled Leon. He was giving a client a tour of the hospital. I couldn't stop now. Anton was showing signs of warming up.

"Hey, guys," he said. "Got a minute? I've got a guest I want you to meet."

With Anton's organ still firmly in my grasp I turned my head. In front of my nose were the finest pair of legs I had ever seen. Smooth and sensual, they rose from the floor, disappearing within the confines of a skirt. I pictured them merging into thighs and hips.

"Don't get up, fellows," said Leon. "This is one of our better clients. I thought I'd show her around the hospital."

I let go of Anton's now disinterested penis and stood up. I blushed.

"I'm Arlene Francona," she said.

It was Arlene, the mafia queen, in the flesh. I felt weak in the knees. She was amply proportioned with short, blonde hair that she brushed backwards. She had flashing blue eyes and an impish nose set above provocative lips.

I stuttered. "Nice to meet you, Arlene."

She raised her finger to her lips and said, "Do you mind if I ask you a question, Doctor...uh?"

"Doctor Everson," said Harry, beating me to the punch.

"What were you and that other doctor doing on the floor?"

"Just trying to ejaculate this little male," I said. "He's eleven years old and won't breed naturally."

"Oh, really," she said. "Are you boys good at that sort of thing?"

"Actually it's our first try," said Harry.

"Would you like a suggestion?" she asked.

"Yes ma'am," said Harry, who had taken a fix on her behind.

She cocked her head sideways and then advised, "Try stroking a little faster."

"We've got to be going," interrupted Leon, grinning widely as he ushered her back into the hall. "See you guys later."

"I wonder where she learned that?" said Harry.

"Probably from Leon," I said.

"Wow!" said Harry. "I'd give anything to have a date with her."

"How about your life?" I said.

Harry and I resumed intimate contact with Anton.

"You've got the magic touch," said Harry. "He's getting an erection."

Encouraged by Anton's response, I pumped his organ with increasing fervor, but just as it reached full size, Anton went limp, and so did his penis."

"Oh, my God, you've killed him," said Harry.

"Quick!" I said. "Give him some oxygen. He's turning blue." Hands trembling, I put Anton on the table and felt for his heart. It was beating wildly. I pumped on the dog's chest while Harry hooked up the gas."

"Oh, please, Anton," I cried. "Take a breath!"

"If it's any consolation," commented Harry, "that's a helluva way to go."

"Dammit, Harry. Cut it out. This is serious."

Anton coughed, gasped and then inhaled normally. His color returned and his respiration became regular. "Jesus. He almost died," I said.

"Now what are we going to do?" said Harry. "Mrs. Mouton expects results."

I placed Anton in a cage, for observation. Poor Ella waddled over and stuck her nose through the bars, obviously expressing her sympathy.

Again, I trooped into Gene's room for advice.

"Don't you have any imagination?" he said. "What you need is another male. Go in the kennel and see if you can find a substitute."

"You mean to..."

"To mate with the female," he said, confirming my supposition.

"But we can't do that," I said.

"Who says we can't?" said Dr. Gene.

"But she's bound to find out," I said.

"Who is?" he asked.

"Mrs. Mouton," I said.

"And who's gonna tell? You or the dog?"

Confronted with Gene's argument I accepted his decision and left to find a replacement.

Once back in the kennel, I went cage to cage, searching for the right volunteer. There, depressed and hidden in the rear of his small prison, was Fritz Benoit. As I approached, he stood and wagged his tail. I fastened a leash to his collar. He was overjoyed. He thought he was going home. Discreetly we entered Ella's room and she ran to greet him.

First the two eyeballed each other, then they sniffed noses, then behinds and then the more intimate areas. It was love at first sight. In a flash Fritz had mounted and was pumping for dear life. The affair was consummated in minutes and I waited until the two disengaged. "We've got it made," I said. "Fritz is staying all week. Mrs. Mouton can bring her dogs back for two more visits."

The liaison was a complete success. Mrs. Mouton was especially pleased. "Anton hasn't been the least bit exhausted," she marveled. "He was just wearing himself out at home."

Fritz had a change of heart. He didn't sulk in his cage and his appetite stayed good. Unfortunately, I didn't get to see him leave. Arthur said he had to drag him from his cage.

Ella had seven adorable puppies. Mrs. Mouton observed this was the first time she had bred two silver dapples and had gotten all reds.

I didn't see Mr. Benoit again until two months later. "What did you guys do to Fritz?" he said. "He's a new dog. Now, when I send him to bathe or board, he hops right in the car." He winked. "What do you guys got going, an escort service?"

"I'll never tell," I said. And neither will Fritz.

CARDIAC KIDS

D epending upon the whim of mother nature, a pet born with a congenital defect usually faced an uncertain future. A minor defect like an umbilical hernia was easy and inexpensive to correct, but a more severe problem, like a cleft palate, required sophisticated and costly surgery that was well above the means of the average client. As a rule, animals with the severest of congenital abnormalities mercifully died at birth or soon after, but occasionally they survived, and a decision had to be made whether to treat them or not.

"The LeBreton girls are here," said June, stopping me in the hall. "They've brought a new puppy, and Leon's busy in surgery. Will you examine it?"

The LeBretons lived on a private street adjoining the New Orleans Country Club. Mr. LeBreton was a director of the Whitney National Bank and had major interests in oil and gas. His wife was a socialite, and her picture could often be found in the society section of the New Orleans *Times Picayune*.

They had twin daughters and one aging French poodle, Jean Pierre. I saw the girls infrequently, since Mrs. LeBreton had given orders that only Dr. Gene or Dr. Bob should treat their pet, but today, the two of them were playing golf, and the daughters, who had purchased a new puppy, were given permission by their mother for another doctor to see it. June gave me their card.

The girls were either seventeen or eighteen, possibly college freshmen, and they dressed alike, with walking shorts, deck shoes and lots of gold jewelry. The taller of the two had her sunglasses pushed back in her hair.

"I'm Michelle," said the taller girl. "And she is Lynette."

"And this is Juno," said Lynette as she offered up a rather large puppy, white with black spots. It was a harlequin Dane. A notation on the record said it was twelve weeks old.

"We saw an advertisement in the paper, and we just had to have him. We think he's neat. How big do you think he'll get?"

"Oh, by the size of his paws he could go over a hundred pounds," I said. "But he's got a ways to go. Are you sure you wouldn't rather have another poodle?"

"Like Jean Pierre? He's no fun. Besides, he's Francine's dog."

"Francine?"

"That's our mother," said Michelle.

I wasn't accustomed to children calling their parents by their first name. Somehow it sounded less respectful and I wondered if these modern girls would be responsible pet owners. "Are you girls ready to be parents?" I asked. "Having a new puppy is almost as demanding as having a new baby."

"That's no problem," said Lynette. "Lee Yin looks after him."

"Who's Lee Yin?" I asked.

"That's our houseboy. He's Vietnamese."

I was impressed. I thought houseboys went out with slavery.

"How long have you had Juno?" I asked.

"About two weeks," said Michelle. "The breeder gave us

a seventy-two hour guarantee, provided we had him examined, but he was doing so well we didn't feel it was necessary. Lee Yin said Juno quit eating, so we want you to check him over."

From a distance Juno appeared fine, but as I weighed him, I felt a steady vibration coming from his chest.

"He weighs fourteen pounds," I said. I took him off the scale. "That's a tad light. Have you noticed anything else besides loss of appetite?"

"He seems a little short of breath," said Michelle. "Coughs at night."

I placed my stethoscope at the middle of Juno's ribs. Instead of the rhythmic lub dub of a normal heart there was a constant whoosh, whoosh, audible against the background of fluid crackling in the lungs. The dog was in congestive heart failure.

"Come over here, Lynette," I said. "Put your hands onto Juno's chest and listen." I placed the stethoscope onto her ears and put the bell on Juno's chest again. After she had listened, I did the same for Michelle.

"What's wrong with him?" they asked.

"Juno has a heart murmur. Probably a patent *ductus arteriosus.*"

"You'll have to explain that," said Michelle.

I took a piece of scratch paper and drew a pear-shaped picture representing the heart. "Actually the heart is composed of two pumps," and I drew a line dividing my diagram in half. "The right side of the heart pumps blood to the lungs and the left side carries the oxygenated blood to the rest of the body. Before Juno was born he received enough oxygen from his mother's blood, so he didn't need to use his lungs to breathe. His fetal heart pumped blood directly from the right side of his heart to the aorta, by sending it through this shunt; it has that fancy name, *ductus arteriosus.* When he was born, in fact when all of us are born, this vessel closes and blood flows from the right side of the heart to the lungs, where it absorbs oxygen. Then it returns to the left side of the heart, which pumps it out the aorta and on to the rest of the body."

I elevated Juno's lips. "Just look. A normal pup his age should have rosy gums."

"They certainly aren't pink," said Lynette.

"That's because Juno isn't getting enough oxygen. His *ductus* is still open, or patent, and he's failing to oxygenate properly. Human babies with this same condition are called blue babies."

"But why does he cough?" asked Lynette.

"Because of poor circulation," I said. "The blood stagnates in the lungs and fluid accumulates."

"I still don't understand," she said.

"Have you ever stood for a long period and had your ankles swell?"

"No," said Michelle. "But it happened to my mother. She told us her feet swelled when she was pregnant."

"It's the same thing," I said. "When blood stagnates in your feet, like when you've been standing for a long time, serum seeps into the surrounding tissue, causing the swelling. It's called edema. The same process occurs in Juno's lungs. He feels a heaviness there, so he coughs."

"Last night he coughed so bad I was awake all night," said Michelle. "I had to put him outside."

"Wouldn't you know it?" said Lynette. "Of all the pups we could pick, we chose a dud."

"So what are our alternatives?" asked Michelle. "We can't take him back."

Juno was such a handsome pup, long legged and seemingly growing every second. He had short, sharp puppy teeth that seemed so out of proportion for a dog his size. Except for the extra effort to move air in and out of his lungs, he was perfect. I held him in my arms. It wasn't his fault he was born that way. His hopeful eyes seemed to say, fix me. I took the plunge.

"He needs an operation," I said. "It's risky, but I think we can do it. But it'll be expensive. I guess over three hundred dollars."

The girls looked at each other then agreed on a remedy. "Mother will pay for it," said Michelle.

"So when will he be ready?" asked Lynette.

"Not so fast," I said. "First, we have to confirm the diagnosis, and that means some tests, and of course there's the surgery, and he'll have to convalesce, so it'll be at least two weeks before he goes home, provided everything goes well.

"Can you try to have him ready by the thirtieth?" asked Lynette. "We're having a party and we want to show him off."

"If Juno's not well by then," I said, "he's not going to be ready, ever."

With that understanding, they gave Juno a perfunctory hug and wished him good luck and left. I gave Juno Lasix for the congestion, put him in a cage and went to see June.

"People buy pets for the darndest reasons," I said.

"What are you talking about?" asked June.

"The LeBreton girls," I replied. "They've just bought this new puppy and they treat him as if he were just a novelty."

"Well, Michelle did say they'd bought him because the neighbor up the street has one," said June. "I guess it's fashionable.

"Like gold beads," I said.

"Sure," said June. "Some people just want a pet that'll be the biggest or the weirdest in the neighborhood, and if Juno doesn't meet their standards, they'll buy another. By the way, what's wrong with Juno?"

"Congenital heart defect," I said. "But don't worry. We're going to fix it."

"I didn't know you were a heart surgeon," she said.

"I'm not, but it's a straightforward operation, and I'll get Leon to help."

Actually, I'd never repaired a patent *ductus* before, but I had read of other doctors successfully completing the operation so why couldn't we? It would be good public relations and we'd get a lot of referrals, like Doctor DeBakey.

"I hope you know what you're doing," said June. "The LeBretons are real important clients. "Money talks. You know what I mean?"

"No sweat," I said. "I've got it all under control. Just have Harry and Leon come up and check with me."

"He certainly has a murmur," said Leon as he removed his stethoscope and handed it to Harry. "And it's probably a patent *ductus*," he continued. "But how, Joel, are you going to be sure? You know our x-ray isn't equipped to take serial pictures. What if he has some other defect, like a hole in the septum. You should have consulted me before you told those girls we'd do the surgery. Now they'll expect miracles."

"C'mon, Leon," I said. "You've listened to his heart. What else could it be? We've got to play the odds."

Technically, Leon was correct. Juno could have some other defect, but the dog met all the criteria for a patent *ductus*. In fact, just two plain films of Juno's chest would suffice for a confirmation, yet Leon was being difficult. I was convinced this was the type of operation we younger doctors should attempt. I appealed to his vanity.

"Listen, Leon. Of all the doctors here, only you have the surgical expertise Juno needs to pull him through. How about it?"

Leon grinned. I thought he was coming around. "All right. I'll do it," he said. "But on one condition. That we have serial x-rays of Juno's chest."

I didn't have the slightest idea where to get that done.

"I know where we can get them," said Harry.

"Where?" said Leon.

"At Hotel Dieu," said Harry. "I have a doctor friend, Ron Longley. He's a resident in radiology. I take care of his dogs on the side. He owes me a favor. I'll get him to do it."

"Harry," I complained. "We need a hospital. Not a motel."

"Hotel Dieu is a hospital," said Leon acidly. "It's run by French nuns."

"Pardon me," I said to Leon, in my best Charles Boyer imitation. "Harry, how do we pull this off?"

"Easy," he said. "We'll sneak Juno into the hospital, snap a few pictures and then get the hell out. I'll arrange everything."

"Well, you guys can go ahead and get the pictures," said Leon. He leaned against the wall and folded his arms, "I'm staying here."

"Where's your sense of adventure?" asked Harry. "You're coming, aren't you, Joel?"

"You bet," I said, though without as much enthusiasm as I initially felt. This was getting more complicated than I anticipated. But it was my fault. I said we'd do the surgery, and we couldn't back out now.

That evening Harry and I gave Juno a sedative and an hour later the dog was sleeping soundly. We put him on the rear seat of my car, drove down Tulane Avenue, crossed Jefferson Boulevard and headed for downtown New Orleans. Hotel Dieu loomed straight ahead as Harry and I finalized our plans.

Harry would go in the emergency entrance and commandeer a gurney. Then we'd strap Juno on, connect him to an I.V. and hide him under a green drape. We wore our usual surgical garb: green pants and tops, name tags, radiation monitors and stethoscopes. Radiology was in the basement, and we'd have to ride the elevator down, but it would be smooth sailing after that.

We arrived at RECEIVING and Harry exited while I parked the car. With envy, I watched my accomplice confidently march to the entrance and boldly pass through. I checked the time and waited. Five minutes ticked by. I walked in circles around the car, peering through the window, checking on Juno. I was getting antsy and felt a chill. I had to suppress a desire to use the restroom. At last the doors swung open and Harry reappeared, casually rolling a stretcher back to the car. I was relieved. Suddenly, a voice boomed, "HEY! YOU! WHATTYA DOIN' WITH THAT COT?"

I froze instantly, expecting searchlights and sirens to go off any minute.

"WE'RE BRINGING IN A REFERRAL FROM CHARITY," yelled Harry.

"DO YOU NEED ANY HELP?" the voice thundered back.

I fashioned my hands into a megaphone and drew a mighty breath. "No," I croaked. "We can handle it."

The orderly waved an acknowledgment and retreated inside.

I was shaking as Harry rolled the cart to the car. "Say, Harry," I said, "I'm not so sure about this. What do we do if we get caught?"

"It's too late for cold feet," he scolded. "Besides, you do want to get this dog well, don't you?" Harry waited for my response and then reached in the back seat, lifting the sleeping canine out of the car and onto the stretcher.

"And what about Leon? You're not going to let him off the hook? Look. Just act like you know what you're doing and it'll be a snap." Harry threw me a green drape and I covered Juno over as if he were a corpse.

"See how good that looks," he said. He fixed the I.V. "C'mon. The elevator should be on the right. You push and I'll pull."

Inspired by Harry's pep talk, I rolled our patient to the entrance, on through the swinging doors and into the building.

Just past the foyer, a nurse glanced up at us from an admitting desk, but she asked no questions as we went by, so we pressed on, uninterrupted, down the corridor and over to the elevator, where two other people were waiting – a boy about ten, on crutches with a cast on his leg, and a maintenance man who was polishing the floors. His machine droned around him in lazy, circular patterns.

"Ya'll going up or down?" the man asked.

"We're going to radiology," I said.

"That'd be down then." He pressed the button to summon the elevator. Then he made a sweep with his buffer.

"Y'all must be new," he said.

"Right," said Harry. "We've been on obstetrics all week."

Harry's ability to lie just amazed me.

The boy pointed to the gurney with his crutch. "What's wrong with the kid? He sure is tiny."

"Born deformed," I said, biting my lip. "You wouldn't want to look."

"He doesn't even look human," added Harry.

The youngster cringed. I laughed to myself. Children will believe anything.

DING. The elevator doors retreated into the walls and a nurse stepped off and rushed toward the emergency entrance. Harry followed her progress down the hall until she disappeared. Then we maneuvered the cot onto the elevator. I thought we would be alone, but the kid decided to hop on just before the doors started to close.

The elevator lurched as it started down and I felt Juno shift to one side. I glanced nervously at Harry, who smiled back and gave me a thumbs up sign, and then I looked at the dial which designated the floor, hoping it would hurry up and do its thing. Finally, I looked at the kid. His eyes were big as moons. Juno's tail was protruding from under the cover.

"Say, mister," he said suspiciously. "Do you really...?"

DING. The elevator bounced to a stop and the doors reopened. "C'mon, Harry. This is where we get off."

We angled the stretcher across the threshold and cruised down the hall, leaving the kid behind. Radiology was two doors down. We flew into the waiting room, where a young man wearing a white coat was filling out records. When he saw Harry the two of them leaped in the air, swapping high fives. Harry had a medical clone.

"We made it!" he said.

"I told you you could do it," said the gentleman. "Where's our patient?"

I pointed to the lump under the drape.

"I'm Ron Longley," he said.

I introduced myself as Harry and I positioned the gurney alongside the x-ray table.

"Did you guys have any trouble sneaking him in?" asked Ron.

"Just right at the – "

"It was a cinch," interrupted Harry. "You're lucky this place isn't a bank."

I uncovered Juno, who was still sleeping soundly.

"He's beautiful," said Ron. "My uncle raised Danes when I was a kid. They're wonderful dogs."

While Ron flipped switches to activate the machine, Harry and I placed a catheter in Juno's jugular, connecting it to a syringe filled with radiopaque dye. We would inject the dye right into the vein, which would carry it directly to the heart, all the while the machine would take pictures, out-lining the course of blood through Juno's heart. We put on lead aprons and took up our positions.

"Are ya'll ready?" asked Ron.

I signaled we were.

"Okay," said Ron. "Shoot!"

Harry squeezed in the plunger as the x-ray hummed and clicked and then whined down and shut off.

"The film develops automatically," said Ron. "We'll have pictures in five minutes. You can relax."

I felt silly as I blew out a chest full of air.

"It's a patent *ductus* all right," said Ron, as we viewed the pictures together. "Looks the same way in babies. See. Here's the connection. Right between the pulmonary artery and the aorta."

"That's what we came for," I said. "Pardon us for not stay-ing, Ron, but we need to get out of here." Juno had began to tremble, which meant the sedation was wearing off.

"Oh, sure," he said. "Just go back the same way you came." He handed us the films.

Harry and I returned Juno to his cot and I covered him again with his drape. Ron stuck his head out the doorway and indicated the coast was clear, so we sped to the elevator and pressed the page.

DING. The doors rolled back once more revealing a pas-senger, the kid with the crutches. Seeing us, he decided not to get off. We ignored him and pushed the cot onto the ele-vator. Then we closed the doors and waited for the inevita-ble, which came right away.

"Say, mister," asked the kid. "Is that a dog under there?"

I didn't know how to answer, but Harry had a way with children. He took a pencil from his pocket and snapped it in two as he said, "If you say one word I'll break your other leg."

DING. We were back on the emergency floor. My heart was pounding. We were going to do it. I was thrilled. I gave the kid a threatening last look, and Harry and I barreled down the hall, heading for the exit, which loomed larger and larger. Suddenly a figure all dressed in white floated out of a side room and blocked our way.

"Oh, Jesus," moaned Harry. "It's a nun."

"Excuse me," she said, holding her hand like a traffic cop.

We put on the brakes.

"Could one of you interns assist us? We're swamped with deliveries and all our residents are busy."

"Here's your volunteer," said Harry, pushing me to the front. "Dr. Goldman just got off obstetrics.

Dumbfounded, I followed the nun as Harry and Juno passed safely through the swinging doors. "You'll be assisting Dr. Rosenberg," the nun advised, and she conducted me into an emergency room. We threaded our way around infant incubators, I.V. stands, instrument trays and cardiac monitors. Then a scrub nurse pointed me in the direction of a sink. "Wash your hands over here," she ordered, "and put this on." She threw me a surgical cap and gown. After I scrubbed my hands and arms she helped me put on gloves and led me to Dr. Rosenberg, who was standing by a woman in labor.

Dr. Rosenberg read my name tag. "Are you related to Danny Goldman?" he asked. Danny Goldman was a prominent New Orleans OB-GYN. I was always getting his calls.

"No relation," I said.

"No matter," he said, and he apprised me of the situation. "Mrs. Lewis's baby is making normal progress, but it's been slow, so we're giving pitocin to speed things along. Excuse me a second. Bear down, Mrs. Lewis, you're doing great. Now, Dr. Goldman. Here, put one hand under the baby's head and get ready to put the other under its arms after I turn its shoulders."

With some misgivings I started to follow his instructions, but what I saw next stopped me dead in my tracks. Mrs. Lewis was naked.

"What's the problem? asked Dr. Rosenberg.

"None, sir," I said, trying not to get rattled. "No problem at all."

Keeping my eyes squarely on the baby, I stepped into the inner sanctum between Mrs. Lewis's thighs and pretended I was pulling a calf. I cradled the child's head. It was wet and slippery, just like all newborns.

"How am I doing?" grimaced Mrs. Lewis.

The baby's shoulders popped through.

"You're doing fine," I said. "I can see the head and front legs."

"We don't think much of comedians," growled Rosenberg. Then he asked, "How much pitocin would you give to induce contractions?"

I stuttered and stammered and spit out the first dosage I could remember. "Uh . . . at least a hundred units."

"God damn!" he bellowed. "That's enough for a horse!"

Dr. Rosenberg slandered the L.S.U. med school and then returned to Mrs. Lewis, who was straining once more. "One more good push, Mrs. Lewis. That's it . . . you're doing fine . . . a little bit more . . . you're almost there . . . support the baby with both hands, Doctor Goldman . . . there we go . . . It's a boy! Let's have someone tell Mr. Lewis."

"I'll do it," I said. I handed the baby to the nurse and sped out of the delivery room, raced down the hallway, through the exit and into the parking lot. Harry was waiting in the car. The man was hysterical.

"What did she have?" he asked between laughs.

"It was a boy," I said.

"Do you think she'll name it after you? Ha, ha, ha, ha, ha."

"I don't know about that," I said, "But I can tell you one thing for sure."

"What's that?"

"If I get sick, don't take me to that hospital. They got some crazy doctors working there."

The next morning a sense of forboding pervaded the hospital. Even the kennel boys were subdued. Normally we would exchange jokes and small talk, but today everyone was somber and serious.

"The old man has Doc Leon on the carpet," said Arthur. "Best be careful what you do."

When Bob was in a bad mood, everyone steered clear, since the slightest error could provoke a tempest on our heads as well. I had often been the target of his wrath, but Leon always managed to stay out of trouble. I could hear through the door.

"Leon," growled Bob, "when Gene and I are gone, you're supposed to be in charge. Is that too little to ask?"

"Of course not, but – "

"Let me finish!" snapped Bob. "Don't you think I should be informed of critical decisions that affect me and my clients?"

"Yessir," whimpered Leon.

"Then why is it that every time I take the day off, someone else has to tell me what's going on at my hospital?"

"Who told you – ?"

"Wait 'til I'm through!" roared Bob. "Are you aware that I was playing golf with Mr. LeBreton, when out of the blue he tells me we're doing heart surgery on his daughters' great Dane, and I know we've *never* done heart surgery in the history of this practice!"

"But – "

"Don't interrupt!"

Bob stopped to catch his breath. "When he told me I nearly had a heart attack! Is that what you want? Speak up!

I want an answer!"

I drew closer to the door.

"That was all Joel and Harry's doings," whined Leon.

"JOEL and HARRY!" Bob became even more animated with the prospect of fresh meat. He got on the intercom. "June! Have Dr. Everson and Dr. Goldman report to the office! Immediately!"

I waited for Harry and we walked in together, like two condemned prisoners.

"What in hell have you clowns been up to?" barked Bob.

"Dr. Williams says you're going to operate on Mr. LeBreton's Dane."

"The dog has a patent *ductus arteriosus*," I placidly explained. "He needs an operation, or else he's going to die."

"And I guess that you budding Denton Cooleys are going to do the surgery?" added Bob.

"Together with Leon," I said. "He volunteered to help if we confirmed the diagnosis."

"And we have the films right here," said Harry. "We took them at Hotel Dieu." Harry dangled them in front of the boss, like a matador waving his cape in front of the bull.

"I must be going crazy," shouted Bob. "I've hired two complete lunatics!" He threw his hands up in the air and shook his head. Then surprisingly he said, "All right. Let me see the pictures."

I put the films on the viewer and Bob studied them intently. "What's this line here, Joel?" He pointed to a streak outlined on a film.

"That's the patent *ductus*," I said proudly.

Bob paged Gene over the intercom and moments later Gene ambled in. "These are films of one of our client's dogs," said Bob. "Give me a second opinion."

Gene scrutinized each film one by one. Then he went over the group again, but this time more quickly, sort of shuffling them like cards, and then a final check, again one after the other.

"These are great films," said Gene. "Where'd you get them?"

"We took them at Hotel Dieu," said Leon. "We have a friend in radiology."

I looked up at the ceiling.

"So what do you think?" asked Harry.

Gene cleared his throat and answered, "Cardiac hypertrophy . . . ummm, secondary to a patent *ductus*. Bob and I always refer these to the veterinary school."

"Why refer it when we can repair it?" I argued. "We've got all the surgical equipment. I know we can fix it."

"Whose dog is this?" asked Gene.

"Edwin LeBreton's," said a sanguine Bob. "Joel admitted it for surgery."

"Uh oh," winced Gene. "That's not an easy decision." He thought it over then reexamined the radiographs for the longest time, and finally, gave his opinion. "As long as the owners are aware of the risk and it's agreeable with Bob, it's fine with me. But this has to be a major team effort."

Bob rubbed his hand on his forehead, pondering the situation. Then he made his move. He gave instructions to June. "Get on the phone and cancel all of tomorrow's surgery, and if anyone asks why, tell them we're doing a heart operation."

I drifted out of the office, content with the verdict, and walked back to the kennel to give Arthur instructions on how to prep Juno for surgery. Arthur was fiddling with his grooming shears.

"I hear Bob's going to let ya'll operate on Mr. LeBreton's dog," he said. "That shows what the old man really thinks of you . . . and Leon and Harry," and he winked at me and got on with his chores.

Arthur's comment was more than welcome news, but my

accountability seemed to weigh even heavier that ever.

Beep beep beep beep beep beep beep beep. The heart monitor assured that all was well with Juno. He was lying left side up, completely covered with surgical drapes, with a tube down his trachea and I.V.s in his veins. Harry monitored the anesthesia, Leon acted as chief surgeon and I was assistant surgeon. Standing by in advisory capacity was Gene, while Doctor Bob alternated between exam rooms and surgery, seeing walk-in patients and checking on our progress.

Leon had made a long incision between Juno's third and fourth ribs. Only the thin, clear pleural membrane separated us from Juno's thoracic organs. Leon alerted Harry, "Start breathing for Juno...now!"

Leon cut through the pleura, breaking the vacuum, and the lungs shrunk down like a compressed sponge. Harry began rhythmically squeezing the air bag, and Juno's chest rose and fell in time with his efforts.

I gently moved two lung lobes aside, so we could see the heart. It was beating normally as waves of contractions rippled down its base and over its surface. The *ductus* should be just above the heart, in the middle of a maze of other major vessels that carried blood either to the lungs, the aorta or back to the heart itself. Adding to the crowded conditions, the esophagus and branches of the trachea were in the same area. A thick band of connective tissue held everything in place. Leon carefully peeled that covering aside. It took about fifteen minutes. He was sweating. "I can't find the damn *ductus*," he said. "Take a look, and see what you think."

I peered into the gap. I couldn't distinguish one vessel from another. "The diagrams in the book never look anything like the real thing," I said, disgusted.

"So where do we go from here?" asked Harry.

"I've got a suggestion," said Gene. "Put your finger on a

vessel and see if you can tell if it's causing the thrill. It should come off here," and he pointed in the direction of the pulmonary artery.

Leon reached in with his hand as Harry and Gene and I leaned over to get a better view. I was so tense I almost quit breathing. The constant beeping of the monitor only added to the suspense. We waited while Leon searched. Beep beep beep beep KWHAM!

"How's he doing, how's he doing?" It was Bob. He'd slammed the door open, and it had bounced off the wall.

"Damn!" said Leon, shaking like a nervous pup. "Next time, please knock." Harry suppressed a chuckle, and then we regrouped.

Again, Leon reached in and felt for the *ductus*, while we waited expectantly. The corners of Leon's mouth arched upwards behind his mask. He was smiling. "I've got it," he said. "Here, Joel. Put your finger on it."

Leon guided my hand to the source of Juno's trouble. The artery shivered with each pulse as it conducted its tremors throughout the chest wall. I pinched the vessel closed and the vibration stopped.

"That's it," I said.

"Good work," sighed Bob.

"Now all we have to do is tie it off," I said.

"Use umbilical tape," said Bob, handing us the ribbon-like suture. "It won't cut through."

Leon took the suture, which was used more often for large animals and tied off the *ductus* in two places. Then he picked up his scissors. "Here goes," he said, and he snipped the vessel in half, in between the two knots. A trace of red welled into the cut ends, but then subsided. The sutures were holding. "Let's close up," said Bob. "I think we've got a winner."

Harry, Leon and I completed the operation while the Burruses left to tend to outpatients. We sutured Juno's chest closed and reinflated his lungs. Then we placed him in intensive care. After we'd finished, June came to see me.

"There's someone here to see Juno," she said.

"Who is it?" I asked.

"Some man and, I guess, his son," said June. "They're Oriental."

I had June send them back to the office.

They were dressed alike, very neat and clean with short sleeve white shirts and khaki pants. The man was in his early thirties and the boy was seven or eight.

"I'm Lee Yin," the man said. "This is my son, Lee Diem. We would like permission to visit Juno."

I was pleasantly surprised. "Certainly," I said. "He's fresh out of surgery, so he'll still be asleep, but you're welcome to come with me and see him."

I led them to Juno's cage, where the two of them crouched down to get a better look. The boy spoke rapidly. He gestured and pointed, ooing and aaahing over the dog, and then after checking with me, reached through the bars and began petting Juno's face.

Lee Yin then spoke. "Ever since Michelle and Lynette get this dog, my son become very attached. I fond of Juno, too. He will be all right, yes?"

I nodded that he would.

"Oh, very good," he said. "We worry about him a lot."

I was genuinely pleased. At least someone in the LeBreton household really cared about the dog, and with Lee Yin, I could feel more confident about Juno's future.

"Juno'll be here for a week," I said, "and then he'll go home, but you can visit as often as you like." Mr. Lee passed the message to his son, which served to initiate another round of excited chatter, so I went into the office. Bob was on the phone, talking to Mr. LeBreton.

"Edwin," he said, "you can tell the girls everything went well and they can expect to take Juno home in a week.

Noooo. It all went off without a hitch. You bet. We do
everything the M.D.s do...yep...uh, huh...see ya at the
club."

He hung up the phone and leaned back in his chair, folding his arms behind his head. Bob was pleased as punch,
and so was I.

Juno healed quickly, as all youngsters seem to do, and
his cough disappeared. Lee Yin and his son visited every
afternoon, and I had Diem take Juno for walks. Juno would
run around in circles, dragging Diem over the hospital
grounds or getting him entangled in the leash. Diem
squealed each time Juno licked him on the face or knocked
him down. They were fun to watch.

Michelle and Lynette called to say they were going across
the lake to spend time at their summer house. They hoped
to do some skiing and would I please deliver Juno whenever he was ready. Two weeks before the girls' deadline, I
took Juno home.

The LeBretons lived close to Long Vue Gardens, in a
swanky part of town. I drove into their circular, pebble-
stoned driveway and parked behind a BMW. Between the
house and the drive was a live fountain, flanked by Grecian
statuary. The entrance was bordered by abundant growths
of azaleas and gardenias. The house was built French country style – two story, with a mansard roof and a shield
carved above the front door. I rang the front doorbell and
Lee Yin answered.

"Oh. Doctor Goldman, you bring Juno home. I have
everything in order. This way, please."

Juno tugged at his leash and dragged me inside to a foyer
lined with Italian marble. Then Lee Yin led me past stately
panelled rooms graced with oil paintings and on through a
long hallway floored with polished cedar and highlighted
with Persian rugs. Eventually, we passed through the
kitchen and into a large laundry room.

"This is my office," said Lee Yin. "I have Juno's food and water right here. You tell me what I need to do. Hokay?"

"There's nothing special you need to do," I said. "Just feed him normally." I gazed through a window into beautiful gardens and a gorgeous swimming pool. I was dazzled.

"Are you the only one here?" I asked.

"Yes, Doctor Goldman. Mr. and Mrs. LeBreton gone to farm near Hominy."

Hominy? I didn't know of any town in Louisiana named Hominy, but it seemed plausible. I thought for a moment, and then laughed.

"Oh. You mean Harmony." Harmony was a small town on the Mississippi, north of Baton Rouge, in Feliciana parish. There were lots of old homes and plantations around Harmony.

"Pardon my English, Doctor Goldman. I still working to speak better."

"That's all right," I said. "You're doing just fine."

I had liked Lee Yin from our first meeting, and his faulty pronunciation only made me like him more. Curious about his background, I asked, "How did you wind up in America?"

Lee sat down next to Juno, who paused from eating just long enough to give his caretaker a lick on the hand. "My family fishermen in Saigon," he said. "We escape to Singapore after Viet Cong take South. I work very hard and apply for visa to come to United States. It was very difficult."

"I bet it was," I said. "Are you settled in now?"

"Oh, yes," he said. "We have small house in New Orleans East, near Chef Menteur Highway. My wife and older daughter work in seafood plant. They clean crabs and crawfish. We good at that."

"How does Lee Diem Like America?" I asked.

"He have hard time in school and not have many friends," he said. "The children make fun of him because of the way he talk, but he like Juno very much. Juno good friend for Lee Diem."

As if to second Lee Yin's comments, Juno glanced up from his dish, catching my eye, but just as quickly he returned to eating.

I knew there was a large Vietnamese community in New Orleans. The climate, the proximity to the gulf and the opportunity to get in the fishing business attracted them.

"One day I earn enough money to buy boat," he said.

"I bet you will," I said, and I got up to leave. "Tell the girls to take good care of Juno," I said. "If you notice anything out of the ordinary, call me right away."

"I tell them," he said. "They still across lake, but they be home this weekend. They planning big party at end of month. It's for birthday."

I gave the house a final once over. "I'm sure it'll be quite a bash," I said. I walked to the front door and out to my car. "Say hello to Diem," I said as I waved goodbye.

The end of the month fell on a Sunday and I had the weekend duty. I had just completed morning rounds when Michelle called about an emergency. She said Lynette was coming right over with Juno and wanted to be sure a doctor was available. I told her I would wait outside in case her sister needed help.

I watched Lynette's car swerve onto our parking lot and skid to a stop. I opened her car door and found Juno lying on the back seat, limp, cold and soaking wet.

"Is he dead?" she asked, a tremor in her voice.

"Damn near," I said, gritting my teeth. I could feel a faint heartbeat, but the dog's tongue was blue and his eyes were dilated – an ominous sign. I hauled him inside as Lynette hurried to keep up. I yelled to Arthur, "Give me a hand!"

We placed Juno face down on a tilted table and cupfuls

of water ran out of his mouth. "Bring me a suction bottle and a trachea tube. Quick!"

I closed Juno's mouth and breathed into his nose. His chest rose and fell, and now water started pouring out of his nostrils, too. "Hurry, Arthur!" I screamed. I injected a respiratory stimulant into a vein. Then I passed a tube down Juno's trachea, so Arthur could administer oxygen. I continued giving artificial respiration, raising and lowering Juno's chest, up and down, up and down.

"Breathe, Juno, breathe... please," whimpered Lynette. She clutched her hands together and started to cry.

I had almost given up when, abruptly, Juno retched, and then vomited, gurgled and finally took a deep breath. I suctioned out more water, and by then his color had improved, though his chest rattled every time he took a breath. I dried him thoroughly, injected him with a massive dose of antibiotic and finally placed him in a heated intensive care cage. I watched over him for signs of consciousness, but he remained comatose. I had done all that was possible and now it was a question of time.

"He'll be all right, won't he?" sniffled Lynette.

"I don't know," I said. "It's out of my hands. Could you tell me what happened?"

"Last night was our party," she said, wiping her eyes, "and we let Juno run around. We wanted everyone to see him. I guess it got a little wild." She reached for a chair and sat down, a blank expression on her face. "I really can't remember. I must have passed out."

"Where were your parents?"

"They went out for the evening," she said. She sniffled. "They never stay home anymore."

She reached in her bag for some Kleenex.

"I found Juno floating in the pool," she said. "He must have fallen in and couldn't get out." She blew her nose and dabbed at a tear.

I was in no mood to sympathize. I wondered how long Juno struggled just to tread water, hoping he'd be spotted before he became exhausted. Then I looked at Lynette. Where was her common sense? Without realizing what I was doing, I said what I was thinking.

"Don't you girls have any brains? A four-month-old pup has the maturity of a six-year-old!" I banged on the table and Lynette's eyes opened wide. "YOU were responsible for this dog's welfare, and YOU blew it!" She rose form her chair, backed away and cowered in a corner, while I continued blasting. "If Juno were human YOU'd be liable for CHILD abuse! You ought to have your butt kicked."

That made Lynette cry even more, and before I could apologize she ran out of the hospital. I heard her start her car and drive away.

"It's been nice knowing you, Doc," said Arthur. "When Mr. LeBreton tells the old man how you treated his daughter you'll be joining the ranks of unemployed."

I didn't care. Lynette and her sister had been irresponsible. I had gone to extraordinary efforts to get the dog well, and she and her sister had thrown that all away.

I stayed at the hospital all morning observing Juno's status. At noon I sent out for lunch. By six that evening the dog had started to whine and was shaking all over. He was slowly regaining consciousness. When Duane came on for the nightshift I instructed him as to what to expect and then I went home.

That evening I planned my rebuttal to Mr. LeBreton's charges, but nothing I thought of seemed appropriate. I had violated the first rule of merchandising: "The customer is always right." But we weren't running a store, or were we? I decided to see the boss early in the morning and get my two cents in, before the LeBretons did.

"What happened to our Great Dane?" asked Harry.

"Yeah,"said Leon. "He's just barely hanging in there.

"I'll tell you later," I said. "Is Bob here?"

"He's in the office," said Harry. "He's talking to Francine LeBreton. She called first thing this morning."

My heart sunk at the news.

"Did I say something wrong?" asked Harry.

"I've probably lost my job," I said. I explained what happened to Juno and my blowup with Lynette.

"You can always go back to teaching," said Leon.

Harry was more sympathetic. "As far as I know you still have a job. Why don't you check on Juno?"

Harry's optimistic approach cheered me, so I walked back into the wards. Juno was lying on his side. He blew bubbles from his nose and coughed incessantly. The dog had pneumonia. I was just thinking how unnecessary it all was when I heard a voice from behind.

"How's he doing?" It was Bob. It was nice of him to ask about Juno, just before he gave me the axe, but I dismissed his civility as coincidental and steeled myself for the final blow.

"I heard he had quite a night," he said.

"Yessir. The LeBreton girls found him floating in their pool. I guess you know..."

"I know all about it. What are you doing for him?"

"He's on cephalexin four times a day, plus a vaporizer, heating pad and oxygen."

We discussed other facts of Juno's treatment and then Bob said he'd have Leon x-ray Juno's chest. He wanted to determine the degree of pneumonia and note any changes since the dog's recent operation. Satisfied, he went about his business, postponing my dismissal until closing time. Late that afternoon, Lee Yin came to visit.

"Mrs. LeBreton tell me about Juno," he said. "My son very upset and want to come, but I make him stay home until I talk to you."

I motioned for him to follow me back to Juno's cage. The

dog was surrounded by oxygen tanks, vaporizing equipment and other medical paraphenalia adding to an already dismal picture.

"Juno no look good." said Lee Yin, sadly.

"He may not survive," I said. "He's got a severe case of pneumonia."

"He no going to die," he said. "You good doctors. You save him. Now I say prayer for Juno." Lee Yin began chanting in a monotone. I felt self-conscious and left.

Juno spent the next week in the intensive care cage. Each day he progressed, bit by bit, but it was a struggle. The slightest exertion would provoke Juno into violent fits of coughs and hacks, but with time this diminished, and – as Juno's radiographs visibly confirmed – his lungs began to clear. Again Lee Diem was allowed to visit, and soon he and Juno were taking their walks as before. Bob still hadn't fired me, but I knew he hadn't forgotten. The man had the memory of an elephant.

Strangely enough, I never saw or heard from the LeBreton girls until the day Juno was to go home.

"Bob wants to see you," said June. "He's in his exam room with Juno and the LeBreton sisters. Their mother is with them, too."

I was perplexed. Why would Bob wait until now to nail me? Perhaps he wanted to be sure Juno would recover, and then he'd have me canned. Apprehensively, I walked in. Bob spoke first.

"Joel. Except for Mrs. LeBreton, I think you know everyone."

I turned to face Mrs. LeBreton, a tall, striking woman, with sharp, pointed features. She wore a hat and gloves.

"Lynette and Michelle have something to say," she said. She flashed her eyes in their direction. "Isn't that right, girls?"

"Yes ma'am," they said obediently.

Lynette, acting as spokesperson, coughed nervously. She never looked up. "Michelle and I have thought this over," she said. "Since we don't have time to care for Juno the way we should," she licked her lips and swallowed hard, "we've decided to give him to Lee Yin."

"That's wonderful," I said, trying to be restrained. "I know he and his son will be thrilled. His boy just dotes on the dog. I think they'll be perfect for each other."

"Well, I guess that's about it," said Michelle, who was fidgeting with her sunglasses.

"Not quite," said Mrs. LeBreton. "There's one more thing."

"And we want to apologize for being so irresponsible," said Lynette. "Next time we'll try to be better parents."

I nodded my head in acceptance, and the five of us stood there, mired in awkward silence, until Bob, sensing an end to the conversation, indicated the meeting was over. He escorted the family outside.

I was vindicated. I went to the front desk to tell June, and maybe get some answers. "I still can't figure why I didn't get in trouble," I said.

"It's simple," said June. "Mrs. LeBreton's no fool. Bob threatened to tell Mr. LeBreton how Juno got sick in the first place. And if you think Bob has a temper you should hear Mr. LeBreton, especially when his kids mess up."

Just then, Lee Yin and his son came in. Diem was carrying a brand new leash and collar. He ran to the back, where Juno was kenneled. I've never seen a kid more excited.

"Oh, we very happy now," said Lee Yin. "This best hospital in whole state, and you doctors...best in U.S.A."

"That's right," I said, as Bob returned from outside. I took our senior vet by the arm. He seemed befuddled as I led him to Lee Yin, who was beaming. "And this man here," I proclaimed in pidgin English, "is smartest doctor in whole world."

Lee Yin and his family still live in New Orleans East, where he operates a shrimp boat. Last I heard, Juno is still alive and doing well.

CROSSED
CIRCUIT

The average bitch will come in heat twice a year, gloriously announced by a bloody vulvar discharge and grossly swollen genitalia. It's the uncommon female who undergoes a season without showing some of these signs, but whenever one does, she poses significant problems for breeders and veterinarians alike. Gretchen LeDoux was one of these, a three-year-old female schnauzer who suffered from silent heat cycles.

Gretchen's owners were anxious to have puppies, so Bob suggested I try a new oral estrogen, hoping it would induce an estrus cycle that would be easy to detect. I prescribed the medication with guarded expectations and waited to hear from the owners. Harry and I were in the pharmacy filling out prescriptions when I finally got the call.

DOCTOR GOLDMAN. DOCTOR GOLDMAN. PICK UP LINE ONE. DOCTOR GOLDMAN, YOU'RE WANTED ON LINE ONE.

"This is Doctor Goldman," I said, balancing the phone between my head and neck.

"This is Mrs. LeDoux," the voice answered.

I switched her to the intercom so my hands would be free.

"I've been waiting to hear from you," I said. "How are

we doing?"

"Terrible," she said. "I've never seen such spotting."

Estrogen therapy stimulates vaginal bleeding, sometimes to excess, so her complaint wasn't unexpected.

"It's a side effect of the hormone," I said. "Cut the pills in half."

"I can't break them, she said. "They're hard as rocks."

Did I ever feel stupid. The pills had been sealed in an aluminum foil wrapper and I wasn't at all familiar with their coating. Harry made a face at me as if I was the village idiot. I grasped for a remedy.

"Then crush them up and use the powder. You can sprinkle it on some food – use something sticky – like peanut butter." I scanned the shelves for a medicine bottle while I waited for her reply.

"Smooth or crunchy?" she said hesitantly.

"Either one," I said. "It doesn't make any difference." I filled a vial with tablets and snapped it closed.

"Is this related to some medical breakthrough?" she asked.

"Oh, no," I said. "We do it all the time."

"You're the doctor," she said. "But I'm getting tired of changing Kotex."

Some clients diapered a bitch in season with sanitary pads firmly positioned by a lady's undergarment, but as a rule most dogs don't tolerate them. Nevertheless, I was fascinated with her success and asked, "How do you get the pads to stay?"

"With a sanitary belt," she said. "What else?"

"Beats me," I said. "Most of my patients tear them off and eat them."

I thought the line had gone dead. At last she replied, "Is there anything else you need to know?" She sounded impatient.

Harry leaned against the wall, arms folded, intent on

catching her every word. I turned around so I didn't have to look at him. I went on with my questions.

"Have you noticed any nausea?"

"No."

"Umm . . . puffy skin?"

"No."

"Breast enlargement?"

Mrs. LeDoux tittered. "Yes," she said. "But my husband thinks it's great."

Harry was beyond stopping. He shoved me aside, facing the intercom as he blared, "He's got to be a weirdo!"

"I beg your pardon!" croaked Mrs. LeDoux.

Harry and I laughed so hard we had to put the woman on hold.

"I'm sorry, Mrs. LeDoux. We got cut off. Listen. Are you the Mrs. LeDoux with the Schnauzer named Gretchen?"

There was a period of quiet followed by Mrs. LeDoux's tentative response, "No, but we do have a Peke-a-Poo named Susie."

Harry doubled over in hysterics while Mrs. LeDoux was demandingly indignant.

"Aren't you Doctor Danny Goldman, the OB-GYN?"

"No, ma'am," I said. "This is Doctor Joel Goldman, the veterinarian."

"Oh, my God. I've called the wrong number."

CLICK.

HOW I
GOT TO TEXAS

The practice in New Orleans was demanding. I left the house by seven in the morning and didn't return until seven at night. I stood emergency duty every Wednesday plus a Saturday and Sunday stint every fifth weekend. But in spite of the rigorous routine, I was enjoying my work more than ever. First, I was being adequately compensated, and second, the praise of satisfied clients was feeding my ego. The practice became an addiction. As I spent less time at home, Kay began to resent my workaholic attitude, especially when I tended to glorify my role to the detriment of hers. She argued that she was raising the children alone and they'd grow up without knowing their father. I believed I was only doing what a good father should do, work hard and earn a living. And I was perfectly happy with my professional arrangement. She wished I had a practice of my own. For a while our differences led only to minor quarrels, but eventually our squabbles reached a crisis.

"I'm taking the children to visit Mother," she said.

"Is your mom sick?" I asked.

"No," she said. "You've been so busy with your work I decided to spend a few weeks with her until you decide who comes first. The practice or us."

Kay had made idle threats in the past. I didn't take her seriously.

"When are you going?"

"This weekend," she said. "I've made reservations."

I was shocked.

"How long are you going to be gone?"

"Six weeks," she said.

"Six weeks?"

"Yes. Do you think you can handle it?"

"I don't know why not," I said. "I managed before we got married." The moment the words left my mouth I was sorry, but inside I was steaming and I wasn't in the mood to apologize.

On Sunday I took the family to the airport. The girls were excited, but I acted as if it were like a funeral. All along I thought Kay and I would be reconciled, but now I knew she really meant business. After a wistful hug, she told me to get my priorities in order, and when I did, she and the girls would come home. Then the three of them boarded the plane for Texas while I went home to a house full of pets: three Shetland Sheepdogs – Wendy, Duke and George – and three cats – Sunshine and Rummager, a mother and daughter calico pair, and A&P, a gray-stripe shorthair that Kay found wandering in a grocery store parking lot.

Sensing I was lonely, the animals did their best to console me. The dogs lay on the floor on either side of my chair, occasionally rising to paw at my feet and whine, while the cats draped themselves over the edge of the sofa or jumped in my lap, begging to be petted. They were helpful in their own special way, but things weren't quite the same. The days dragged on aimlessly. I was glad to see Monday, even though I overslept.

"Where have you been?" asked Harry. "You're almost an hour late. Leon's been asking about you."

"Kay's gone to visit her mom. I forgot to set the alarm."

"I told him you called in with car trouble," said Harry.
"He'll buy that," I said. South Louisiana's high humidity was always causing havoc with my points and condenser. I perused the hospital roster. "Anything exciting happen this weekend?"

The usual," he said. "Two dogs with broken legs, a Poodle with a crushed chest – it fell from a second story balcony and a pet shop pup with Giardia. And we lost Jeanie, the Mulligan's Beagle."

"Do the owners know?"

"I've been calling since Sunday. They were supposed to go out of town."

Jeanie's kidneys had been failing for some time. With dialysis treatments and diligent nursing, the dog had overcome several life-theatening crises, for which we of course were thankful, but unfortunately the animal's tenacity for life only spurred false hopes that ultimately she could be cured. I had been realistic and told the Mulligans that Jeanie's future was bleak, yet they persisted in maintaining an optimistic outlook and fervently believed their pet would eventually get well.

Once, when Jeanie first suffered a kidney attack, Dr. Bob advised that the dog would not survive, but Mrs. Mulligan remained oblivious to the prognosis, requesting us instead to cut the dog's toe nails before we sent it home. I thought she acted stupidly, but Dr. Bob said it was Mrs. Mulligan's way of coping with the inevitable. She practiced self-denial. Now her pet was dead. I groaned.

"You look like you had a rough night," said Harry.

"With the kids gone, all the animals wanted to sleep with me. They kept jumping on and off the bed."

"Bob and Gene won't be in 'til nine," he said. "Get a cup of coffee and you can start the front. Leon and I can handle the in-patients."

Seeing clients was what I enjoyed most. I filled my cup,

walked past the admitting desk, where June handed me the first client's card, and escaped to my exam room to study the record. The admitting history indicated that the patient was a ten-week-old Norwegian Elkhound puppy and that the owner, a certain J.L. Foret, lived across the river in the New Orleans suburb of Algiers.

"Aiyaiyai!" announced the arrival of Fidel, my assistant for the day. "Doctor Goldman," he said. "What a weekend I had at the dog show." Fidel was a single, exuberant, macho twenty-one-year-old who raised show quality Salukis. He worked for us as a kennel boy. His parents were refugees from Cuba.

I was only half interested as I asked, "Did your dog score lots of points?"

"We both did. Natasha made it to the finals and I scored big time with a broad that showed English Bulldogs."

I asked nonchalantly, "Did she look like one?"

He turned up his nose. "You know me better than that."

Then he outlined the shape of an hourglass with his hands. "She was a fox."

I sighed. "You and your one night stands."

"Everybody does it," he said. "It's free. All you have to do is ask."

"Grow up," I said.

"I have," he said. He strutted like a banty rooster. "That's why the girls like me."

I threw a paper wad at him but Fidel ducked and left to call in the client. Moments later he returned with a tall, slender brunette who said, "I'm Jacqueline Foret."

I was speechless. Finally she said, "Is something wrong?"

I held the card up so she could see it. "The front desk abbreviated your name. I guess I was expecting someone else." I smiled and she smiled back.

Jacqueline wore a skin-tight leotard top and snug blue jeans that displayed her lithesome figure without being lewd. She was animated and fresh and wore her hair in a page boy. I guessed she was in her mid to late twenties. In her arms she carried her silver Norwegian Elkhound pup, whose impish tail curled over its butterball frame. It resembled a miniature Husky. Jacqueline handed the pup to Fidel. Only then did I realize the young woman wasn't wearing a bra. "A friend of mine brings her pets here," Jacqueline said. "She says if anyone can get my Elsa well, you can."

An ego builder. Just what I needed. I took a sip of my coffee and motioned Fidel away. Then I shook the thermometer down and reached for her pet. "What's this baby been doing?"

"Elsa's been throwing up," she said. "And she didn't eat this morning.

The dog's temperature was normal, so I listened to its heart. It was normal too. "What are you feeding her?" I asked.

"Purina and some scraps." She thought for a minute. "And Charlie gave her a bone to chew on last night."

"Charlie?"

"That's my husband," she said.

Fidel flashed a sign of disappointment.

"Never feed her scraps," I said. "Nutritionally it's unbalanced and it encourages bad habits."

"Oh, Elsa," she said. "Your mommy didn't know."

"You're not to blame," I said. "Most owners aren't aware what type of diet is proper. I bet she's chews your shoes and socks, too."

"She's demolished two pairs of my Nike's," she said.

I took a sample of the pup's stool. It was stained pink and had red fuzz throughout. "I bet you have a red carpet," I said.

"That's right," she said. "How did you know?"

"Because the fibers are coming through in her bowel movement."

"So that's why I have holes in my rug. I thought it was moths."

"Well," I said, "if she's eating the carpet she'll vomit for sure, but I'll check her for worms just in case."

"That's not necessary," she said as she shook her head to get the hair out of her eyes. "I've seen them."

I showed her some specimens. "Were they white and flat? Like this?"

She wrinkled her nose. "I didn't get that close," she said. "But it was alive and it moved."

That narrowed it down to either roundworms or tapes, so I offered a tie breaker. "Did it curl up in a circle or did it inch along like a caterpillar?" I took my finger and arched it at the first joint, pretending it was a worm crawling along the counter.

She laughed at my parody and offered one of her own. "It was more like this." And she began a slow sensual gyration that started at her knees, progressed to her thighs, spiraled to her hips and ended with an earth-shaking shimmy that scored 8.0 on the Richter. I was spellbound.

"Definitely tapeworms," I said.

Just then, Harry burst through the door and asked, "Have you seen my surgery scissors?" He searched through my instrument tray, ransacked the cabinets and looked under the sink, taking a good ten minutes to go through my room. Finally he searched his own pockets. "I'll be darn. Here it is." Then he backed out the door, winking at me and Fidel as he left. I apologized to Jacqueline for the interruption and continued.

"Fleas transmit tapeworms," I said. "Elsa must have accidentally swallowed a flea to get them. I'll worm Elsa, but you'll have to keep her powdered and free of fleas." I liberally dusted Elsa with flea powder and followed that with the pup's first vaccination. Elsa howled from the inoculation, so I held her in my arms, trying to console her.

"Let me hold her," said Jacqueline," extending her arms. I started to make the transfer, but Elsa struggled during the exchange and started to fall. Instinctively, I reached forward to catch her, but in the process Jackie's arms became entangled in mine and we rescued the pup together. Then our eyes met, if only for an instant. I was embarrassed. She seemed intrigued. Again the door opened. This time it was Leon.

"Have you seen the bone saw?" he asked.

"I'm sure it's in the surgery," I said. "With the orthopedic equipment."

"No," he said. "I think I left it here."

I watched in amazement as Leon repeated the process Harry had just performed, thoroughly examining every nook and cranny for the missing item while taking every advantage to examine Jackie as well. When he decided he had looked enough he finally admitted, "Maybe you're right. I'll try the surgery."

Whenever a good-looking woman was in the hospital Harry and Leon would mosey in on some pretense to make an appraisal or look for something. Usually their unscheduled visits went unnoticed but today they'd been so obvious. Again I apologized for their aberrant behavior and said, "Harry and Leon go wacko whenever our clients are attractive...like you."

Jacqueline was petting Elsa, sliding her hand down the dog's back and straightening its tail, watching it spring back into its normal half circle.

"I bet you say that to all your lady clients."

"Usually the older ones," I said. We laughed. I could feel the doctor-client barrier melt away. It was a nice feeling.

She paid her bill and I walked her to the door.

"Remember," I said. "Don't let Elsa eat the carpet."

"I'll do my best," she said. "We're not home all day, so it's hard to keep her out of trouble."

I returned to the room, where Fidel was waiting. "And you think I'm a womanizer," he snickered. "You made a first class move on that broad. I couldn't have done better."

"I was only being nice," I said.

"You were making a pass," said Fidel. "Admit it."

I didn't know if I was flirting or not. Some people hit it off the first time they meet. Jacqueline seemed to like me and I enjoyed talking to her, so what could be wrong about that? We had met completely by chance. Whatever this was, it was fun, and I had enjoyed it. Fidel was trying to make me feel guilty.

"Besides, the girl's married," I said.

"So what?" said Fidel. "Most of the married couples I know cheat on each other."

DOCTOR GOLDMAN. DOCTOR GOLDMAN. REPORT TO DOCTOR BOB'S ROOM. DOCTOR GOLDMAN. REPORT TO DOCTOR BOB'S ROOM.

I hustled down to see Bob. He was standing by the phone, red-faced and impatient.

"I've got Mrs. Mulligan on the line," he said. "She wants to know how Jeanie is doing. What should I tell her?"

"Didn't Harry tell you? Jeanie died over the weekend."

Bob exploded. "I can't tell her that. Don't you understand? This woman is a step away from a mental breakdown. Why didn't you tell me so I could've prepared her?"

"I've been busy seeing clients. Harry and Leon knew about it, too."

"Don't give me that. Leon's been in surgery. In fact he came by looking for the bone saw. And Harry is still treating patients."

I knew right then that any defense would be useless. I waited there, meekly, while Bob gave the situation some thought.

He took a deep breath, punched in the talk button and in a soothing voice more appropriate for an analyst began explaining to Mrs. Mulligan what had happened to her pet.

"Jeanie was doing so well," he said, "but I'm sorry to tell you she's suffered..."

He halted for a second, and I whispered, "Kidney failure."

He only glared at me and said, "A stroke." Then he added, "And she's been unconscious ever since Saturday night." Then he stood back as the speaker poured forth heart-rending wails of deep anguish. I felt like two cents.

"We're doing everything we can," he told her. "We've got her on artificial support systems." He paused once more. "Yes, ma'am. We won't do anything until you get here." Then he hung up.

"Where's Jeanie?" barked Bob.

"She's in the cooler," I said.

"Then get her and take her to surgery. I'll meet you there."

"Yessir," I said.

As a service to clients we kept deceased pets until the owners decided what to do with the remains. I ran to the rear of the kennel where a decrepit refrigerator doubled as a make-shift morgue. The kennel boys used it to store their sack lunches. I cracked the fridge open and peered inside.

Jeanie's head was wedged between a carton of Cokes and a pack of Oscar Mayer bologna. Small brown paper bags were perched on her belly. I set those aside and began pulling the dog out, but condensation had made her coat slippery and she fell to the floor. I ran to the front and got Fidel.

"You Anglos are crazy," he said as we stumbled along. He didn't stop grumbling until we unloaded the corpse on the surgery table.

"Fidel," ordered Bob, "Fill some empty jugs with hot water and bring a blanket. And Joel, shine the surgery light directly on Jeanie." I switched the lamp on. The beam felt hot to my hand as I positioned it over Jeanie's head. "Now help me with this tracheal tube." He opened Jeanie's mouth while I held the dog's clammy blue tongue and pulled as far as it would go. Then he slipped the tube into Jeanie's windpipe.

Fidel returned with the jugs and Bob arranged the hot-water bottles on either side of Jeanie's body. Then he covered her with a blanket.

"Now bring over the I.V.," he said, and he ran the tubing under the blanket allowing it to drip uselessly into the catch basin under the table. "All right, Fidel, roll over the oxygen tank and start giving oxygen."

Jeanie was warm and life-like. Her chest inflated and deflated as Fidel alternately filled and then emptied the respirator air bag. Except for the hissing of the life-sustaining gases, all was peaceful. Then there was a commotion in the hall.

I heard June shout, "You can't go in there." The voices grew steadily louder until the doors flew open and Mrs. Mulligan burst in crying. Bob stopped her before she could get close to Jeanie.

"We just lost her," he said dejectedly. "We can't raise a pulse."

Mrs. Mulligan froze at the news. Fidel sucked in his cheeks. I expected her to go completely beserk, but instead of becoming hysterical the woman took on an air of calm. She softly walked over to Jeanie and stared at the body, which continued to heave up and down, thanks to Fidel's ongoing efforts. Bob placed his stethoscope on the dog's chest. He listened intently, then removed the instrument from his ears and put his hands on Fidel's shoulders, signifying he could stop. Then, with all due solemnity and head respectfully bowed, he officially proclaimed, "It's all over."

Mrs. Mulligan sniffled. Bob handed her his handkerchief. "I couldn't bear putting her to sleep," she said. "I feel better that she died here, with you, knowing that you did all you could." Then she tugged at the blanket and drew it over the dog's head, assenting as Bob closed the dog's eyes. Quietly, the two of them left.

"Did you see that? Did you see that?" Fidel was dancing about the room, gibbering like a maniac. He popped his fist into his cupped hand. "What a performance."

"I saw it," I said.

"Then why aren't you excited?"

"Because I feel like a whore."

Indeed, I had been an accomplice to the whole business. It went against my grain.

The surgery doors flew open once more as Bob returned. He was beaming. "The pet cemetery is going to pick up the body this afternoon," he said. "Good work." Then he started to shake hands.

"I think it stinks," I said.

Fidel slunk down behind the oxygen tank. I stood my ground.

"Why?" asked Bob. "Because we pulled off a sham?"

I nodded yes.

Bob folded his arms and lectured me like a father. "Would you have rather told Mrs. Mulligan that her dog died suddenly, in the middle of the night, without anyone being able to do anything about it? This woman would never forgive herself. Now she can grieve without having any guilt. We did her a favor." Then he left, leaving me alone with Fidel.

"He makes good sense," said Fidel, shaking his head affirmatively.

"If I want your opinion, I'll ask for it," I said. "Put the dog back in the fridge. We've got other work to do."

That evening I went home to my dogs and cats. They were glad to see me, especially after I filled their food bowls. I heated a T.V. dinner and shared a silent meal with my animals. After dinner I lay on the couch and in that hazy area of consciousness between wakefulness and sleep I thought about Bob and what he had said. He was probably right, but I was still miffed. I didn't like being a party to his dishonesty. If I had my own practice maybe I would have done differently.

Then I dreamed of Kay and the girls, but another figure kept appearing. It was Jacqueline Foret. I curled my knees to my chest and thought how nice her visit had been. I dozed off and woke up the next morning, late again.

The next two weeks were a drag. I was happy to go to work just to see people and have someone to talk to. At night my routine was the same. A walk with the dogs, who went wild when I arrived, and a petting session with the cats, who stretched and yawned with typical feline indifference. Then it was frozen dinners and a full night of television culminating with the late show and sleep. I was suffering from an extreme case of boredom. Harry had the solution.

"Let's go to Fat City," he said that Friday after work. Fat city was Jefferson Parish's answer to the French Quarter. Young singles who worked in the suburbs went there for entertainment. Harry was a Fat City regular. I had never been.

"It's just what you need to cheer you up," he said.

"I don't think so," I said. "It's not my kind of place."

But Harry was persistent, arguing I needed a change in routine, so I agreed to go. That evening I put dinner in the oven as usual, but this time, while it heated, I showered and shaved. Puzzled, the dogs watched me dress in a suit and tie. Harry arrived dressed in loafers, sport shirt, gold chains and designer jeans.

"We'll go to the Trade Winds," he said. "It's a hangout for singles. Maybe we'll get lucky."

"Harry," I chided. "We're only going for drinks."

"We'll do that, too," he said.

Fat City was crowded. Groups of young people, many with drinks in their hands, drifted on the streets with no apparent destination. Fancy cars cruised the blocks, their occupants looking for action, while couples strolled down the center of the road daring the drivers to hit them. The smell of stale beer floated in the air.

Harry steered us past gaudy nightspots whose flashing lights and extended canopies beckoned like sirens. Raucous hawkers extolled the pleasures of what we would find inside. Through a doorway I saw a tan carnal goddess writhing on a platform. I tugged at Harry's arm, but he dismissed me by saying, "Female impersonators."

Finally, we stopped in front of a club with the distinctive decoration of a Spanish galleon garishly portrayed in pink neon. "This is it," announced Harry. He opened the door. A band blared a deafening rendition of "Tie a Yellow Ribbon Round the Old Oak Tree." I couldn't see a thing. I was beginning to regret my decision.

"How do you know where you're going?" I hollered.

"What didya say?" he yelled in return.

"Never mind," I said. Like a blind man I clutched Harry's belt and we shuffled along. We climbed a staircase and the music abated. By now my eyes had adjusted.

At one end was a bar – at the other a circle of tables. A small dance floor was in the middle. An entwined couple wandered on the parquet, pretending they were dancing. They drifted in and out of view as layers of wispy smoke wafted across the room. We stood and stared until a bar-maid asked us for our order.

She was dressed in a skimpy black excuse of a skirt. Fish-net hose latticed her legs and a lacey white top revealed most of her cleavage. We mounted our bar stools.

"Scotch and water," said Harry like a veteran.

"Seven-Up for me," I said.

Harry looked at me with disdain.

"Scotch and Seven," I responded. We swiveled our bar stools half circle and examined the layout more closely. A girl at the opposite end of the bar smiled at me, so I smiled back, just trying to be polite, but Harry cautioned, "She's a hooker." Then he spied two singles sitting at a table.

"That's what we're looking for," he said. He grabbed his glass, slid from his seat and escorted me to where they were sitting. "Do you ladies mind if we join you?" he asked.

They gave us the once over from top to bottom as if we were meat on the hoof. Then they turned a chair outwards so it faced us, and Harry sat down. I was uneasy but found a chair for myself and sat next to Harry. Harry introduced us and offered to buy drinks.

The younger of the two women said her name was Angie. I figured she was in her late teens to early twenties. She wore a tight yellow skirt, a wide belt and a frilly silk blouse.

"What sort of work do you do?" she asked.

"We're veterinarians," I said.

"Oohh," she said wistfully. "Ever since I was a little girl I wanted to be a veterinarian."

Her answer wasn't unexpected. Most of the people I meet have harbored hopes of being a veterinarian. I wondered if anyone was really happy doing what they do. I replied in a similar vein. "When I was little I always wanted to be an accountant."

Harry patted Angie on the arm. "He's only kidding," he

said.

Reassured, Angie put a stick of Spearmint in her mouth. "Do you mind if I ask you a professional question?"

Anything to break the ice, I thought.

"It's about my Toy Poodle, Mitzie," she said. "My vet says she's neurotic – she gets jealous real easy."

Angie spoke with a New Orleans twang and she smacked her gum. I could have thrown up. I stirred my drink, expecting a question clients have posed countless times before.

"Is it true," she asked. "if Mitzie has a litter, that'll calm her down?"

I gave my stock answer. "Remember the little old woman who lived in a shoe – had so many children she didn't know what to do?"

"Uh, huh," said Angie.

"Do you think one more kid would help settle her nerves?"

Angie wasn't impressed. The older woman guffawed.

Before I could insult them further Harry interjected, "What do you ladies do?"

"I'm a legal secretary," said Angie. "Rita works for D.H. Holmes department stores."

I chimed in, "One of my clients works for Holmes. He's in upper management."

"I work in Ladies Ready-to-Wear," grumbled Rita.

Rita was older, in her mid to late thirties. Telltale creases etched patterns under her eyes and gray streaks ran through her black bouffant hair. Her lips were obscenely red. She and I watched as Harry led Angie onto the dance floor. Then Rita turned to me and said, "You're married."

I felt as if I had just been caught stealing. "How can you tell?" I asked.

"It's easy. You're dressed for church."

Rita removed her compact from her purse, snapped it

open and scanned her face. Then abruptly clamped it shut.

"Where's your wife?"

"Back in Texas," I said. "She's visiting her mother."

"So what are you doing here?"

"Harry didn't want to come alone. I tagged along for the ride."

She lit a cigarette and studied my face. "I bet you and your wife aren't getting along." she said.

"Sort of," I said.

"Why not?" she asked.

"She says I spend too much time at work. But if I don't work we don't eat. There's only so many hours in a day."

"You found time to come over here. What's the problem?"

"No problem," I said. "I enjoy my work and don't want to quit."

Rita blew a cloud of smoke in my face. "You dodo," she said. "She doesn't want you to quit. Just slow down. Take time for your family. The practice won't suffer." She leaned forward. "Your clients can learn to live without you. Your family can't."

"And what makes you so smart?" I asked.

"Experience," she said. She straightened my tie. "You're just like the last guy I dated. He was married, too. Had the same excuses. His wife worked her fingers to the bone raising his kids while he ran around. When she found out about us she divorced him. Can you believe that scum had less time for me after his divorce than while we were dating."

I shuddered. I wasn't after a divorce.

"Do you have children?" she asked.

"Two girls," I said. A seven-year-old and a two-year-old."

Thinking of them made me feel sad.

Rita sucked on her cigarette, then angled it wisely. "Why

don't you go home, call your wife, tell her you miss her and patch things up? If she's the kind of woman I think she is, she'll understand."

That sounded wonderful. I ran on the dance floor and collared Harry.

"But it's early," he whined. He held his finger on point as Angie pirouetted about, bobbing and dipping with the music. I thought she looked spacey.

"We're just getting started," she said. Harry gave Angie a twirl, moving further away on the floor.

I insisted we leave, but Harry only agreed after Angie said she'd meet him later that night.

We walked to his car. "I was totally out of place," I said.

"Rita's not your type," he said. "I'll ask Angie to find you somebody else."

"Don't do me any favors," I said.

We took a shortcut through an alley when we heard the sound of a breaking bottle. Then, a meow.

"Hey, Harry. It's a kitten. Must be a stray."

"Or abandoned," he said.

Partially kneeling, I balanced on the balls of my feet as I called, "Here, kitty, Here, kitty." A fuzzball of orange ran out of the shadows. It waited suspiciously, tantalizingly close. I scooted nearer and extended my hand. When the kitten came to investigate, I grabbed it.

It was a domestic shorthaired cat, orange striped, skinny and bedraggled. I thought it would be wild, but it didn't seem to mind that I held it. I was pleased. I was back in my element.

"What are you going to do with him?" asked Harry.

"Take it home," I said. "Kay would want me to." Once, on a trip from New York to New Orleans, Kay and I rescued a stray from the parking lot of the Roanoke Holiday Inn. We jammed the surprised feline in our cold drink cooler, where it rode during the day. At night we smuggled it into motels where it slept on clean sheets and dined from room service. Later we found it a home with a lady down the street.

Harry, myself and the refugee cat climbed into Harry's car, but just as we were about to leave Harry burst out, "There's Your Lady With The Norwegian Elkhound!" and he pointed to a Porsche. I started to wave, hoping to catch her attention, but I only saw the side of her face as she passed. Again there was a strange thrill of anticipation, then this twinge of disappointment. I wanted Harry to chase her, yet I didn't want him to know I was interested. Instead, he took me home. It was after twelve. The dogs were waiting.

They sniffed the new visitor, imbibing and assimilating the new scent. Then I put them outside while I prepared a place for the cat in our downstairs bathroom. I provisioned it with food and water, requisitioned a hot-water bottle to keep it warm and a soft towel to sleep on. The kitten licked its plate clean and meowed, so I added more food. After finishing that portion it washed its face and feet and curled around the hot-water bottle. I closed the door and walked to the phone. I was anxious to tell Kay about our latest stray and that I had had a change of heart. The phone rang a long time before someone answered.

"Hi, honey," I said.

"Where have you been?" she demanded. "I've been trying to get you all night."

"Harry and I went for dinner together."

"My God," she said. "How long does it take two people to eat?"

"The restaurant was crowded. Full of tourists."

"Where'd you go?"

I couldn't tell her I was at a bar. What would she think?

"Commander's Palace," I said. Commander's was pretty ritzy, but it was the first decent place I could think of.

"That's nice," she said. "Maybe you'll find time to take me."

I knew I had lost that round, so I tried my ace in the hole.

"I brought home a stray cat. Found him by the restaurant. I thought you'd want to know."

"Honey," she groaned. "It's almost one o'clock. Couldn't that have waited?"

Kay had an answer for everything. I tried the romantic approach.

"I miss you," I said. "When are you coming home?"

"Not for another month. The girls are enrolled in day camp and Mother and I have plans to go shopping in Austin and San Antonio. Besides, this is the first chance I've had to get in some sewing."

"Sounds like you're staying busy," I said.

"Oh, yes. What about yourself?"

"The same," I said. "Work, you know."

"It's late," she said, "and I'd like to go back to bed. Next time don't call so late. You'll wake up Mother."

That ended our conversation so I allowed the dogs to come back in. They immediately ran to the bathroom door and stuck their noses along the crack, hoping to establish some communication with our new visitor, I left them there as I trudged upstairs, thoughts racing through my head.

Kay had begrudged my one evening with Harry. You'd have thought I was running around. And she wasn't even excited about the cat. And I had called her special. I heard the dogs pawing at the bathroom door knob. Wouldn't you know it. They were more concerned about the kitten than Kay was. I undressed, crawled into bed and lay there just thinking. I had had a change of heart and wanted Kay to come home and she turned me down – at least for a month. While I slaved at the hospital she had other things to do –

like having a vacation. It's true, the girls were a handful, and she probably deserved some time off, and I appreciated that, but what about me? I could use a little vacation, too. The more I brooded the more confused I became. At last I concluded that what was good for the goose could be good for the gander. If she could enjoy her vacation away, so could I.

I arrived at work early next morning and arranged for the kennel boys to bathe and dip the new kitten. Leon was glad to see me.

"You're the first one here," he said. "You even beat Harry."

"He'll probably be late," I said. "He had a heavy date."

Leon and I had finished medicating most of the patients when the exit door slammed and Harry poked his head into the treatment room. But he just as quickly vanished. I went searching for him, arriving in time to see him stagger in the office, where I found him cupping his hands around a mug of hot coffee. His eyes were bloodshot, and he needed a shave.

"Is it safe to take aspirin with chicory?" he asked hoarsely.

"For a man in you condition, it's indicated," I said. "How did you and Angie make out?"

"Miserably," he said. "It was all Mitzie's fault." Harry fumbled with an aspirin bottle trying to get it open. Failing that, he handed it to me. Gene came in to put on his smock.

"Who's Mitzie?" he asked.

"She's a snotty, three-year-old bitch," said Harry.

"He's talking about a Poodle," I said, handing Harry two pills.

"Is she a client of ours?" asked Gene.

"I was hoping to make her one," moaned Harry. He looked at me. "After I dropped you off, I met Angie back at the Trade Winds, but it took most of the night just to get rid of Rita. That woman can hold her liquor. She cost me a bundle."

Harry swallowed his pills with his coffee and continued. "After I dumped Rita at her apartment, Angie invited me to her place."

Fidel came in the office and handed me a card with my name clipped to the top. The card belonged to Jacqueline Foret. She had specifically requested to see me.

"Hurry up and finish," I said. "I've got someone waiting."

"Not so loud," said Harry. "I've got a splitting headache." He took a deep breath and put his hand to his head. "While Angie changed clothes, Mitzie wanted to play. She'd drop her ball at my feet, wanting me to throw it. Then she'd retrieve it, and we'd have to go through the whole thing again, and again, and again. The dog drove me crazy."

Harry gagged and swallowed, making a face as if he'd tasted lead. "After Angie changed clothes she came back and sat next to me on the couch."

"And you hit a home run," said Fidel.

"Hell, no," said Harry. "Mitzie kept squeezing in between us. When I tried pushing her away, she bit me." Harry held a mangled finger for us all to see. "So we went into the bedroom and shut the door." He groaned, "Then the dog started barking. She wouldn't shut up."

The frustration was beginning to show in Harry's voice.

"Mitzie was in the living room, standing on her hind legs, looking out the window, barking like crazy, but when I tippy-toed over to see what she was barking at, she ran to the bed and jumped in with Angie." Harry pulled down his pants and mooned us, revealing a large hole in his shorts. "I had to sleep on the couch. The dog spent the night chewing a hole in my drawers.

"That's pathetic," said Fidel. "You Anglos let a ten-pound Poodle boss you around."

"You don't argue with a dog when you're naked," said Harry. "I'm lucky she wasn't a Doberman."

I left Harry to recuperate while I prepared to see Jacqueline. I combed my hair, straightened my tie and smoothed my smock. Fidel said I looked perfect. So did Jacqueline. I felt warm all over.

"How's Elsa?" I asked.

"She's doing so much better," she said, "and look how much she's grown."

I put the dog on the scale. "She's doubled," I said. "She's up to twelve pounds." I bubbled over Elsa as if I were the owner.

June stuck her head in the room. "Can you take Mrs. Franks? I think her cat is obstructed."

"Isn't anyone else available?" I asked.

"Harry is in no condition to do anything, Leon is in surgery, and Gene has a patient."

I didn't want anything to disturb my visit with Jacqueline, but a cat with an obstruction was a genuine emergency. I apologized. "I have to see this cat now. If it's blocked it'll need immediate attention."

"I don't mind," she said. "Can I stay and watch?"

I couldn't have wished for anything more. I found her a chair and she sat down, holding Elsa on her lap. Fidel brought Mrs. Franks and a large gray and white tom into the room.

"His name is Grayson," she said.

I grasped the cat's abdomen to feel its bladder. Finding it was easy. It was the size of a grapefruit and very turgid. The diagnosis was simple.

"Grayson's unable to urinate," I said.

Mrs. Franks clasped her fingers into a fist and put them to her mouth. "He's been squatting in his litter box all day.

I thought he was constipated."

"Has he been vomiting?" I asked.

"No. But he goes to his water bowl like he wants to take a drink, but then he walks away."

I smelled Grayson's breath. The odor of ammonia nearly bowled me over. "He's toxic," I said.

"Does that mean he'll die?"

"Doctor Goldman is a wonderful vet," said Jacqueline. "I'm sure Grayson will be fine."

"I'll need to sedate your cat," I said, "and relieve the obstruction."

Do I have to stay?" asked Mrs. Franks. "I'm squeamish about this sort of thing."

"Of course not," I said. I glanced over at Jacqueline and asked, "Why don't you take Mrs. Franks to the waiting room and come back?"

Jacqueline left with Mrs. Franks while Fidel and I sedated Grayson. Then we placed the cat on its back, flexing its knees until they pointed to his chest, somewhat like a woman in position for a vaginal. Jacqueline returned and watched as I extruded Grayson's penis and began massaging the tip. Within seconds a yellowish gritty substance began oozing forth.

"What's that?" she asked.

"The urethral plug," I said. "It's a conglomeration of mucus, pus cells, and fine ammonium phosphate crystals. A cat makes these crystals like people make bladder or kidney stones."

I took Jacqueline's finger and rubbed it in the grit.

"It feels like sandpaper," she said.

"Of course, these aren't as big as stones," I said, "but when Grayson urinates, the crystals scrape against the urethral lining, causing it to bleed."

"Just like a sand blaster," said Jacqueline.

"That's a good description," I said.

She took an abbreviated bow. I thought she was cute.

"When Grayson urinates it stings, so he licks the tip of his penis and sends germs the other way. Then he gets cystitis, an infection in his bladder."

"I had cystitis once," she said. "It was awful. I felt like I had to go every second, and it burned."

"Same thing with Grayson," I said, "but a male cat's urethra is narrow at the end, so pus, mucus and these crystals get jammed at the tip of the penis. That's why male cats are prone to obstruct. Once that happens, the bladder gets distended, the cat becomes toxic, and if he doesn't receive attention, he dies. Occasionally, an owner won't realize what's happening, and their cat's bladder gets so big it bursts."

"How horrible," she said. She looked up at me, and once more our eyes met, but this time she didn't look away. My heart skipped a beat as we stood there entranced. Then I remembered Grayson.

I massaged his penis some more, hoping that would relieve the obstruction.

"You'd better stand over here," I said. I took Jacqueline by the hand. She held on to mine tightly, even squeezing back.

Then with her safely behind me, I pressed Grayson's bladder, very slowly, gradually increasing the pressure.

Suddenly, the plug gave way, and urine shot across the room. "He's open now," I said. I threaded a catheter up the urethra and into the cat's bladder, and urine began steadily dripping from the free end. Then I sutured the catheter to the cat's sheath. "We'll leave this in overnight," I said. "It'll give his bladder a chance to rest." Then I hooked Grayson to an I.V. and sent Fidel for Mrs. Franks.

"We relieved the obstruction," I told her, "but Grayson has to stay. Hopefully, by tomorrow he'll be able to urinate on his own. And he'll be on fluids for a couple of days. His kidneys need time to recover."

Tears welled in Mrs. Frank's eyes. "I knew something was wrong," she said, "but I didn't know what."

"You did well just to realize he was sick," I said.

"There's no way I can thank you enough." Then she motioned toward Jacqueline. "And thank you, too. You both are very sweet."

I had Fidel show her out. Then I double-checked to be sure my drip and the catheter were still working.

"You're so nice to your clients," Jacqueline said.

"I enjoy them," I said. "I'd like to know them all better."

"That might be possible," she said," if you ask the right questions."

If that meant what I thought it meant, the next move was up to me. I needed an opening without being too forward. I relied on my veterinary background. "Do you like cats?"

"I love cats," she said. "I've had cats since I was little." Jacqueline playfully rubbed Elsa along the dog's ribs. "We got Elsa because Charlie wanted a dog. Of course, I love Elsa very much and wouldn't trade her for anything." She squeezed Elsa so hard the dog yiped.

I whispered to fidel to get my foundling, and he returned with the kitten, all fluffy and clean.

"Oh, how cute," she said. "Look, Elsa," said Jacqueline. "Wouldn't you like to have a friend?" Elsa stood on her hind legs so she could see it, too.

The kitten mewed twice and settled in Jacqueline's arms, just purring away. "Oh, I just love him" she said. "Who does he belong to?"

"He's yours if you want him."

She looked up at me and then down at it, pursing her lips. "Charlie will kill me," she murmured. Jacqueline hesitated, then said, "But I'm going to take him anyway." She petted the cat lightly. "But I need you to do me a favor."

"Just name it," I said.

"I have to run some errands. If you'll keep the cat I can pick him up later?"

"I have a better idea," I said. "Let me deliver him."

"Why not?" she said.

"Are you sure it's okay?" I crossed my fingers.

"I'd like nothing better."

"Good," I said. "I have tomorrow off."

"Make it after two," she said. She prepared to leave.

"Wait a minute," I said. "You can't leave now. We haven't given Elsa her shot."

Jacqueline held onto Elsa as I slipped the needle under the dog's skin. This time Elsa didn't make a sound.

"She didn't even cry," said Jacqueline. "I told her you were a very nice man and wouldn't hurt her. I'll see you tomorrow."

My unnamed cat was content to sleep as we drove downtown, passing the Superdome and the Trade Mart. He dreamily stirred, changing positions as we entered the lanes for the Greater New Orleans-Mississippi River bridge. Up and up we went, high above the water. I could see tankers, side-wheeler party boats, barges, and tugs, plus a fleet of other assorted craft cruising the river. On the other side was the old city of Algiers and Jacqueline's house. It was on an alley-size side street off General McMullen Boulevard. I stopped at number 6 Beauvoir.

I climbed the front steps and rang the bell – then my insides went liquid while I waited, wondering what I'd do if someone else came to the door. Finally it opened. It was Jacqueline. She wore yellow shorts and a white, loose top that exposed her trim midriff. God she looked good.

"Hi," she said warmly. "I've been waiting."

She led me to a sofa and we sat down together. "Can I get you a drink? I have just about anything you might want," she said.

"No, thanks. I'm fine." I fiddled with my fingers.

"Did you have any trouble finding your way?"

"No, it was easy." I felt retarded. At the hospital, conversation came easy, but now we were alone and my mind was going blank.

I gazed around the room. There were oriental rugs, tall, leafy-green plants grown in gaily colored pots, and many carved pieces of furniture. Over on a sideboard were photographs, and I went to examine them. Jackie followed and explained, "That's me and Charlie," she said. "And this one was taken in Guadalajara, and this one in Bordeaux, and this one here, let's see, this one was in French Morocco."

"You've been everywhere," I marveled.

"Charlie's on the road a lot. It's part of his job. Right now he's in Colombia. Won't be back for two more weeks."

She looked at me, checking my reaction. A shiver ran up my spine.

"Have you and Charlie," my voice sounded squeaky and I had to clear my throat. "Have you and Charlie been married long?"

"Actually we're not married," she said. "We've been living together. It's less confusing if we tell people we're married."

"I'm married," I said, as if it were criminal.

"I know," she said. "June told me. And you have two little girls. One day, I'd like to have two little girls."

Suddenly from the hallway came a clattering, as Elsa, slipping and sliding against hardwood floors, burst in. Gaining traction, she revved up to speed and jumped on my lap, turning herself over so I could rub her stomach.

"Get down, Elsa," said Jacqueline. "You're getting your doctor dirty. Let's meet your new playmate." She put Elsa down while I took the kitten from his box.

"What are you going to call him?" I asked.

"I don't know," she said. "Where did you find him?"

"In Fat City," I said. "In fact, Harry and I saw you right after we found him."

"Charlie has accounts over there," Jacqueline said. "I service them when he's out of town."

She held the kitten at arms' length, puzzling over a name. "I'll call him O.C.," she said. "For Orange Cat." Then she took me by the hand and said, "Let me show you what Elsa and I fixed up."

With Elsa at our heels, we walked into a den where a small wicker basket stuffed with a pillow was lying on the floor. "This is for you, O.C.," said Jacqueline as she set O.C. in his bed.

O.C. began kneading his paws, catching his nails in the pillow threads, but when he saw Elsa, his hair stood on end. Elsa had only wanted to say hello, and after a few seconds of mutual sniffing, the two scampered away into another room. I became concerned.

"Don't worry," said Jacqueline. "They can't get out. I've closed the doors."

She leaned against the wall, her arms behind her and one knee raised. No sooner had I turned around than she caught my eye and asked, "Why did you come?"

I shuffled around with my hands in my pockets, mustering up courage.

"I know this is ridiculous...but...you see...I..."

"Yes?"

I was afraid she might laugh.

"Ever since I met you I had this feeling. I can't explain it. I just had to see you."

"Isn't that strange?" she said. "Ever since I met you, I've had that feeling, too."

"But I'm married."

"Lots of people are."

My skin began to tingle. I was dying to touch her. Her mouth looked so tempting. I wavered. What would she think if I forced my attentions. I was always a gentleman.

I reached for her hands and pulled her gently away from the wall. She put her arms around my neck, watching me with wonder, contemplating my next move. I cradled her head as her hair mingled through my fingers. Then our lips touched, a first kiss. We shivered, and then drew apart.

"That was nice," she said, keeping her eyes closed. "Can we try that again?"

"I'd better go," I said.

Jackie opened her eyes. She sounded confused and maybe a little hurt. "But there's plenty more where that came from," she said.

"I know," I said. "That's what I'm afraid of."

"Don't be afraid. It's perfectly natural."

"But I don't understand what's happening."

"I do," she said.

"It must be hormones," I said.

"You know better than that," she said. "It was something special."

That made me even more apprehensive. I headed for the door.

"Wait," she said. "You're forgetting something." She handed me the cat carrier. I took it and skipped down the stairs. "Call me," she said. I quickly drove away.

I was confused. I had just spent part of the afternoon with a woman other than my wife, and we had kissed. It was something I wanted to do even though my conscience had told me no. I needed advice, good advice, so after driving back across the river, I headed for the French quarter and Myron Landauer.

Myron owned an antique store in the quarter. I had treated his dogs and ever since then he became a good friend and mentor. Over coffee at the Monteleone Hotel, I told him what happened.

"I can't explain it," I said. "It's like I was eighteen all over again."

"How old are you?" he asked, stirring his coffee.

"Thirty-three," I said.

"And the girl?"

"Twenty-seven or twenty-eight."

"And how long have you been married?"

"Over eight years," I said.

"It figures," he said, knowingly.

"What's that got to do with it?" I asked.

"Finish your story and I'll tell you," he said.

"I've told you everything," I said. "I'm attracted to this girl, but I don't know how to handle it."

"What about her?" he asked.

"She has the same feelings, even stronger than mine, but we barely know each other. The best way I can explain it is that we have the right..."

"Chemistry," he said. He sounded as if he had heard it all before. "Listen," he said. "You're lonely and bored. Your wife's away and your marriage is a little stale. This gal happens to come along when you're most susceptible, feeds you the right vibes, and bingo, you're infatuated. It'll pass."

"But what do I do in the meantime?"

"That's up to you," he said. "But I can tell you one thing. Don't be seen with this girl or it'll get all over town. You owe your family that much. Hang in there. This happens to all of us."

Myron was right. My family came first, and Jacqueline came second. Regardless of how much I was attracted to her, I resolved to put her out of my life. But O.C. had other plans.

"I have to see you," said Jacqueline, calling me one night after hours. "O.C.'s bleeding from the rectum. The hospital said you weren't on duty, but I don't want anyone to see him but you."

I debated whether to risk inflaming the fire of passion or suffer from the agony of suppressing desire. It was no contest. "I'll meet you at the hospital," I said. "It'll take me twenty minutes."

Duane was all eyeballs and teeth as he grinned his greeting. "Your client's here, Dr. Joel. And Dr. Harry's just called, checking on things. I told him Mizz Foret was here to see you special, but he said he'd come down anyway, to help you out."

The last thing I needed was Harry, but just seeing Jacqueline made me forget him. She was rocking O.C., crooning him a lullaby.

"O.C.'s not himself," she said. "He even won't play with Elsa."

O.C.'s temperature was mildly elevated, but more importantly, a spot of blood was left on the tip of the thermometer. I smeared the bloody feces on a slide and put it under the microscope.

"He's got Coccidia," I said. "It's a protozoan parasite that lives in the bowel. He probably got it while he was running loose. He'll be all right."

I started O.C. on oral sulfa and showed Jacqueline how to administer the medicine. Then, with Harry's arrival being imminent, I escorted Jacqueline to her car where she said, "I hope you don't mind me calling you at home."

"It was all right," I said. "Actually I would have had my feelings hurt if you'd called someone else." I was surprised how easily I said that. I put my arm around her waist as we meandered in the parking lot, walking in circles.

"I'm having a small party this weekend," she said. "Just a few close friends. I want you to come."

That was the ultimate invitation, but I knew it couldn't be. "I can't," I said. "It wouldn't be right, with circumstances being the way they are."

"You're old fashioned," she said.

"But I'd feel funny. Especially with Charlie there."

"He'll be out of town," she whispered. Then she kissed me. "Try to make it," she said. Then she drove away, leaving me in a quandary. No sooner had she left than Harry arrived. He parked his car next to mine, got out and came over.

"Is Jacqueline still here?"

"You just missed her," I said.

"But I was on duty. She should have called me."

"She didn't want to see you."

"What makes you so special?"

"I can't explain it. I wish I knew."

"I don't believe that," he said. "Damn. I wish I had your luck."

"If you did, you'd be going to her house for a party."

"She's invited you to her house!"

"For better or worse, yes."

"You are going, aren't you?"

"I haven't made up my mind."

"Go for it," he said.

"I wish it were that simple," I said, and then I drove home.

The phone was ringing as I walked in. It was Kay.

"You're never home when I call," she said. "Where were you?"

"I was on an emergency."

"But this isn't your night, is it?"

"No. It's Harry's."

"Don't you have enough to do?"

"I did someone a favor. They didn't care to see anyone else."

"I thought you'd want to know. Alvin Daniels has his practice in San Marcos for sale. He's moving to San

Antonio."

"How come?" I asked.

"He and his wife are getting a divorce."

"And you want me to buy him out."

"It'd be perfect," she said. "We can live on the ranch with Mother. She'll give us ten acres to build a house."

"Let me think about it."

"What's holding you back?"

"I'm not holding back. I said I'd think about it."

"I don't understand. Here's an opportunity to be your own boss. I thought you'd jump at it."

"Can't we discuss it later?"

"Are you all right?" You sound tired."

"Right now I have a lot on my mind."

"Well, think about what I said. I just hope you're in a better mood when we talk next time." And our conversation ended.

All the following week I was preoccupied with Jacqueline's invitation. It was tough to concentrate.

"Joel," said Gene. "Is there something bothering you?"

"No, Gene. I'm just fine."

"But you've seemed snappy lately and especially after what you said to Mrs. Gaille."

Mrs. Gaille's cat had spent the night sleeping under the hood of her car. When she started the engine, the cat had been mangled. I thought I handled the case well.

"Did I do something wrong?" I asked.

"Sorta," he said. "You asked her whether she drove a V-8 or a 6." Gene was sympathetic. "I know your wife's been gone, and you're doing without," he gave me a paternal pat, "but once she gets back, you'll be your old self. Oh, one other thing. Do you have plans for Saturday and Sunday?"

Except for deciding about Jacqueline's party I didn't have any, but I couldn't tell him that. He'd ask too many questions. I said I didn't.

"Then you won't mind if we switch duty weekends," he said.

That took care of that. I couldn't go to Jacqueline's even if I decided to.

"But if you have someplace to go," he added, "We'll have these. With these nifty gadgets you can go anywhere and still be reached." He reached in a box and brought out a pager.

Pager? Pagers. I worked five years for this hospital and finally, today of all days, we have pagers. That meant Jacqueline's party was viable. What luck. I caved in to fate and decided to go.

At last the big night arrived. I hitched my pager onto my belt and swaggered outside, jumped in the car and headed for the west bank and Algiers. I had just entered Orleans Parish when I was startled by an electronic alert. "BEEP BEEP BEEP BZZZ. BEEP BEEP BEEP BZZZ. DOCTOR GOLDMAN. DOCTOR GOLDMAN. PLEASE CALL THE HOSPITAL. PLEASE CALL THE HOSPITAL."

It was the pager. It frightened me so bad I almost had an accident. I swerved onto the access road and drove straight for the hospital. Luckily it wasn't far. I barged in quite agitated.

"What's the problem?" I hollered.

"It's Mrs. Franks," said Duane. "She thinks that tomcat of hers is stopped up again. She's already on her way."

I fumed over my rotten luck but after I called Jacqueline to tell her I'd be late I felt better.

"Take your time," she said with reassuring smoothness. "I'm not going anywhere."

That's what I liked. She was so understanding.

By now Mrs. Franks had arrived and Duane had placed her cat on the table. "Grayson has started squatting again," she said. "Just like the last time."

I felt the cat's bladder. This time it was small and contracted. I managed to express a small amount of bloody urine. I felt relieved. I could handle this quickly.

"Grayson's not blocked," I said, "but he's having a severe bout of cystitis. He feels like he has to go, but actually his bladder's empty. We'll keep him tonight and send him home in the morning."

I promptly escorted Mrs. Franks to the door and bade her goodbye. Then with all due speed I treated Grayson, put him in a cage with a litter box and set off in a whirl for Algiers. Unaware of traffic, I cruised the interstate while fantasies played in my mind. I thought about Jacqueline and the first time we kissed. I dreamed about her hair – how it felt as my hand had run through it. My nose tingled with the scent of imaginary perfume. I envisioned her body pressing closely next to mine. Each successive picture heightened my pulse and quickened my breathing. I was on a spaceship rocketing to the moon. It was exhilarating. I careened onto Jacqueline's street and smashed right into a barricade. A policeman shined a flashlight in my face.

"You in a hurry to go somewhere, son?"

"I guess I was going too fast, officer. What's happening?"

"Drug bust," he said.

"Which house?"

"The one with the Porsche." He studied my face. "Do you have business in there?"

"Not me," I said. "Just taking a short cut." I swung the car around and slowly drove home.

Jacqueline and Charlie made the headlines. Their house in Algiers had been a distribution center for illegal drugs. She and six of her friends were charged with possession and intent to distribute narcotics. Charlie was arrested the same night in Miami. The Porsche was full of hidden compartments where bags of hashish were stashed. The paper said the house had been under surveillance for weeks. Even the phones had been bugged. I was scared stiff that I was under suspicion. The following Monday everyone was discussing the case.

"Was she a friend of yours?" asked Bob.

"Just a good client," I said.

"I knew there was something fishy about her," said Leon.

"How would you know?" I said. "You only saw her once."

"You'll never see her again," said Gene. "They'll put her away for a very long time."

Myron called to tell me I was damn lucky. Harry was more philosophical. "Just think," he said. "You might have made the Ten Most Wanted List."

I worried that O.C. and Elsa might have been abandoned, so I called the pound, figuring the police would have taken them there, but the animal wardens had no record of them. I scoured the papers daily, hoping to find more information about Jacqueline's fate, but none was forthcoming until a month later, when I had a visit from Sandy Johnson, who identified herself as one of Jackie's friends. To my relief, Sandy brought O.C. with her. "Jackie's not allowed to have pets," she explained. "She said you'd take good care of him."

"What about Elsa?" I asked.

"I'm looking after her," she said.

Sandy handed me the kitten. I looked fondly upon O.C. He had filled out and his tummy wasn't quite so rotund. He sniffed my fingers, oblivious to the fact he'd lost his mistress to a felony charge. Then Sandy said that Jackie was doing as well as could be expected and her attorneys were trying to arrange bail.

"There's one more thing," said Sandy. "Jackie wants to be remembered. She asked me to give you this." Sandy stepped up and kissed me.

I kissed her in return and said, "Tell Jackie I'd like to be remembered, too."

That evening I took O.C. home. Again I called Kay.

"I'm ready to make a change," I said. "Find out about that practice in San Marcos."

My curiosity got the best of me. Instead of waiting for the family to come home I took a plane to Austin, where I met Kay. As she drove us on to San Marcos I weighed the consequences of moving to Texas and owning my own practice.

For one, I'd be giving up the benefits offered by the hospital in New Orleans – mainly its multi-faceted caseload spread among the four other doctors. In return I'd have autonomy, but all responsibility would rest squarely on me. I would miss my old clients and the friends we had made, but surely, as Kay said, we could make new ones. And of course no town in America could compare with New Orleans for excitement, but I had had enough excitement for a lifetime. A change would do me good. As for my family, Rachelle was two and Dorie was seven; they could certainly adapt. Kay was all for the move. She would be closer to her mother. Even now she lobbied hard as she briefed me on cash flow, down payments, average charge per visit – everything I hated to discuss. But that's how it's always been. I was the medical romantic while she was pragmatic, though she always had an interest in animals. When we dated, Kay had pets of her own, a collie named Pudgy and a shorthaired yellow house cat named Taffy, so naturally we gravitated to each other, though I suspect her blonde hair and blue eyes played part in the romance. And we've been together ever since, which I attributed to our willingness to be flexible, but this time I sensed she wasn't ready to concede. She dropped me off in front of Alvin's building and drove on to her mother's, eight miles further up the road.

Alvin conducted his practice out of a modest cinder block building with a rock masonry front. I had seen it before on previous visits to San Marcos, but this would be my first time to view it from the inside. I followed as he gave me a tour. His hospital was small, pint sized compared to the one in New Orleans, but it had everything a veterinary clinic would need, a waiting room, exam room, a combination pharmacy-lab and x-ray room, a surgery, treatment wards, and a dozen kennels to board dogs and cats. Then he took me outside to show me the large animal facilities. He had a squeeze chute for cattle, docks and stanchions for horses, plus an assortment of stalls and pens. Seeing that aspect of the practice made me uneasy – it had been years since I treated large animals – but as Alvin said, if I made the transition from research to practice, I could adjust to large animals as well. Then we returned to Alvin's office, where he told me how he ran his business.

He said the clinic opened at eight though he didn't get there until eight-thirty. And he didn't take appointments. You just called to be sure he was in. He had two employees. Patty, a veterinary technician who helped mostly with small animals, and Travis, a local cowboy who assisted on large animal cases. Alvin said Patty was nurse, receptionist, medical technologist and groomer all rolled into one. Her only drawback was she liked to speak her mind. Travis's talents were, as Alvin put it, indescribable. Since Travis was away at a rodeo, I spoke to Patty about staying on. She answered by saying that before she worked for Alvin she worked for another vet, but she quit that doctor because he was too bossy. Finally, she said she might stay, which I interpreted as she would if I met her standards. I wondered if I'd ever be in charge. Personnel problems aside, I got on to a more basic consideration. Money.

My experience in New Orleans conditioned me to worry about collections, so I asked Alvin about his clients' economic status. He said his people generally paid their bills, but if they were short of cash he extended credit. I told him my present employer swore only by Master Card or Visa, but Alvin said if money was my main consideration this practice wasn't for me. However, if I was interested in meeting friendly folks who cared about their pets, this place was it. Then he told me he earned enough to make a good living while having time for his family. I found that statement rather strange since he had recently separated from his wife, but before I got to question him further, he had patients to tend to.

I stood by as Alvin treated dogs with skin sores and cats with runny noses, ailments similar to the ones I had seen in New Orleans. Then he invited me to help him treat a cow with mastitis, a common bovine disorder. It was routine for Alvin, but for me, a novel experience. Deftly, Alvin injected antibiotics into the infected udder without incident and prescribed medication for the owner to use at home. Then Alvin examined a dog with a bad eye, a problem he quickly remedied by removing a cactus thorn from its cornea. Alvin was professional in everything he did, but what impressed me the most was the rapport he had with his clients. As he ministered to the animals he treated the owners like neighbors, chatting with them about items of local interest, while they related to him as if he were family, discussing events and patients past that he had been involved with. Everyone appeared to be having a good time. Even the pets. Alvin may have had a smaller piece of the veterinary financial pie but his was a more intimate slice – something I couldn't measure in dollars and cents.

That evening Kay and I debated this practice's pros and cons. After I enumerated the economic facts, Kay's enthusiasm waned, while I, after spending a relaxed day practicing medicine with Alvin, was encouraged about proceeding with the purchase. We went to bed without reaching a decision, but by the next morning we were of one mind, so we drove on to town and signed the necessary papers. The practice was ours.

RABIES

O ther than AIDS, no disease strikes more fear and anxiety among people than rabies. Caused by a virus, and spread by the bite of an infected animal, rabies is invariably fatal. The disease is endemic in wildlife, where it occurs most often in skunks, foxes, bats and raccoons. They pass the virus among themselves, occasionally carrying it to livestock, but when the infection spreads to dogs and cats, transmission to man becomes more likely.

Rabid animals exhibit variable behaviour, ranging from aggression and irritability to depression and somnolence. The virus inflames the muscles of the jaw, making swallowing painful, and the animals drool and salivate. Considering the symptoms, exposure may not be evident and vaccination of susceptible pets is a must. That was especially true in San Marcos, where the occasional rabid animal was a seasonal occurrence.

In 1982 southern Texas experienced a rabies epidemic. It began in northern Mexico, spread to Laredo and worked its way north towards San Antonio. In Nuevo Laredo, a Mexican border town, free-roaming dogs were shot on the spot and leash laws were strictly enforced. I followed the epidemic with interest, as did most folks in the central Texas area. In the beginning the public remained calm and acted rationally, bringing in pets for rabies vaccinations and commenting on the epidemic as if it were commonplace, but after a rabid skunk was discovered in a local neighborhood, all sanity disappeared under a wave of paranoia.

I was in the surgery, docking the tail on a Weimaraner pup, when the foul odor of skunk assaulted my nose.

"Good grief, Patty! Have you seen skunks around the clinic?"

"Only Mr. Rawson's" she said. "He brought it in a sack."

"But it's stinking up the place! I thought you'd know better."

"I told him to wait in the parking lot," she said. "I don't know how he stands it."

I bandaged the pup's tail and put him in a cage. Then I grabbed an aerosol deodorant and sprayed every room in the hospital and went outside to see Ralph Rawson, an occasional client who owned an old-time barbershop. He catered to the older crowd who remembered barbers before they became hair stylists.

Ralph was sitting on the tailgate. Next to him was a black plastic garbage bag neatly tied at the top with wire.

He untied the sack, allowing it to open wide. The odor was overwhelming. "Gotcha a polecat," he said. "I want you test it for rabies."

"Sure thing, Ralph. Be glad to." I peered into the depths, looking for the victim's head. I gagged. "Where'd you shoot him?"

"Right square 'tween the eyes," said Ralph. "Blew his head kuh-leen off. Used my 30-06."

Using a .30-.06 on a skunk was like using a howitzer on a mosquito. Ralph hiked his pants and puffed out his chest, expecting a commendation.

"Darn it, Ralph. You're not supposed to shoot 'em in the head. The lab needs the brain to run the test."

Without comment, Ralph silently retied the bag and got back in his pickup. He seemed insulted. I leaned on the door and said, "I appreciate everything you and other folks in town are doing, but next time call City Animal Control. They'll destroy the skunk and send off the head. It's their job."

"Hell, nobody told me," he said, and he drove away, tires squealing.

I returned to the office where Patty was waiting with my next client, Allen Shelton.

Allen lived in a rented house across the highway opposite the clinic. He worked nights at a fast-food restaurant and attended college during the day. We had met over a year ago when Allen, needing money, came by looking for a job. At that time I hired him to do yardwork, yet knowing his schedule and financial situation, I was surprised to see him with a dog, and a large one at that.

"Meet Bear," said Allen. "Arrived a month ago. Just wandered to the house. I felt sorry for him and gave him something to eat. Of course then he wouldn't leave. But don't you think he looks good?"

Bear yawned and moaned simultaneously, stretching on the table before closing his eyes. He had a tail like a Collie, a body like a Lab and a face like a German Shepherd. His coat was a mixture of brown, yellow, black, and tans – the texture like a Wire Haired. Still, it was shiny and his ribs didn't show. The dog bordered on plump.

"He looks great," I said. "What do you use for dog food?"

"Big Macs, large orders of fries and medium shakes," said Allen. "But his favorite is Egg McMuffin."

I laughed at this underhanded endorsement for the golden arches, then said, "But has he had any shots? We're in the middle of a rabies outbreak."

"Yes, sir, I know," said Allen. "I would've brought him sooner but I've been broke."

"We'll work that out later," I said, "but for now let's

check Bear for parasites and heartworms, and I'll vaccinate him, too."

Bear had hookworms, a very light load and his heartworm test was negative. After treating for intestinal worms I gave the injections under the skin for distemper and parvovirus. The dog hardly flinched. He even wagged his tail while I stuck him in the thigh to vaccinate him for rabies. Bear didn't seem to mind anything.

"He's real layed back," said Allen.

"That's the kind I like," I said. "Let me see him in a couple of weeks and we'll reworm him."

With all the publicity about rabies, business was booming. I was fully occupied, vaccinating pets and giving advice about what a person should do in case of exposure to a rabid animal. The outbreak had entered its seventh week when I began my day with a sixteen-week-old male kitten who belonged to Mrs. Garza, an elderly lady who lived on Zarzamora Street.

It was a domestic short-haired cat, gray stripe with yellow eyes, narrow of body and face. Its ears were burnished brown, almost seal point, and I suspected it was part Siamese. It rested, trance like, on the table happily purring and staring into space.

Mrs. Garza stood to one side, nervously fingering her rosary, watching my every move. She couldn't speak good English and I hadn't spoken Spanish since high school. Luckily, Angela, a granddaughter, had come along to help with the translation.

"Where'd she get him?" I asked.

"*De donde le obtuvo?*" said Angela.

"*De Gutierrez,*" said her grandmother.

"From the next door neighbors," said Angela. "Their cat had a litter about five months ago and this is one of the babies. She says they're half wild. They live under the house."

"Ask her how long the cat's been sick."

Angela repeated my question in a torrent of Spanish. Mrs. Garza gave it some thought and then rattled off the answers, machine-gun fashion, expressing her dismay with her hands.

"Grandma says the cat hasn't eaten for days," said Angela. "She says it just sits there and purrs. If you ask me, I think it's stoned."

I put my hand close to the animal when suddenly it whirled and bit me on the finger. I suppressed an obscenity and uttered instead, "Wow, he's quick!" quickly washing the blood from my finger. Then I drowned the wound with a flood of antiseptic. I shook my finger.

"Ask your grandma if the cat's had shots."

"*Tomo'el gato para vacination?*" asked Angela.

"*Oh, no. No podia pescarle,*" said her grandmother.

That I understood. The cat hadn't had shots because she could never catch him.

"Tell her I'll treat the cat, but since he bit me he'll have to stay at least ten days. It's required by law. If she wants, she can visit, or maybe you can call, and we'll tell you how the cat's doing and you can tell grandma."

As Angela relayed the message her grandma broke into a smile and nodded her head. I donned the lead gloves we used for taking x- rays, grabbed the cat behind the neck and put it in a cage. After I returned, Grandma Garza poured forth another round of Spanish.

"She wants to know if the cat's going to get well," said Angela.

"I hope so," I said, and I put my hands together and raised my eyes to the ceiling. Angela giggled. Mrs. Garza seemed lost. But just as the two of them were about to leave, Mrs. Garza faced me and said, "Thank you, doctor," in broken English and I responded with "*De nada*" in gringo lingo. With that, both Mrs. Garza and her granddaughter started laughing and left.

"What do you think's wrong with her cat?" asked Patty.

"I'm not sure," I said. "Could be encephalitis, possibly a stroke, maybe a tumor... This cat's pretty young for a tumor."

"Could be rabid, too," said Patty.

"Could be," I said reluctantly.

Animals whose vaccine status was questionable had bitten me before, but as a precaution I kept them in quarantine for the required ten days. Then I vaccinated them for rabies. I was confident as long as I had the offender in my care, though I didn't sleep well until the trial period was over. I gave the cat food and water and stuck a HANDLE ONLY BY DOCTOR sign on the outside. Then I scrubbed my wound and followed that with a second antiseptic rinse.

"When did you have your last rabies booster?" asked Patty.

"A year ago," I said. I remembered it well. It was a new intradermal vaccine that didn't leave my arm sore like the old duck embryo shots.

"Oh, then I don't have to worry about you foaming at the mouth."

"Very funny,"I said. "Don't you have things to do? Like preparing a surgery set or writing reminder cards?"

Patty left to file case records. On impulse I returned to the ward to see how the cat was adjusting. It hadn't moved at all and was purring like a turbine. I watched him intently, trying to match his symptoms with any benign illness. It was impossible. My mind was only in gear for rabies. I walked into the surgery, stepped to the sink and scrubbed my finger again. I went home early.

That night I watched baseball while soaking my finger in a basin of saltwater. It was late, after ten, and the game was in extra innings. Then the phone rang. Late night phone calls could be tiresome, especially after a busy day, and I was in no mood for something trivial, but most people who call me at home have genuine concerns, so I listened sympathetically. A gentleman introduced himself as Mr. Hardin.

"I know you're gonna think I'm crazy," he said, "but I have a question about my dog, Delilah. She hasn't been herself. She's been acting rather strange."

"What do you mean strange?" I said.

"She's spying on me," he said.

"You mean she works for the C.I.A.?"

"Oh, Doc, you know. When I sit in the living room Delilah lies in front of me, on a rug. It's her special rug and she likes to lay on it."

"Um, hm," I said.

"She just sits there, head on the floor and every time I look at her, she looks at me. And if I get up and go to some other part of the house, she follows. Its weird. She's never done this before. I'm worried something's affected her brain."

At this point I had to wonder who was the patient. "Okay. What kind of dog is she?"

"She's a Bassett."

"Has she been spayed?"

"No, sir. In fact she was in heat six weeks ago."

"And I presume Delilah's up to date on her shots. Rabies, distemper?"

"Well, not exactly. She's late for her booster. I just haven't had the time. Could she have rabies?"

At last the real reason for the call had surfaced. With the epidemic every animal was suspect, even household pets. The contagion was affecting everyone.

"I don't think so, Mr. Hardin. It's probably hormonal. Why don't you bring the dog in for a booster and a checkup. It'll put your mind at ease and I'm sure Delilah will feel better, too."

"Thanks, Doc. I was really worried. Delilah was sleeping in bed with me but now I make her sleep in the living room. She scratches on the door all night, trying to get in. I thought she was planning to attack me."

"I think it's safe to allow her in," I said. "She'll leave your door alone and both of you can get some rest."

"Thanks again, Doc. Sorry to have bothered you. Good night."

"Good night, Mr. Hardin. And tell Deliliah good night for me, too."

I hung up the phone and returned to the television. By now the game had ended so I turned off the tube and crawled into bed. Kay, who was only half asleep, yawned and then mumbled, "Who was that?"

"Mr. Hardin," I said.

"What's his problem?" she asked sleepily.

"He needed a psychiatrist. Someone strong to hold his hand."

"Look who's talking," she said. "You've washed your finger enough times to make it fall off."

My finger was looking terrible. Between swelling and scrubbed, the skin around the wound appeared to be corroding. At least it was clean.

"So what was wrong with his dog?" she asked.

"False pregnancy," I said.

Post-heat hormones can alter a bitch's behavior. The animal becomes broody, as if she were pregnant and about to deliver. I'd explain it all to Mr. Hardin when he came in.

"By the way," said Kay. "Any chance that cat's rabid?"

"Not likely," I said, hiding some misgivings.

I rolled in the covers and snuggled next to Kay, taking care not to jam my finger, which was beginning to throb. I lay in bed but couldn't fall asleep, so I went to the kitchen and fixed a light snack. I thought about Delilah and her paranoid owner. Then I rehashed my experience with the Garza's cat and, as an afterthought, washed my finger once more. I crawled back into bed and soon was fast asleep only to be awakened a few hours later by the sound of the phone. Eyes shut, I reached for the receiver and put it next to my mouth. I said hello, but the blasted thing kept ringing. I raised my eyelid. Damn. I was speaking into the alarm clock. Wide awake now, I chose the proper equipment. The voice on the line said it was Allen Shelton. He sounded frightened.

"I know it's late," he said, "but something is terribly wrong with Bear. First he runs around like crazy and then he falls down and gets stiff as a board."

I assured Allen as soon as I dressed I would be on my way and to meet me at the office.

Bear and Allen were waiting on the front steps. Bear was lying down, wide-eyed. I unlocked the door and showed them in. Allen put Bear on the table, but just as I began my examination, Bear cried out, jerked his head back, stiffened his legs and began to shake violently. His jaws snapped wildly, whipping his saliva into froth. Bear was convulsing.

Allen grabbed Bear to keep him from falling, while I reached for my bottle of pentobarbital.

"You've got to hold him steady," I said. With Allen barely holding on I clamped the dog's cephlic vein and then slowly injected the sedating fluid. Gradually the muscles in Bear's body relaxed and his breathing slowed to a more normal pace. The drug was taking effect and I motioned to Allen that he could relax his hold.

"What's happening?" asked Allen. "Is he dying?"

"Of course not," I said. I raised Bear's lip to check his color and I touched his eye, ever so lightly, in order to check his reflexes. Bear responded normally by blinking.

"He's doing just fine."

"What was that stuff?"

"Pentobarbital," I said. "It's a long-acting general anesthetic. It eliminates the seizures while giving Bear's system time to recover. The drug supresses the electrochemical transmissions in Bear's brain and causes him to fall asleep."

"What caused him to seizure in the first place?" he asked.

I shook down a thermometer and explained, "Some area of his brain became overly excited and gave off irregular electrical signals. That caused adjacent brain cells to discharge their signals, too. In an instant the signal spreads over the entire brain and the end result is a convulsion or seizure."

"Like an epileptic attack," said Allen.

"Most likely," I said.

Most seizures in dogs are epileptic type spells, but occasionally they can be caused by certain poisons. I questioned Allen about that possibility.

"Does the dog have access to chemicals?" I asked.

"No, sir."

"Do you know of anyone that would want to poison the dog? Strychnine poisoning can mimic epilepsy."

"No, sir. Everybody just loves Bear. And he's been with me all day."

I gave Bear a little more drug to be sure he slept all night, then turned to Allen and asked, "Has he ever had a spell like this before?"

"I've seen him do it...maybe once or twice a month. But never this bad."

"Why didn't you tell me?"

Allen patted Bear's head. "I was afraid you'd say he was sick and I'd have to put him to sleep. But it didn't happen often. He always came out of it after a few minutes and then he was perfectly fine."

"Well, sometimes they don't come out of it," I said, "and they go directly from one seizure to another. Then their temperature begins to rise, they become exhausted and they die from cardiac arrest." I removed the thermometer from Bear's rectum. It read 104. Bear had started to overheat but it wasn't serious. I took some towels and immersed them in water. Then I placed them across the dog's chest and abdomen.

"I'll keep Bear here overnight," I said. "To sleep off the anesthetic and cool off. Tomorrow I'll start him on pills to prevent seizures. You'll need to give it every day."

Bear was in a deep sleep now and Allen helped me carry the dog to a cage.

"Are those pills expensive?" he asked.

"No. And don't worry. Your credit is good."

I saw Allen to the door. Then I returned to the ward to peek at Mrs. Garza's cat. He was lying down and wasn't purring. The food wasn't touched and he still had that vacant stare. A flash of apprehension ran through me. If this cat was rabid, it would die before the ten-day quarantine ended. I wondered if I could stand to wait the entire ten days. Neurological signs in a cat usually indicated serious illness anyway, so even if the cat wasn't rabid, the prognosis was poor. I decided to call Mrs. Garza's granddaughter and discuss it with them in the morning. We would allow a reasonable time for improvement and if there was none, it might be best to euthanize the animal and have the brain examined. I locked up and went home.

The next morning I arrived early. Patty was waiting at the door. She seemed grim.

"The Garza cat's dead," she said. "He's in the Safeway bag in the refrigerator."

"Call the lab," I barked, "and tell them we're sending a

head on the bus. It should arrive by eleven. And advise there's human exposure involved and to call us as soon as they have the results."

"Anything else?" asked Patty.

"Yes. Call Angela and have her contact her grandmother. She needs to keep in touch. And get me a pair of gloves and the autopsy knife."

"I've got them out already," said Patty.

I walked back to the ward, looking for Bear. "Where's Allen Shelton's dog?"

"You mean the funny looking Heinz 57?"

"That's him."

"He's on the run," she said. "He ate, did number one and number two and looks just fine."

I poked my head outside and checked the dog pens. Bear was pushing his empty feed bowl around his run. After catching sight of me, he stood on his back legs, his front feet propped against the wire partitions. He had recovered well from the anesthetic. No hangover. "Give Bear a Primidone tab," I said. "We'll put him on one pill three times a day to be reduced to two a day after a week. If Allen calls, tell him he can take Bear home, but be sure he has enough medication for at least three weeks. And it's all right to charge."

I went to the refrigerator, removed the little sack and took the chilled feline to the room where I did autopsies. The bag was just a little small for that sized cat and its two hind legs protruded from the top. I turned the bag over and the body slid out. Its eyes were open wide with that everpresent stare, while blood-tinged saliva dangled from its mouth. I cut through the skin, completely encircling the cat's head. Then I arched its neck and with a sickening crunch cut down to the bone, exposing the joint that connects the skull to the neck. Holding the head in one hand and the rest of the cat in the other, I snapped the cat's neck with a pop, and severed the connecting muscle with a knife. Finished, I plopped the head into a clear cellophane bag, twirled the bag shut and put it in a styrofoam box filled with ice. Patty finished wrapping the container and left for the bus station while I stuck the headless body back in the fridge. I saved the body in the unlikely case the lab needed more tissue. I cleaned and disinfected the knife, removed my gloves and scrubbed my hands and arms. Being a veterinarian can be gory.

I checked my desk for messages. There were three. Allen had called and would be in this afternoon. Mr. Hardin had made an appointment and Danny Feffer, a new client, was coming over.

Since I had a few minutes, I went into the office, where I kept a small library. I chose a book on infectious diseases and turned to the section on rabies. It brought back memories. During my senior year I saw a film about rabies. It showed the effect of the disease in all its graphic and tragic consequences. A boy of eleven or twelve had contracted rabies and the pictures documented the disease's entire course, from muscle tremors and exaggerated reflexes to eventual paralysis and death. The child was restrained with straps to keep him from injury during a convulsion, while a circle of doctors wrapped in masks and gowns observed what was for them, a rarity. Everyone knew the outcome, except for the patient. I wondered if the youngster was ever told. And if he was told, did he know what that meant?

At least I had a will. I had insurance. The kids would be taken care of. My wife would be rich. I thumbed through the pages. "The early symptom of most diagnostic significance is some abnormal sensation about the site of infection." My finger was awfully sore but was that abnormal? I read on. "The act of swallowing may precipitate spasm of the muscles of the throat." I poured myself a glass of water but I was so tense I almost choked. I slammed the book shut. I could go crazy just worrying. The front door squeaked as someone came in lugging a cat carrier. I was grateful for the chance to rid my mind of morbid thoughts.

"I'm Danny Feffer," said the caller. "I've got a sick cat."

Danny was a student at the university and he lived near the campus in a large older home that had been converted into a fraternity house. The cat, whose name was Reggae, was an unneutered, unvaccinated black male.

"What's his problem?" I asked.

"Well, he's not eating and all he does is lie around and slobber."

Immediately, I was on the defensive and decided to wait for Patty before attempting an examination. "You're taking a mighty big chance having an unvaccinated cat running loose," I said. "The incidence of rabies in cats is higher than dogs and right now there's plenty of rabid skunks for Reggae to come in contact with."

"I know it," he said, "but Reggae just hates to ride in the car. He howled all the way over here. If it weren't for his being sick I wouldn't have been able to bring him. But now, since he's here, why don't you give him his shots?"

"We will," I said, "if he doesn't already have a disease we'd vaccinate for."

Patty returned and together we planned our strategy. I put on the x-ray gloves. She brandished a leash and a broom. Then I had her tilt the carrier, raising the box until it was nearly perpendicular to the table. Reggae's claws scraped the plastic floor as he struggled to stay inside.

"Shake the box," I said.

Patty gave the carrier a vigorous rattling and a leg fell through the opening. I grabbed the limb and tugged. Squalling and howling, out came Reggae, who, finding himself alone and exposed, curled in a circle, apparently just as frightened of us as we were of him.

"See, Doc," said Danny, pointing at Reggae, "he's drooling all over." Reggae was wet from his chin to his chest and his mouth hung open as if paralyzed.

"Two rabid cats in one week is too many," said Patty. She retreated from the table.

"Just one second," I said. "Don't jump to conclusions." Reggae had pawed at his mouth and then meowed as if he were hurting. Cautiously, I extended a hand, to let him get accustomed to my scent. The cat sniffed me thoroughly until he, feeling safe, arched his back and began kneading his paws. I held him and rubbed him behind his ears. He was purring.

"I want to look inside his mouth," I said. Using a tongue depresser, I pushed on Reggae's jaw, until his mouth was open wide. "There's the problem," I said. "He's got a sticker burr stuck under his tongue. Look here." And I carried the cat, with his mouth gaping open, over to Danny.

"How did he get that?" he asked, peering down his cat's throat.

"When he groomed himself," I said. "The sticker got caught in his mouth, probably while he was trying to pull it out of his fur. Cats are quite particular. They like to stay clean."

"Reggae always likes to look nice," said Danny. "He's a ladies man. The neighborhood's crawling with his kittens."

"I'll have to sedate Reggae to remove the thorn," I said. "I can neuter him while he's asleep. Neutered cats make better pets."

"Then how's he going to have any fun?"

I had a defense for that sort of argument, backed with horror stories of the hell homeless cats endure and the depressing statistics on the number of unwanted kittens and cats that were euthanized by humane societies that I soon had Danny nodding in agreement. He left the cat with us, and I removed the sticker and neutered Reggae without complication.

I saw patients till noon, took a break for lunch and had a waiting room full when I returned. Allen came in and picked up Bear.

"Be sure he gets his pills every day," I said. I stressed the fact it was important for Bear to receive his medication regularly, otherwise the seizures would return, often on a more severe and frequent basis.

Mr. Hardin came in with Delilah. She was the most docile of Bassets, with those irresistible sad eyes, not at all the conniving canine his owner had pictured. And she was in the middle of a false pregnancy. Her breasts were even full of milk. I explained to Mr. Hardin that hormones produced by the dog's ovaries would stimulate her to lactate and make her very moody.

"Like pre-menstrual syndrome," he said.

"Sorta," I said. I vaccinated Delilah for rabies and told Mr. Hardin that Delilah would probably go through a false pregnancy after each heat and if he wanted to eliminate them, he ought to have her spayed.

I had become so involved with seeing patients, I was startled when Patty came in to say the lab was on the phone. Heart pounding, I picked up the receiver. A female voice said, "I have the results of the fluorescent antibody test for rabies on the Garza cat."

"Go ahead," I said.

"It's positive!"

"Positive?"

"Positive. We'll be sending you a copy of the test results. If we can be of furthur assistance please let us know."

"Thank you very much," I said, and I hung up. "Hold everything," I said. "Call Dr. Elgin at the Health Department and tell him I'll need to start the rabies shots. And get hold of Mrs. Garza's granddaughter and have her grandmother see her physician." I filled a cup with water, drank it all down and walked through the waiting room to the surprise of my clients. I wasn't symptomatic so I still had a chance.

The treatment for rabies exposure is five daily injections of a killed rabies virus grown in human cells. The shots are given in the skin of the arm with a very fine needle and are less painful then the old method of subcutaneous injections given along the abdomen. Patty, Mrs. Graza, Angela and I took those shots, but as I was actually the only one bitten, I also received an injection of gamma globulin that was administered just below my hip. The shot sped searing pain down to my toes and the soreness was slow to leave. I felt like a football player with a hip pointer.

The next three weeks were scary as I felt abnormal sensations in my hand and arm and drank extra amounts of water. But with each passing day, my chances of developing rabies diminished and my psychosomatic illness disappeared. Meanwhile, as the rabies epidemic continued, the hysteria in town surged onward.

During a lunch hour, midway through the epidemic, I left the office for Ralph Rawson's barber shop. Ralph's shop was opposite the courthouse on the east side of the square, in the middle of the block, between the Rexall Pharmacy with the working soda fountain and the local savings and loan.

Ralph's barber shop reminded me of the ones I used when I was a kid. Inside, a shoulder-high mirror ran across both walls – so you could chat with the barber while you monitored what he was doing to your hair. At the front was an old bronze register and in one corner were two wooden slats that fitted across the barber chair arms. Ralph used them to boost up kids who were too short to sit in the chairs by themselves. Directly behind Ralph's chair was Ralph's pride, a mounted deer head with the biggest set of antlers I'd ever seen. Ralph was an avid hunter, belonged to the National Rifle Association and had a sticker on the door that said, "If you outlaw guns only outlaws will have guns." He never failed to tell his clients the story of how he bagged that buck with one shot from 1500 yards with his 30-06.

The other fixture in Ralph's shop was Ralph's only employee, Jorge Hernandez, who said he'd been working for Ralph since Truman ran against Dewey.

The sharp, cool scent of shaving cream, aftershave lotion and hair tonic had just settled in my nose when Jorge said, "Nice to see you, Doc. How's your heep?"

"It's a lot better, Jorge. Thanks for asking."

Everyone knew I had been bitten by a rabid cat and my daily condition was of concern to all.

Ralph was busy with a customer, so I climbed into Jorge's chair, which was next to the window, instructed him to take a little off the top and trim the sideburns, and then settled down with the sports page from the *Austin American-Statesman*. Except for the snipping of scissors, the whirring of clipper blades and Ralph's chronic rendering of the slaying of the stag, the afternoon melted into monotony, unbroken until Allen Shelton arrived, followed by Bear.

"You'll have to leave that mutt outside," said Ralph. "This here's a barber shop and not a Poodle parlor."

"Yessir," said Allen. He took Bear outside and told him to "stay." Bear lay on the sidewalk, just below the barber pole. From my vantage point, high in the chair, I could see the dog's sad eyes follow Allen back into the shop.

"I didn't know you came here," I told Allen.

"I don't," he said. "I'm short on money."

Ralph finished with his customer, brushed the gentleman's clothes with a wisk broom and rang the charges on the cash register. He shook the barber's cape and motioned to Allen that he would be next.

"I'm ready for you now," said Ralph.

Allen sat in the chair next to mine and we resumed our conversation.

"Bear doing all right?" I asked.

"Just fine, sir."

"You're keeping up with his medication?"

"Not as often as I should," said Allen. "Some days I forget. Hasn't seemed to bother 'm."

"Stop forgetting," I said sternly. "Still working at McDonald's?"

"Yessir."

Abruptly, Jorge, who had been silently trimming my hair, stood in the middle of the room, pointed to the door with his scissors and let out with an ear-piercing scream, "AEIEEEE RABEED DOG MEESTER RAWSON RABEED DOG."

"Oh, God, Bear's having a convulsion," yelled Allen.

I looked in the direction that Jorge was pointing and there was Bear, in the middle of the street, jerking violently like a drunken Jack-in-the-Box, in the throes of a grand mal seizure.

"I'll take care of him," said Ralph. He drew a gun from a small drawer under his counter and ran outside.

"Wait a minute, Ralph!" I hollered. "It's not what you think." I struggled to free myself from my cocoon-like sheet. It was entangled in the chair's footrest.

"Hey! Whaddaya think you're doing!" yelled Allen. He jumped from his chair and joined the chase, only seconds behind Ralph.

Throwing off the encumbering cape I followed Allen, but just as I reached the door Ralph took aim and fired. BAM!

"I got him, I got him," whooped Ralph. His gun was still smoking.

Allen grabbed Ralph by the arm and whirled him around. "You asshole!" screamed Allen. "You've shot my dog, for chrissake. He's epileptic!"

Ralph was befuddled and stood there, not knowing what to say. "Hell, ain't nobody told me," he said. Ralph shrugged. "You're lucky I didn't shoot him in the head."

"Thanks for nothing," said Allen. He dropped to his knees and bent over Bear, sobbing over the body. In an instant I was right alongside, checking Bear over. Luckily, Bear's seizure was so violent Ralph wasn't able to draw a steady bead, and the bullet entered adjacent to the spine, behind the last rib, exiting the lower flank before lodging in the thigh. Miraculously, the dog was still living, but a steadily enlarging pool of blood was ominous.

"Give me a hand," I said, nudging Allen in the side. "As long as he's breathing we got a chance."

I yelled at Ralph. "Call my office and tell Patty I'm on my way with a gunshot case and be ready to go into surgery. And put that gun away."

Bear left a trail of blood as we rushed the dog inside the clinic to where Patty waited with an I.V. I added anesthetic and antibiotics directly through the drip, while Patty rolled the x- ray to the surgery table and took whole-body films.

"Start warming a bottle of blood," I ordered.

"Don't you need Bear's blood type?" asked Allen.

"It's only important if we have to give him blood more than once," I said. "And if we don't get some blood into him now, we won't have to worry about a second time."

Patty hung the blood bottle from the I.V. stand, ran the tubing over a heating pad and connected it to the drip we had going. From the hole in Bear's back, blood was coming out as fast as Patty had it going in. I gowned and gloved as Patty prepped the dog.

Quickly, she turned Bear on his back, clipped away the hair, vacuumed the stomach clean, scrubbed the abdomen with antiseptic soap, wiped it with Betadine and pronounced the dog ready for surgery.

I suspected that Bear was hemorrhaging from a major abdominal vessel, but if I was going to find it, I needed lots of room, so I made a long incision, from below the breastbone to just in front of the pelvis. I set a retractor and spread the incision wide. The dog's belly was full of blood. I couldn't see.

"Give me some suction!" I yelled. Patty directed the sterile tip of the surgical vacuum into the pool of blood. It gurgled as it aspirated the red fluid.

Cautiously, I entered my hand into the abdomen and gently laid the dog's intestines onto the sterile drapes. By now there was less blood and my field of view was clearer. Bladder, stomach, spleen and liver all seemed okay, but there was a constant pool of blood where the left kidney should have been. In its place was an engorged, dark, semipulpy mass. I clamped the vessels that fed the amorphous structure and the bleeding slowed to a dribble. Fatty tissue made the surface around the damaged kidney slippery, but I managed to seal the vessels with suture and remove the useless organ and its accompanying ureter. With the hemorrhaging controlled, Bear's membranes appeared pinker. It was a good sign.

An inspection of the intestines revealed four small holes, none of which completely penetrated all the layers of the bowel. I repaired them quickly and then turned my attention to the wounds in Bear's back and flank.

The muscles around those wounds were blackened, yet they still oozed blood, indicating viable circulation, so I trimmed the damaged tissue, positioned a drain and closed the wounds as best I could. Finally, after checking the rest of Bear's organs, I replaced the intestines, rinsed the peritoneal cavity with an antibiotic solution, inserted a belly drain and closed the incision.

Bear's leg was next. The x-rays showed the bullet to be just under the skin, and I felt a lump as I ran my finger in the area where the bullet had lodged. Metal ground against metal as I incised the swelling. I probed with a hemostat and found it. The slug came out easily and I handed it to Allen.

"Looks like a .22," I said, as I placed the final stitches.

"We might want to send it to ballistics," joked Allen halfheartedly.

Patty began cleaning as I took inventory of Bear's condition. His color was still poor, but holding, and his breathing and heart rate were adequate. He'd been given a half liter of fluid and an equivalent amount of whole blood. If he survived the initial shocks from the shooting and the surgery, I felt he might have a chance, but, realistically, the odds were poor. He faced the possibility of kidney shutdown, and, if he got by that, an even greater risk of infection.

"What are his chances?" asked Allen.

"About three in ten," I said, removing my gloves and gown.

"Do you mind if I stay with him?" asked Allen.

"You can spend the whole night," I said. "But I suspect Bear's gonna sleep most of the evening and we won't know much until morning. If something comes up, you can call me at home." Patty prepared the bathroom for Bear and Allen. She lined the floor with layers of newspapers and covered them with a sheet. Allen went home to get his sleeping bag. I cleaned up and went on home, where my wife asked me where I'd gotten such a terrible haircut.

The next morning Allen met me at the door. Patty came out of the bathroom. "Bear's holding his own," she said. "He's groggy, but his temp is only 102.5."

I went to see Bear. He shakily raised his head, flapped his tail and laid his head down once more. Patty handed me two syringes and I aspirated the drains. They produced only a scant amount of fluid.

"So far so good," I said. "Maintain him on two I.V.'s with the same antibiotic schedule as yesterday. And let's give some liver-iron with B-12."

"Does that mean he's going to make it?" asked Allen.

"No. I'm just upgrading his chances to five out of ten."

Allen went to class while I got ready to see patients. I spent an uneventful day until late that afternoon when I had a visit from Mrs. Weber and her daughter Lori.

They were cat lovers. They had three cats that they claimed as their own, but I knew they ran a shelter for sick or injured feline transients, nursing them to health and then searching for suitable homes. Mr. Weber, however, wasn't fond of cats at all.

"Actually, Mr. Weber is afraid of cats," confided his wife. "My mother-in-law said that when he was little, a cat scratched him terribly and ever since then, he's been scared of them."

It was unusual that today the Webers had come without any of their infirmed felines. I inquired about the reason for their visit.

"Lori and I were driving down Springs Street when we saw a cat lying in the road," said Mrs. Weber.

"We think it was hit," said Lori.

"Of course, you know us," said Mrs. Weber. "We stopped to pick it up."

"And it bit me on the hand. See!" Lori held her palm in my face. There were two fresh punctures in the webbing between her thumb and her forefinger.

"It was trying to claw us, so we had to leave it," said Mrs. Weber. "But now, I'm wondering if that cat had something we might catch, like . . ."

"Like rabies," I said.

She clutched her purse and shook her head yes.

I looked her earnestly in the eyes and said, "Take Patty, go to Springs Street and bring that cat over here before someone else finds it and takes it home. Patty!"

"You don't have to yell," she said. "I'm right at the front desk."

"Pardon me," I said. "Listen. Go with the Webers and help them find this cat. Uh, what color did you say it was?"

"Orange and white," they said.

"And take the lead gloves and a box," I said. "If we can't find him, Lori will have to take the shots."

Patty collected her equipment and led her group away. Meanwhile, I took two jars of baby food and joined Bear in the bathroom. I put his head on my lap and started to feed him. Using a tongue depressor, I scooped a portion from the jar and smeared it inside his mouth. He let it stay there for a second, determining if it fit his taste, then his decision made, he rolled his tongue and swallowed. Following that, he poked his nose in the jar and began eating on his own. I stroked Bear behind his head and between his ears. He stopped eating long enough to look at me as if to say thanks and redirected his attention to finishing his meal. An hour later the Weber expedition returned.

"We found the cat," said Patty. "It was dead."

I explained to Mrs. Weber there was nothing else to do except send the head to the lab in Austin.

"Let me take it," she said. "Besides, my husband is bringing his mother up from Corpus and I need a good excuse to get out of the house. I'll be sure it gets there. Just give me directions."

Patty drew a map while I duplicated the procedure I had performed on the Garza kitten. Again I plopped the head in a clear cellophane bag, put the bag in a small sack from Safeway, handed it to Mrs. Weber and cautioned, "Be sure to keep it in the refrigerator." Then they went on their way.

In spite of his blood loss, Bear made good progress, no small thanks to Egg McMuffins.

"Everyone at work is chipping in," said Allen. "I have a whole freezer full of Big Macs."

Ralph Rawson apologized and told Allen he could have a free hair cut. Patty said Allen deserved more than that. What Rawson deserved I can't describe in print.

I sent Bear home, but only after I made Allen promise to give the epilepsy medication faithfully.

I assumed all went well for Lori but I didn't know for sure until a few weeks later when I saw her mother in the grocery store.

"Everything worked out fine," said Mrs. Weber. "But that's not the half of it. I told you William and his mother were coming from Corpus. Well, they drove all night without stopping and they were starved when they got here. I was already in bed, so William's mom offered to fix a snack. She rummaged in the refrigerator and opened the sack with the cat's head. When she looked in she fainted dead away. She always said I didn't feed William right, and now she's convinced."

By the onset of fall, the epidemic was waning and as the number of reported rabid animals declined, the intense public participation decreased as well. San Marcos finally got back to normal. But the virus is still present in nature, and as long as people keep unvaccinated pets, rabies will remain a constant threat.

TIME OF
THE MONTH

Who was that on the phone?" I asked as I walked into the office. Travis and I had just returned from a ranch call and I didn't want to handle unnecessary "emergencies". After palpating 150 head of crossbred mother cows for pregnancy, we were sweaty and dirty and ready to go home.

"Some coed from the college," said Patty as she replaced the receiver. "She thinks her dog ate..."

"Just a second," I said. "Hey, Travis, before you make yourself comfortable take my truck to the Seven-Eleven and bring us some cold drinks." I tossed him my key ring. "Now, Patty, what did you say that dog swallowed?

"She thinks her dog swallowed her Tampax."

"Oh, c'mon." Must be some mistake, I thought.

"She says she saw him eat it," insisted Patty.

This was a first. I've removed socks, rocks, Christmas ornaments, corn on the cob, baby nursers and more from the inside of many a canine, but never a tampon.

"Hmmmm. What kind of dog does she have?" I asked, hoping that it might be a Dane or some other giant breed whose size alone would allow the tampon to pass.

"She's got a six-pound Shih Tzu. I told her to come over and we'd do something about it. Was that okay?"

"Yeah, it's okay. Say, are tampons digestible?"

"I wouldn't have the slightest idea," she said.

I stepped into the bathroom to wash my face and to cool off and weigh my alternatives. First, I wasn't sure of the medical significance of an ingested tampon. Could it obstruct the dog's stomach or would it absorb so much water it could cause dehydration or even toxic shock? Would it be possible that a tampon suitable for the average female could be lethal in a six-pound Shih Tzu? Regardless of the scenario, the tampon would have to come out. I would give the dog an emetic to make him vomit and he'd throw it up. I emerged from the bathroom refreshed and prepared. I gave my first order.

"Unlock the narcotics cabinet and get out the bottle of apomorphine." Apomorphine is chemically related to morphine and produces similar effects except for one. A person vomits before the narcosis sets in. The drug was quite useful, since its effect on dogs was similar, but federal law made us keep the drug under lock and key, and we had to maintain strict records as to how much we used and when.

"I'll get it for you," said Patty, "but you haven't forgotten that today I'm leaving early? You promised. Trudi and I are going to San Antonio for Fiesta and the Parade of Flowers."

Patty placed the small bottle of apomorphine on the counter, hurriedly cleaned off her desk, grabbed her bag and yelled, "See ya tomorrow." Then she zipped toward the door. She was taking no chances. On some days it was possible to be trapped all evening seeing patients, and if we didn't close up and leave, we could work till midnight.

I sat in the office to await Travis, who arrived just as Patty was leaving. She held her hand over her nose as they passed each other, and he saluted her by tipping his hat. He sashayed into my office, shoved an opened six pack of beer in front of me, wrested a can from the carton and popped the top.

"Take one, Doc. I'm jest two ahead."

"Put it in the fridge," I said calmly. "You know I don't drink on the job. Besides, there's an emergency coming. Do you think you can handle a Shih Tzu?"

Travis took a hearty swig from what must have been his third can, smacked his lips and said, "What's a Shit Sue?"

"That's Shih Tzu, Travis. They are small Chinese dogs. They look like Pekingese."

He tilted his head and inverted his can, chug-a-lugging the rest of his beer. Then he belched contentedly. "Damn, Doc. If I can handle cows I can certainly handle a Shit Sue."

"Shih Tzu, Travis. Shee Tsu! Get it?"

"Yeah, I got it."

Travis walked to the sink, then as an afterthought faced me and asked, "Whose dog is it?" But before I could answer, he lowered his head over the basin, pressed a finger to a nostril, closing it off, and then snorted, clearing his nares and sinuses. He did the same to the other side, flushing the mucous down the drain with a burst of water from the faucet. Then he returned to his seat, where he sprawled like a slinky.

"Now who'd ya say owned that dog?" he asked.

"A coed at the college," I said. "She's never been here before."

"What's wrong with it?" he asked. He crinkled the empty can with his burly fist and stuffed a chew in his mouth with the other.

"Swallowed his owner's Tampax," I said.

As the full implication of my statement registered in Travis's brain, his lips puckered and his cheeks puffed out as if his chaw had exploded. I thought he looked like a chipmunk with a toothache. Regaining his composure, he angled his cud to one corner, cocked his sweat-stained hat back on his head and said, "Aw, now, ain't that something." His face had mischief written all over it.

Travis was my large animal assistant. He had studied animal husbandry at the college but failed out of school after his freshman year. He worked odd jobs, part time at a feedlot and part time for me. He also broke horses and rodeoed on weekends. His specialty was team roping. Two cowboys on horseback would chase a calf – one would lasso the head and the other the hind legs. The team with the quickest time would win. Travis could handle either position, header or heeler, and he was good.

On Saturday nights I could find him at the Crystal Palace, a popular western dance hall where all the local "kickers" gathered. They'd two-step to music by Willie Nelson or George Strait and put away pitchers of Lone Star beer. The gals would come in singly and sit at a table, while the guys would gather in groups of three or four, stand at the bar and look over the prospects. Travis thought women considered him irresistible, but Patty's reaction was closer to the truth. In my eyes, Travis had drawbacks in his lack of social graces and his sporadic practice of basic hygiene, but he could do wonders with horses or cattle, so I kept him on. This, however, would be his stiffest test.

"Damn," He said. "The dog must be some kind of pervert to eat a Tampax."

"Dogs aren't perverts, Travis. It's just a question of pheromones."

"Farah who?" mumbled Travis. He raised his butt from the chair as he eased out a slow, rumbling fart.

"Pher-o-mones," I said, fanning the air with a magazine. "It's an airborne sex attractant. It brings opposite sexes together. That tampon had a scent the dog couldn't resist, so he ate it."

Travis dragged the wastebasket over, placed it between his knees and let go with a shot of tobacco juice.

"I still think he was a pervert," he said.

"C'mon, Travis," I said. "You've had dogs smell you and the first thing they do is stick their nose between your legs. They're checking out your pheromones."

"And that's all they'd better be checking," he said. He stood up to adjust his crotch and then dropped his empty can in the wastebasket.

"But it's true," I said. "Once I owned a male Sheltie that would drag my wife's panties from the hamper just to lick them, and then he'd pull his lips back every so often and grin like a stud with a mare in heat. When I practiced in New Orleans I even got a phone call from a woman who wanted to know if her Poodle could catch V.D. from licking her panties."

"What did you tell her?" asked Travis, who sat up in his chair, keen on learning a lesson in venereal disease.

"That the dog most certainly would, especially if she had it. You see, it's all a matter of pheromones."

"I never heard of such a thing," said Travis, "Farah Moans?" Chuckling, he took his pen knife and began cleaning the dirt from behind his fingernails, scraping the filth onto his jeans.

"I'll give you another example," I said. "There was Mrs. Fontenot."

"Who was she?"

"Another one of my New Orleans clients. She was about forty and divorced. She had a German Shepherd named Max. She told me Max liked to lick the inside of her thighs." I sighed. "Whenever Max was sick she wanted me to make housecalls."

"Did ya?"

"Travis. There's no way a man's tongue can compare with a German Shepherd's."

"Oh, you know what I mean. Was she good lookin'?"

"Max must've thought so."

"Damn, Doc, sometimes I think you don't have a serious bone in your body." He propped his manure-laden boots up on my desk and stuffed more tobacco in his already swollen cheeks.

I got up from behind my desk and peered through the doorway and out the waiting room window. A baby-blue Mustang was parked in front and a young lady was walking a petite silver and white Shih Tzu to the entrance.

"Our client's here," I said, straightening some papers. "Get your feet off my desk – and you'd better get rid of that tobacco. You might want to ask her for a date."

"Not me, Doc. All they got at the college are a bunch of bookworms. They're not my type."

Travis opened the door while I went behind the counter to fill out the lady's card.

The young woman was lovely. She had blue eyes and long blonde hair pulled back in a pony tail, and she wore a tartan skirt with a white blouse, knee socks and penny loafers. I guessed she was in her early twenties. She was country club material, a young Grace Kelly, a candidate for the Junior League. As she approached the counter I detected the faint odor of perfume. She addressed me softly.

"I spoke earlier to the receptionist. She said the doctor would wait. Is he here?"

Granted, I wasn't dressed like city small animal doctors with their spiffy green or white lab coats, but after sticking one's arm up a multitude of bovine rectums to feel their reproductive organs, one doesn't resemble Dr. Kildare. "I'm the doctor," I replied in a corrective but friendly spirit. "Can I help you?"

"Oh, um, yessir, uh, did your secretary explain Chin's situation?" She reached down and picked up her charge while glancing nervously at Travis, whose eyes were glued to her attractive dimensions.

"Yes, she did, but first let's get your name and address on our records. You are..."

"Lisa Wells."

"Your address and phone number."

"1101 Mill Street. 392-7895."

"And the dog's name is Chin."

"Yessir."

"And how old is Chin?"

"He's nine months."

"And has he had all his vaccines?

"I think so. He was a gift from my boyfriend and he said he didn't need any more shots."

"Okay. Lets bring him into the exam room and you tell me exactly what happened. Travis, hold on to this little guy, will you?"

Travis, whom I suspected was mentally undressing my client, swooped up the hairy bundle with one hand and marched smartly into the room, leaving in his wake the odor of beer, sweat and manure. Lisa gasped as she inhaled the fumes, but she doggedly gathered her composure and trooped in after him. Travis placed Chin on the table, maneuvering him single-handedly like a checker, and with his free hand he reached back into his rear pocket, producing a brown, stained styrofoam cup that doubled as a spittoon. He raised it to his lips, emitting an audible "splurp" as he jettisoned the excess spittle and then quickly hid the cup and its contents behind his back.

Lisa was so absorbed in Chin's fate she missed this repugnant act. I was grateful that Travis, at least, didn't spit in the sink. This case would tax my ability to maintain a sense of decorum and professional propriety, and I didn't want to begin with a scene. I would deal with Travis later, so I began with the basic premise.

"I understand Chin swallowed a, uh . . ." I felt my neck

get hot. I turned to Travis as if to ask him for the correct word. He was delighted, watching me squirm until I finally was able to say, "Uh . . . a sanitary pad or something."

"Yes, Doctor, it was a Tampax tampon," said Lisa.

"Are you sure?" I said. "We don't want to put Chin through any unnecessary treatment."

For the moment Chin seemed perfectly normal and content. His coat was smartly parted down the middle and a crowning blue ribbon kept his hair out of his eyes and perfectly matched his painted toenails. He'd look back and forth, either toward me or Lisa, depending upon who was talking and he seemed to be pleased to be the center of conversation.

"Oh, I'm positive," she said. "He stole it from the bathroom wastebasket. When I tried to take it from him, he swallowed it."

Chin gaily wagged his tail, happily admitting his guilt.

"Splurp!" punctuated Travis, repeating his loathsome act. My eyes darted over to my noncompliant assistant just in time to see him hide his arm behind his back. His apparent aloofness was betrayed by an ill-concealed snicker. I was horrified. I frowned at him and then resumed my questioning.

"Uh, okay, Lisa, Has he vomited or seemed uncomfortable?"

"No, he seems perfectly fine. After he swallowed the tampon he went to his food bowl, ate some of his dog snacks and drank a lot of water."

Certainly, I thought. Nothing like dessert and a drink to top off a meal. I felt Chin's abdomen. It was mildly bloated. Travis and Chin's eyes followed me, anxiously awaiting my next move.

"Well, Lisa, I'm going to give Chin an injection of apomorphine. It will cause him to vomit and I'm sure he'll regurgitate his tampon."

"Splurp!" Travis again added to his collection of tobacco juice. He was deliberately trying my patience and relishing every minute.

I prepared the apomorphine and injected it under the dog's skin. Then I collected some paper towels and placed them in from of Chin, and the three of us hovered over the patient, like parents awaiting the birth of a child.

"Will it take long?" asked Lisa. "I have an evening class that starts in an hour."

"No," I said. "We should have results in five to ten minutes. By the way, my receptionist said you were a student at the university. How are you classified?"

"I'm a graduate student in history," she said. "I'm studying Carolingian manuscripts with Dr. Brinegar at Southwest Texas and Professor Newman at U.T. Austin."

"That sounds very interesting. Right up your alley, isn't it, Travis?

Aha! I had caught Travis in between nicotine volleys. He couldn't reply without drooling like the town fool. Eager to enter the conversation and make an impression on Lisa, he courageously swallowed part of his chaw and responded weakly if not creatively. "Aw, Doc, you know I ain't never been to Carolina."

As Lisa and I pondered that cryptic reply, Chin began to show signs of nausea. He began by drooling, followed by compulsive licking and swallowing, culminating with repetitive stomach pulses and spasmodic heaving. The initial efforts produced the soggy remnants of his doggy snacks, then came two unproductive retches finalized by a grand surge of climactic disgorgement, when the tampon, trailing a streamer, rocketed skywards. We cheered and crowded the table, drawing closer to our quarry, thankful for its deliverance. It rested quietly on the paper towels, its string floating in a pool of yellow fluid. The smell of vomit was everywhere.

"Pardon me, Doc," grunted Travis. "Could I be excused? I don't feel so hot." Evidently the beer, barf, tobacco and tampon had taken their toll. He removed his hat and headed for the restroom. The sound of splashing in the commode was, in this instance, recompense.

Chin had settled into a euphoric stupor, an aftereffect of the narcotic. He felt no pain or embarrassment. I placed him in a cage to sleep off the drug. He would be as good as new in the morning.

Lisa politely exited the room, blushing over this intrusion into her private affairs. Her embarrassment being total, she said she would send her roommate to pickup Chin in the morning. Lisa even paid the bill in advance. I figured there was no way she could ever face me again.

Finally, long after she left, I resurrected Travis from the bathroom. He was green about the gills. I chided him over his weak stomach. "Hey, Mr. Cowboy. That little Shit Sue make you toss your cookies? Try this for your tummy ache." I dispensed him a bottle of bismuth suspension. We gave it to dogs with upset stomachs. He mumbled a half-hearted thanks and staggered out the door. I locked up and went home.

The next day Patty and I had a good laugh over the whole episode. I eventually forgot about the pooch with the depraved appetite until one month later, when again at closing, I heard Patty consulting over the phone.

"Who was that?" I asked.

"That was Lisa Wells, the girl who owns Chin. You know, the dog who ate the Tampax."

"Yeah, so what about her?"

"She's on her way over. He just swallowed another one."

A PIECE
OF CAKE

With the graying of America an increasing number of clients fall into the category of senior citizen. They face an adjustment as children move away or husbands or wives grow old and die. For some the change presents problems, while for others the transition is smooth; yet in either case, it's often a pet who becomes the focus upon which these lives are centered. One such client was Jennie Armistead, an elderly widow who raised Boston Terriers at a kennel just outside of town.

Jennie had moved from Minnesota after her husband died, mainly to satisfy her daughter, who didn't want her mother spending winters alone. Jennie told me she had agreed to the move only on the condition she could bring her dogs, which she did, transporting them in the back of a Ryder truck. Keeping the kennel was no easy task but it kept Jennie young. Her dogs numbered more than thirty, and she was over seventy.

I had always thought one Boston Terrier looked just like the next. However, she would point out subtle differences in size, texture of hair coat, degree of twist to the tail and the shape of the white splashes on faces and chests. She knew each one by name and could easily recite how one dog was related to another.

Even though Boston Terriers made wonderful pets, Bostons were notorious for problem whelpings. A female's pelvis could be too narrow or their pups' heads too wide, so surgical delivery was often indicated. Some pups made the vaginal passage safely, only to be stopped by the bitch's small vulvar opening. Those mothers required an episiotomy, a minor operation. But more often than not, when a pup was turned sideways in the uterus, or if it was too large to pass, a cesarean section was required. Just sedating a Boston was risky, as their extensive tongues and elongated soft palates tended to block their windpipes. And, to complicate matters, the dogs were prone to laryngospasm, an event that completely sealed the windpipe shut.

Today, Jennie had called to say one of her prize Boston Terrier bitches was late in whelping and it was possible that the dog would need a section. From the window I watched as Jennie, a slightly built woman with coal black hair – Patty said it was store bought – guided a chunky Boston to our door. They stopped in front of a tree as Jennie allowed the little bitch to sniff out a proper place to eliminate, and then they walked in. Jennie waited for Patty to place Jasmine on the table and brought me up to date.

"Jasmine's been straining for two hours," said Jennie. "She passed a bubble about noon and still no puppy."

A bubble was a breeder's term for the waterbag. When you saw a bubble, a pup wasn't far behind.

I reached for Jasmine, but Jennie wasn't ready to let go. She hugged the dog as if I were going to kidnap it, kissing it repeatedly. Then she told me, "I gave her oxytocin."

Oxytocin was a useful drug that accelerated deliveries. It worked by increasing the strength and frequency of the uterine contractions. Many breeders had access to the drug, but far fewer used it correctly. I examined the dog's vagina, but there were no pups in the canal. A greenish discharge stained my glove, a sure sign that the placentas were tearing. In this case, the oxytocin only served to tighten the uterus about the pups, making a bad situation worse. I had no other options.

"She's going to need a section," I said.

"I was afraid she would," despaired Jennie. "Better go ahead and do it."

While Jennie sat in the waiting room, Patty and I shaved Jasmine's abdomen and then gave her a bath. Following that I administered Innovar, a narcotic anesthetic that put the dog in a stupor. Then I passed a tube into Jasmine's trachea and Patty placed the animal on her back. The dog was so round we had to use sandbags to keep her on an even keel. Together we finished prepping the dog and following that I opened Jasmine's abdomen. Her uterus completely filled her belly.

The canine uterus is split like a Y – the apex attaches to the cervix and the arms extend into the abdomen. Each of Jasmine's uterine arms was divided into lumps, five in all, each lump containing a pup. Working my hand under the uterus, I pulled one arm up and out through the incision and placed it on the drape. Patty stood by with a clean towel.

"Get ready," I warned.

I made a slit on the lump nearest the cervix and a pup popped out. I cleaned the fetal membranes away from its face and waited, allowing every last bit of placental blood to be pumped into the new life. Then I clamped the umbilical cord and tossed the now squirming newborn to Patty. She vigorously rubbed it with a towel and the pup began to cry.

"I can hear it! I can hear it!" sang Jennie from the waiting room. "I'd better get my basket." I heard her open the front door.

"Jennie!" I shouted. "There's no rush."

"Is it a boy or girl?" she hollered back.

"It's a boy," yelled Patty.

I worked each lump down to the opening where the first pup had exited and delivered four more pups. Then I stitched the uterus closed and returned it to its normal position. Almost immediately the uterus began shrinking and the sutures disappeared from sight.

I sewed the abdomen closed, suturing each layer separately, and finally I administered Nalline, the antagonist that counteracts the anesthetic. Within minutes Jasmine was alert and on her feet. From start to finish it had taken only an hour. Patty put the pups in the basket and we took them in to Jennie, who eagerly waited to inspect them.

Jennie took each pup one by one and counted toes, inspected tails, looked for cleft palates and checked for hydrocephalus. Once assured that a pup was normal, she raised it to her cheek and nuzzled it. Jasmine stuck her nose into the basket and examined them too.

"This one is just like Mr. Boston's Best," said a proud Jennie. "He's the daddy. And this one here is more like Jasmine. See. She has this streak of white on her nose."

I honestly couldn't tell the difference but Jennie knew. Bursting with joy, she squeezed Jasmine and kissed her for the umpteenth time. "I'm so proud of you," she said.

Jasmine grunted more from pain than agreement.

"Not so hard," I said. "You'll pop her stitches."

"But she did such a good job," protested Jennie. "They're just what I ordered. Two boys and three girls."

We sat there admiring the litter, when Jennie's face suddenly turned white. She clutched at her chest. "May I have a glass of water," she said, haltingly.

"Are you all right, Jennie?" I sat down beside her.

"Yes, I'm just a little exhausted." She took two or three deep breaths. "I forgot to take my nitroglycerine." She pointed to her bag. "They're in my purse."

Patty searched Jennie's purse and found the pills. I

brought a glass of water and scolded Jennie lightly. "You never told me you had a heart condition."

"It's just a mild case of angina," she said. She took a sip of water and swallowed her medicine. "It's nothing, really."

"With your heart condition, don't you think keeping a kennel is unrealistic?"

"I don't need a lecture," she said. She scowled as if she'd heard it all before.

"But isn't thirty a bit too many?" said Patty.

Jennie looked betrayed. "Now you sound like my daughter," she said. She searched in her bag for a Kleenex. "My dogs are all I've got," she said as she blew her nose. Jennie reached in the basket for a pup as Jasmine whined and offered a paw.

"I'm sure your daughter only wants to do what's best," I said.

"I just wish everyone would leave me and my dogs alone," she said.

Arguing with Jennie was making things worse. I looked at Jasmine, who seemed to be doing well. "Okay," I said. "Just take it easy when you have an emergency. I'm busy enough just taking care of your dogs. I don't need you for a patient."

She knowingly smiled, and after she felt stronger, Patty helped her load Jasmine and the puppies into the car and they left.

It was a few days after Jennie's visit that I had an unexpected caller. A lady, escorted by a rather obese Chihuahua Fox Terrier mix, arrived by taxi. I watched as the woman slid across the car seat and on to the pavement, but the dog gave me a fright as it misjudged the height and nosedived to the ground. Unhurt, it shook itself, and together the two spryly bounced into the hospital.

I stood by as Patty completed their card. "Your name

is...?"

"Ruby Babcock," she said, "and this is Gina, my baby."

Patty recorded the information while Mrs. Babcock prissied about the room, modeling her hair. Even the dog appeared to be strutting.

"What do you think?" asked Mrs. Babcock.

"It looks lovely," said Patty.

"My beautician called in sick," said Mrs. Babcock. "I wasn't sure if the girl was doing it right."

Mrs. Babcock was petite, no more than five feet, with short silvery-blonde hair and bright red lipstick. I guessed she was over seventy, but I wasn't sure, mainly because she wore a lot of makeup. A bowl-shaped bulge protruded from below her waist line. Mrs. Babcock patted her head, making sure every curl was in place, and smoothed her double-knit slacks. I invited both her and the dog to the exam room.

Mrs. Babcock gazed about the room, taking notice of the instruments and shiny counters. I underwent inspection as well. "Mr. Hopson recommended you," she said. "He told me what a nice man you were and that you just loved animals."

"That's very kind," I said. "But what can I do for you, Mrs. Babcock?"

"Call me Ruby," she said with a lilt to her voice. She reminded me of a wren, perky and a little bit sassy.

"All right, Ruby, but what's wrong with..." I looked at the card again. "With Gina?"

"Her bottom's all red." She pointed at Gina's behind. "See where she's rubbing her butt on the ground. It's those glands by her rear end, those uh, uh..."

"Anal glands," I said.

Anal glands are sac-like structures common to carnivores. They lie under the skin on either side of the anus where they produce a malodorous semi-liquid substance.

Normally this material sprays forth whenever an animal is excited, has a bowel movement or marks its territory, but when the glands become clogged, the animal feels uncomfortable and it scoots its rump on the ground. To provide relief, I massaged the gland between my thumb, which I placed just outside the anus, and my forefinger, which I inserted in the dog's rectum. Then I squeezed the sacs and the contents would be extruded to the outside. Gina's glands were bulging.

"They certainly need to be emptied," I said.

I examined Gina closer. She was ten years old, spayed and like many older dogs, overweight. Ruby knew what I was thinking because she patted Gina's behind and said, "She's got love handles, Doc. It comes with age. I know."

Without warning Gina tensed and started to growl.

"She doesn't like you to mess with her bottom," said Ruby. "When she first had this problem I thought she had hemorrhoids. I tried giving her a suppository but she fought me tooth and nail."

Gina squirmed and snapped. "Don't let her bite you," cautioned Ruby.

Patty wrestled Gina into a hammer lock and I slipped my gloved finger inside the dog's rectum, squeezing the gland as gently as I could.

"It's all right, Gina," consoled Ruby. "It's no worse than having your prostate massaged. Isn't that right, Doc?"

I felt as if my privacy had been invaded.

"Gina doesn't have a prostate, Ruby."

"But you do," she said. She gigged me in the side. I was flustered so I changed the subject.

"Do you live far?"

"On East Mulberry," she said.

It was only five minutes by auto but too far to walk.

"How come you took a cab?"

"I don't drive," she said. "My husband took me

everywhere."

"Why don't you take lessons?"

"It's too dangerous," she said. "Besides, I sold the car when he died."

I angled my finger to express Gina's other gland.

"What about your neighbors, Ruby. Won't they give you a lift?"

"They only come around when they want something," said Ruby.

"You've lived there long?"

"Over twenty-seven years," she said.

"Why don't you move?"

"Can't afford it," she said.

"How about your family?" asked Patty.

"Got a stepson in Harlingen. That's about it."

Gina squealed like a pig as I squeezed her other gland empty.

"They were pretty full, weren't they, Doc?"

"Not too bad," I said. "How are you getting home?"

"Same way I got here," she said smartly. "By taxi."

"I'll be happy to have Patty take you," I said.

"Ain't that a kick, Gina. Doc here's gonna have his nurse take us home." She turned to me. "The stinkin' cabbies charge full fare just for the dog. Everybody's after a buck, right? Now how much do I owe you?" Ruby placed her purse on the counter. "Go easy," she said. "I got doctor bills of my own."

"It's twelve dollars," I said.

"Twelve bucks!" Ruby took her purse off the counter. Gina began barking.

"Make it six," I said, "and we'll be even."

"That's more like it," she said, and once more she set her purse on the counter.

Gina pawed at Ruby's ankles, urging her owner to hurry, but Ruby brushed her aside. "Just a minute," she said. "I've got to pay." From her wallet she counted six one-dollar bills. Then she rummaged in her purse, producing a piece of cake neatly wrapped in Saran. "I hope you like it," she said. "It's banana pecan. Made it fresh this morning."

"I'll have it for lunch," I said.

"What's the matter, Doc? Don't you like cake? How about cookies? I make good chocolate chips." Ruby had planted her feet as if she were making a goal line stand so I removed the wrapper and took a bite.

It was delicious. "Umm. It's great." I took another bite.

"Don't say it's good unless you really mean it," she said.

"No. It's good. Honest."

"Then next time I come I'll bring you some more," said Ruby. Then Patty took the two of them home.

About a month later I received a call from Ruby. She wanted Patty to drive her and Gina to the clinic. Since Ruby lived so close I agreed. Ruby arrived wearing a heavy coat and Gina was wearing a sweater. I noticed Ruby was sneezing.

"Aren't you sweltering?" I said. "It's the middle of June."

"I've got a terrible cold," she said nasally. "I'm all stopped up."

"Have you been to the doctor?"

"Three times already," she said, "but now Gina's caught it. Look at her eyes."

The chances of Gina catching an infectious disease from Ruby were miniscule. Nevertheless, Patty hoisted the dog onto the table while I got out my ophthalmoscope. Gina had her eyes half shut. Two brown tear stains made a trail from the inside corners of the dog's eyes down the side of the face. I checked for irritants or extra lashes that might be the root of the problem. Then I sniffed Gina's hair.

"What's that smell?" I asked.

"I think it's menthol," said Patty.

"It's Vicks," said Ruby. "It helps me clear my sinuses. I use it to steam up the bathroom. Gina keeps me company."

"No wonder Gina's eyes are so red," I said. I put some salve in the dog's eyes and handed Ruby a fresh tube of medicine. "Put this in her eyes and keep her out of the bathroom."

"There's got to be something else, Doc."

"Not that I can find," I said.

"Well, she's rubbing her butt on the floor again and she's got her tee-tee all red. It must be her anal glands."

It hadn't been long since I emptied Gina's glands, but I felt them anyway. As expected, they were normal, but the skin around the dog's vulva was red. I watched a flea run down one of Gina's hind legs and hide itself between the dog's toes.

"She's biting at fleas, Ruby. She's made a sore spot in her private area."

"And I thought she had prickly heat," said Ruby. "All week I've made her sit in a tub of baking soda and water."

"Staying wet only makes her feel more itchy," I said. I smeared zinc oxide around the affected area and dispensed some for Ruby to take home. Then, once more, I began to set the dog down when Ruby pointed at Gina's feet and said, "Her toenails look awfully long, Doc."

I took the hint and picked up Gina's paw and began trimming the nails. I clipped the first two then asked, "What's new in your neighborhood, Ruby?"

"Nothing," she said. "Everybody minds their own business."

"So what do you do all day?"

"Keep house," she said.

"For just the two of you?" said Patty.

"That's right, honey," said Ruby. "Just me and my baby. I spent all morning scrubbing floors and shampooing carpets. My husband always enjoyed a clean house." I finished one paw and started another. "Don't you ever go out, to the movies or shopping?"

"I would if somebody would ask me."

"That's depressing," said Patty.

"Don't feel sorry for me, honey. Gina and I get along by ourselves just fine."

"It must get awful lonely," I said.

"You learn to live with it," said Ruby. "But you know, Doc, when my husband was alive, he'd barbecue in the back yard and we'd invite the neighborhood. We'd have a backyard full. But no more. Single women my age are like fifth wheels. The married ones think you're out to get their husbands."

I didn't think she was a threat, but she was twice my age. I put the nail trimmers away.

"You are going to check her glands, aren't you, Doc?" Ruby said.

"I already did, Ruby. They feel fine."

"But you didn't check them from the inside," she said.

I figured I might as well humor her, so I put on my rubber gloves, and Gina, anticipating what was to follow, automatically tensed up.

"What about your church, Ruby? Don't they offer programs for single senior citizens?"

"I went once," she said. "All they got there is a bunch of old fogeys who do nothing but sit and spit."

I turned my finger sideways to express a gland and Gina squealed.

"Ooo," said Ruby. "I know that hurts."

I squeezed Gina's other gland, and then put the dog down. She immediately ran to Ruby and hid behind her legs. "Say, Doc," said Ruby. "Do you have the time?"

"It's three-thirty," I said.

"I'd like to stay and talk," said Ruby, "but I'm gonna be late for my soaps." She pulled out a package from her purse. "Here's your cake," she said. "I made it fresh this morning. Thanks for everything. Gina! Thank the doctor."

Gina ran to the door and bared her teeth. Patty took the two of them home.

The ten-minute round trip took Patty an hour and a half. By the time she returned I was steaming.

"But I've got the perfect excuse," said Patty. "Ruby made me come in and watch soaps with her."

"I wish I could watch soaps at six bucks an hour."

"Doctor Goldman, you don't understand." Patty started filing records. "Ruby's lonely. She enjoys having someone to talk to."

"What did you two talk about?"

"Mostly about her husband, Homer. She showed me all her wedding pictures. It's sad," said Patty. "She was married so long she's forgotten how to live for herself. All she ever did was cook and keep house."

"How long was she married?"

"Thirty-five years." Patty put the records aside. "Isn't there something we can do?"

"I guess she needs a friend," I said. "Next time she wants a ride, just go pick her up."

The highlight of our summer social season was a dinner dance held in July by the Tri-county Veterinary Association at the St. Anthony Hotel in San Antonio. Kay had bought a dress especially for the occasion and I had rented a tuxedo. I had just finished zipping closed the back of Kay's dress when the phone rang. I reached for it automatically, but Kay grabbed my hand away from the receiver and took the call instead. I watched the disappointment grow on her face as she said, "And I'll have him call when he gets in."

"It never fails," she said, after she hung up the phone.

"Who was that?"

"Jennie Armistead. She has a bitch that's having a problem whelping. She thinks it needs a section. Can't she call someone else?"

Kay was just showing normal frustration. She knew Jennie would only see me. "Call her back and tell her we'll meet at the clinic," I said. "We'll just have to be late."

Formally attired, Kay and I drove to the office. I went into the surgery to be sure I had a sterile set and Kay waited up front for Jennie. When I heard Jennie come in I started for the front, but Kay, with a pregnant Boston in tow, blocked my way.

"You can't go up there," Kay said.

"Why not?" I asked.

"Jennie doesn't care to talk to you."

"Is she all right?"

"She's fine."

"Did she forget her nitroglycerin tabs?"

"No. She's exercising a woman's prerogative. She handed me this message." Kay stuck a note under my nose.

It read, "This is my Jennie's Sweet Sue. She's the sister of my Boston Baby Special by my good male, Boston's Best Bobby. He's the father of Jennie's Jewel, the one who won Best of Show at All Texas Dog Breeders' Finals in Waco. I thought she was going to have a pup an hour ago, but she still hasn't delivered. Please examine her and let me know what you plan to do. Take care of her. Jennie"

I was trying to hurry and I wasn't in the mood for games. "Do I have to write back my findings, or is it all right if you go in there and tell her?"

"Don't be ridiculous," said Kay.

"Is it ridiculous to want to speak with my client?"

"Jennie's only doing what any woman in her circumstance would do," said Kay. "Now are we going to look at this dog or not?"

I hung my tuxedo jacket on a hook, undid the cufflinks and rolled up my shirtsleeves. Then I inserted a gloved finger into Sweet Sue's vagina. A pup was in the canal but its head was stuck just inside the vulvar lips. Jennie had probably gotten a glimpse of the pup when Sweet Sue was straining, but it apparently slipped back inside when she couldn't complete the delivery.

"We may be in luck," I said. "Tell Jennie we're going to do an episiotomy and hopefully we'll avoid a section."

I stripped off my shirt while Kay passed on my message. When she returned I gave Sue a local and split the vulvar lips, exposing a fat, roundish puppy head. Sweet Sue bore down and the pup's shoulders came free. Quickly, the rest followed. It was lifeless. I gave it to Kay.

"It's not breathing," she said. She shook it up and down and cleaned the mucous from its mouth.

"It's still not breathing," she said, anxiously.

"Put a drop of Dopram on its tongue," I said. Dopram is a potent respiratory stimulant.

The pup gagged but still didn't breathe. "Try artificial repiration."

"What I don't do for you," she said. She closed the pup's mouth and breathed for him through his nose.

The little rib cage lurched in and out and then settled down into a regular cycle of normal respirations. "I think it's all right now," she said, and she took the pup in to Jennie.

I x-rayed Sue and found there were two pups left, so I gave some oxytocin and within forty-five minutes Sue produced two more pups. Kay took those in to Jennie as well, and I sewed Sue back up.

"Remember. You have to stay in here," Kay said as she led Sue to the waiting room. I could hear Kay and Jennie bustling around, then the door opening and Jennie saying goodbye.

For the second time, I started getting dressed. Kay came back in. "I'm so proud of you," she said.

"What for?" I asked."

"For the way you take care of your old ladies," she said. Kay put her arms around me and kissed me on the cheek. "Jennie says she just adores you." Kay batted her eyes and pretended to pout. "I'm going to be jealous."

"It's no contest," I said, returning the kiss. "Any woman that can give artificial respiration through a dog's nose is a winner with me."

"I told you I was talented," she said coyly. "Let me help you with your tie."

I stood there patiently until she finished. Then I put my arms around her waist and drew her close. "Would you mind telling me why I had to carry on a long-distance conversation with my client?"

"It's a simple case of woman's vanity," she said, purring like a cat.

I whispered in her ear. "Did Jennie forget to put on her lipstick?"

"No," she said as she put a finger to my lips. "She forgot to put in her false teeth."

By summer's end, Ruby was taking full advantage of our taxi service. Every other week she'd call to have Gina's anal glands massaged and I would send Patty to pick Ruby and Gina up. The dog really didn't need her glands checked – Ruby just needed an excuse to come and talk. As Ruby became a regular visitor I felt a certain responsibility for her and I encouraged her to talk about herself. I thought, perhaps somewhere hidden in Ruby's past, lay a resource other than Gina that would help the woman reenter society. Our conversations became more direct.

"Say, Ruby," I said. "Do you mind if I ask you something

personal?"

"How personal?" she asked suspiciously.

"Are you afraid to be with people?"

"Me, afraid? Not on your life. I've been on my own since I was sixteen. I waited tables at a cafe next to the old San Francisco navy yard. It doesn't get any tougher."

"When were you in San Francisco?"

"During World War II," she said. "Those sailors could be right fresh, but I put 'em in their place – " she snapped her fingers – "just like that."

I raised my eyebrows.

"I was in demand," said Ruby. "I'd go dancing every weekend. I could really cut a rug."

She did a little two-step as she hummed a tune. All the while Gina barked.

"Homer took me dancing when we were courting," she said as she pattered about the floor. "Even after we got married, he'd take me out. We'd go with other couples, maybe once or twice a month. We were part of a gang."

For a second I imagined her and Homer dancing together, doing a foxtrot to a Glenn Miller tune while a smaller, younger Gina barked at their heels.

"Of course when Homer died," said Ruby, "the phone stopped ringing." She ended her solo performance and Gina stopped barking as well.

"Maybe you ought to get married again," I said.

"Look, Doc. When you go through what I did with my husband, you think twice about getting married. My Homer was a big, strong man. Never sick a day in his life. And to watch him go down like that...it wasn't any picnic. The medicine for the cancer was worse than the disease. Every time he took a treatment it was two days before he could keep anything in his stomach. I don't need a husband, Doc. All I need is an escort. Someone to take you places. You know what I mean?"

"Then what you want is a date," I said.

"Not even a date, Doc. Once a man finds out you're looking he'll expect you to deliver. Right, Gina?" Gina turned her head sideways and looked at her sympathetically. "And in this day and age you never know what you might catch."

Patty giggled under her breath.

"Surely there's somebody you'd care to go out with? I bet there's plenty of men who would be glad to take you out."

"Well, there was this one old coot who came by every afternoon. Said he wanted to borrow some sugar. But I know what he was really after."

"Ruby, you've got a one track mind."

"You can't be too careful," said Ruby, "what with AIDS and all."

"You're one tough broad."

"I gotta be, Doc. Listen. Quit trying to set me up, and give Gina the treatment."

Poor Gina. Her lowly anal glands had become Ruby's ticket to freedom, even though it was limited to trips to the vet. Patty lifted the dog onto the table, but this time, instead of backing away, Gina stood firm, resigned to the indignity she knew was sure to follow. Perhaps she understood the sacrifice she was making.

I mercifully finished the anal gland ream-out on Gina. Then Patty prepared to take Ruby and the patient home. They were halfway out the door when Ruby rushed back in. She reached in her purse.

"I almost forgot your cake!" she said.

"My mouth was watering."

"Made it fresh today, Doc. It's still hot."

It felt good to be special.

By September Ruby was now calling twice a week for transportation. Meanwhile, Jennie had had three bitches whelp. It was inevitable the two women would meet.

I had just completed Gina's usual posterior treatment and she and Ruby were getting ready to leave. Since Jennie was sitting in the waiting room with Boston's Bobette, the latest of her females to deliver, I introduced the ladies to each other. Gina ran up to Bobette and the two dogs sniffed noses. Ruby pulled Gina away.

"Is your dog contagious?"

"No," said Jennie. "She had a C-section. It's her second."

"I had Gina spayed so we wouldn't have to worry about that," said Ruby.

"You don't know what you're missing," said Jennie. "I just love having puppies."

"How many do you have?" asked Ruby.

"Thirty-three," said Jennie.

"God. How do you find the time?" asked Ruby.

"It's easy," said Jennie, "especially if you're doing something you enjoy. Would you like to see the puppies?" She took one out, cooed in its face and rubbed it against her cheek. She offered another to Ruby. "Why don't you hold this one?"

Ruby backed away. "No. I couldn't. Gina will get jealous."

"Try it," insisted Jennie.

Ruby chose a pup and stroked it with her fingers. "It's so soft," she said. Gina came over to sniff it, but Ruby held it up, out of the way.

"She might hurt it," said Ruby.

"No, she won't, said Jennie. "She's just curious. I bet she'd make a good mother."

"How could she?" said Ruby. "She's never had a litter."

"Go ahead anyway," insisted Jennie.

Ruby lowered the pup down to Gina's level and the older

dog began to lick the pup all over.

"What'd I tell you," said Jennie. "It comes naturally."

Jennie patted Gina on her head and asked, "What's her problem?"

"Her anal glands get plugged and Doc has to clean them out."

"I know how to do that," said Jennie "I could teach you. It's easy."

Ruby made a face. "I don't think so," she said. "Besides, I bring Gina here every week."

"Isn't that expensive?" asked Jennie.

"No. We swap off. Doc sends Patty to pick us up, and I bring him some of my banana pecan cake."

"Cooking's a pain," said Jennie. "Especially when you live by yourself. It's so hard to fix for one person."

"I have company every day for dinner," said Ruby.

"Who's that?" I asked.

"The local T.V. anchorman," she said.

"Why don't you come have dinner with me?" said Jennie. "No need for both of us to eat alone."

"But we hardly know each other," said Ruby.

"So what? Is your social calendar full?"

Ruby was flustered. "What am I going to do with Gina?

"What's one more dog?"

Jennie tucked the pups in their basket while Patty fixed the leash to Bobette's harness. Ruby dug in her purse and left a slice of banana pecan cake on the counter. They were halfway out the door when Jennie did an about-face.

"There's something I forgot to tell Doctor Goldman," she said.

"What's that?" I said.

"I don't have to take nitroglycerine pills anymore."

"Why not?"

"Because of this," and Jennie began to unbutton her

blouse. I covered my eyes and turned away. Ruby almost fainted.

"Don't be so bashful," Jennie said.

I spread my fingers and looked through the open spaces. Jennie had exposed a third of her womanhood. There was a circular bandaid just above her bosom.

"It's a slow-release patch for my nitroglycerine," she said.

"That's real convenient," I said. "But you're embarrasing me and Mrs. Babcock."

"Pshaw," said Jennie. "We old ladies are old enough to be your mother."

"Speak for yourself," said Ruby, and she playfully threw me a hip.

After Patty walked them to Jennie's car she came back in giggling.

"What's so funny?" I asked.

"It's Jennie," she said laughing to herself. "She really didn't mean to expose so much skin."

"She did a pretty good job," I said. "You'd think we were running a geriatric burlesque show."

"Jennie couldn't help it," said Patty. "She was so busy feeding puppies she forgot to put on her brassiere."

A couple of weeks later Ruby and Jennie drove up together in Jennie's car. Jennie had a petcarrier in the back seat and Gina was barking out the window. The two ladies came inside. I was at the front desk, where Ruby plopped a whole cake on the counter. "This is for you and Patty," she said. "You all have been so sweet, and if it wasn't for you two, Jennie and I might never have met. And look at this."

She took a photograph from her purse. "What do you think?"

It was a picture of a man, nattily dressed and smoking a pipe. At his side was a beautiful hunting dog. "I met him at a dog show," said Ruby. "He shows German Shorthaired Pointers. Isn't he a hunk?"

"He looks like my grandfather," I said.

"Doctor Goldman!" said Patty.

"I don't mind," said Ruby. "I just won't bake any more cakes for him."

"I'll behave," I said.

Jennie looked at her watch. "Ruby, we have to be going or we'll be late for the judging." She began to hustle her friend out.

"How's Gina's rear end?" I called.

"It's fine," said Ruby. "Jennie's taken over your old job." The two ladies were almost out the door when suddenly Jennie cried, "Oh, my God! I forgot what I did with our entry forms."

"I got them," crowed Ruby. "You gave them to me for safekeeping."

"So I did," said Jennie, and the two exited laughing.

"What a pair," said Patty. "They'll keep each other busy. They seem so happy."

"I bet Gina is, too," I said. I munched on a piece of cake, leaned back in my seat and smiled.

The door opened once more, and a client walked in with a Cocker Spaniel. It was Kenneth Dixon, the optometrist's son, and their dog, Tippy. He walked to the front and peered over the counter.

"Hi, Kenneth," I said. "Something wrong with Tippy?"

"No," he said. "He just needs his rabies shot."

"We can handle that. How's your father?"

"He's fine," he said. "He's got me working at the office."

"It'll be good experience," I said. "By the way. Would you like a piece of cake? One of our clients made it special." I sliced a wide portion and held it in front of his face. He studied it momentarily, then shook his head no.

"Go on and take some," I said. "It's really quite good."

Kenneth reexamined my offering. "That's Ruby Babcock's banana pecan cake," he said. "I think I'll pass."

I was stunned. This man had just made a positive identification on a cake, and he hadn't even tasted it.

"How did you know?" I asked.

"Ruby wants her eyes checked every other week, so dad sends me to pick her up," said Kenneth. "She always gives me cake to take home."

A WISE
OLD GOAT

Wimberley is a hill country village, hidden along the banks of the Blanco River, twelve miles northwest of San Marcos. Due to its remoteness and narrow economic base, Wimberley remained insulated for most of its hundred plus years, but finally, its natural beauty and laid back life-style caught the eye of migrants who were escaping to the sunbelt, and newcomers began coming in droves. The enterprising natives subdivided their ranches in parcels of five acres or less, selling what was previously two- hundred-dollar-per-acre grazing land for thousands of dollars per acre of what was now termed vacation hideaways. Not that anyone was upset, mind you. The realtors were happy because they were earning commissions. The ranchers were happy because their land was finally becoming productive. And the new Wimberleyites, many who hailed from the Northeast were happy, because now they owned part of the wide open West. They shucked their suits for jeans and boots, hoping to blend in as natural born Texans, but in spite of their efforts, in one way or another, they could always be recognized for what they were, a completely different breed.

Today, Travis and I were on our way to Wimberley. We headed down Ranch Road 12, turned north at Wimberley

Junction, wound our way over an extension of the Devil's Backbone, a serpentine limestone ridge that forms the south wall of the Blanco River valley, and zipped down the big hill coming out on the floodplain. Just across the river we turned west, down Flite Acres Road.

I checked Patty's instructions and said to Travis, "There should be a row of mailboxes, two miles down. Turn left there."

"Where're we headed?" he asked.

"Lonesome Acres Ranch."

"Never heard of it," said Travis.

"Me neither," I said.

"Whatta we gonna treat?" he asked.

"Goats," I said.

"Goats! Aw, Doc. There ain't nothin that stinks worse than one of those four-legged lawn mowers." He unloaded a moist cloud of yellow spit out of the side window, just as a car passed going in the opposite direction. I looked in the rearview mirror to be sure we weren't being followed when Travis said, "Here's the mailboxes," and we turned onto a caliche road.

We rumbled down the road, passing dreary brown pastures dotted with green clumps of cedar and live oaks. Then I spotted the sign, Lonesome Acres Ranch, painted on a board hung between two tall cedar poles. A bleached cow's skull was hanging from the middle.

"This is it," I said, and we drove up an asphalt driveway. A Jaguar and a Mercedes were parked in front of a typical hill-country house, built of cedar and native rock and roofed with tin. An overhang over the front porch ran the length of the building. Off to one side was a portable metal shed shaped like a midwestern barn where a palomino horse grazed placidly in the yard.

"Anybody home?" yelled Travis.

I heard a door slam. "Watch out for the dogs!" cried a

voice from the back.

Travis dived into the truck while I stood my ground. The dogs raced around the corner, snarling and snapping, whipping their saliva into a froth. But just as they reached me, I stomped my foot in front of my body and raised my arms and shouted, "Heeyah! Heeyah!" They wheeled right about and ran off in the opposite direction, their tails tucked between their legs.

I opened the truck door and Travis sheepishly crawled out, rear end first.

"I sure got to hand it to you, Doc," said Travis. "You knew just how to handle 'em."

"It was easy," I said. "They were only Toy Poodles."

A man ran up to meet us. He wore alligator skin cowboy boots with his Levis tucked inside, a western shirt with pearl snaps, a Resistol western hat with flycatcher feathers, a bandanna around his neck and a leather belt with the name Arnold tooled on the back.

"I hope you pardon the dogs," he said. "They haven't been the same since we moved from the apartment."

"They're harmless," I said. I shook the man's hand. "I'm Doctor Goldman. This is Travis, my assistant. We're here to see about the goats."

"I'm Arnold Cline," he said, "but you can call me Arnold." We ambled past the metal shed as Arnold led the way.

"How big a spread is this?" I asked.

"It's a four-acre ranchette," said Arnold. "Don't you just love it!"

He raised his arms over his head, took a deep breath of the Wimberley air and turned around, just in time to see Travis take a plug of tobacco out of his mouth, examine it and then stick it back in.

I quickly asked Arnold, "How long have you lived here?"

"About five months," he said, still gaping at Travis. "I was transferred from Chicago."

"Who do you work for?" I asked.

"Lehman Brothers," he said.

"They live around here?" asked Travis.

"They're Wall Street underwriters," said Arnold, quite haughtily. "I work in their Austin office."

We traipsed on. "Why'd you decide on goats?" I asked.

"I thought they'd be easier than cattle," said Arnold. "And their babies are so cute. I was letting 'em run loose until they started jumping on my cars."

We stopped at the entrance to the pen. Inside it was wall-to-wall goats. There wasn't any grass, and the few trees that had the rotten luck to be included in the enclosure were stripped of branches up to the height a goat could reach by standing on its hind legs.

"How many goats are out there?" I asked.

"Thirty, now," he said. "Two weeks ago I had thirty-five."

Arnold raised Spanish goats, a breed noted for their milk and meat. Folks around here swore the milk was better for you than store-bought cow's milk. The meat was prepared as barbecue known as *caprito*. But here was Arnold, raising goats for fun.

I checked the feed trough. It was sanded smooth by countless tongues.

"What are you feeding them?"

"I give them a little hay."

"That's all?"

"Yessir," he said. "They wouldn't eat the tin cans."

I wasn't in the mood for humor.

"Just kidding," said Arnold.

I looked the flock over. Most had their ribs showing. A few were pawing at the rocks, turning them over, looking for a bite to eat. I continued my questions.

"How do they act when they're sick?"

"First they quit eating," said Arnold. "Then they get down and won't get up. Like that one there."

He pointed to a small female lying in a corner of the pasture. She was wobbly.

Travis and I opened the gate and walked over to the doe, who tried to stand as we approached. We caught her easily. She sat there trembling, pathetically bleating, while the others milled together and watched from a safe distance, waiting to see what we were going to do with our captive.

"Ain't nothin' here but skin and bones," said Travis.

I peeled down the lower eyelid. It was white.

"She's bled out," I said.

Travis took her temperature and I listened to her chest.

"Are they scouring?" I asked.

"Scouring?" repeated Arnold.

"Do they have diarrhea?" I said.

"Just at the end," he said. "Right before they die." He twisted his face in regret. "And speaking of dying, I had another one die last night. I saved the body in case you want to do an autopsy."

Arnold may have been a greenhorn, but that certainly showed some foresight. I was grateful.

We set the doe free and marched off to the opposite end of the property. An ominous droning indicated the spot where we found the latest victim, swollen from the byproducts of decomposition. Hordes of insect squadrons made touch-and-go landings on hairy runways. As I got out my knife and bent over the body, the swarm lifted off. The stench was repulsive.

"How do you stand it?" gagged Arnold.

Travis snorted some snuff and chuckled, "I don't smell nuthin'."

I was busy cutting into the carcass.

"See these muscles, Arnold? They don't even bleed."

"I'll take your word for it," he said, turning away.

I opened the abdomen and punctured the bloated stomach. It deflated like a balloon, subsiding with a hiss. Except for a small amount of grit, it was empty. Next came the liver, a critical chemical warehouse. It was abnormally pale, a sign it had been depleted. And finally the spleen, the last repository for blood. It was small and shrunken, indicating an unresolved anemic crisis.

"This goat just wasted away," I said.

I cut lengthwise down the small intestine and then scraped the inner surface with the autopsy knife. Along the knife's edge I collected a group of tiny, translucent, thread-like objects.

"Here's part of the problem," I said, and I stood up to show them. "It's worms."

Arnold and Travis peered down at the knife, squinting from the reflection while I began my lecture.

"The worms damaged the intestine so badly the goat couldn't absorb any nutrients. Feel how knobby the lining of this bowel is. It's full of scar tissue."

With some difficulty, I sliced a small piece of bowel away.

"See how tough it is?"

Arnold was horrified.

"Of course, while the worms were busy destroying the animal's gut, they also sucked it dry of blood."

I wiped the knife clean. "Your goats are slowly starving to death." I watched Travis pick up a rock and zing it across the pasture while I waited for Arnold's answer.

"Just tell me what to do," said Arnold.

I took a deep breath and began. "First, you have more than twice as many animals as your place can support, so plan on getting rid of half of them. Second, they need to be wormed on a regular basis. And third, you need to supplement their diet. Next time you go to buy hay, get some creep feed and a mineral block. On an overgrazed pasture goats need a steady source of quality protein."

"I'll get right on it," he said. "Now what else can I do?"

"You can help us catch them," said Travis.

We spent the next hour corraling goats, worming them and injecting them with a vitamin-iron preparation. Travis was at his best, lassoing some of the wilder ones and chasing down the baby kids. It was getting hot, so after we finished Arnold invited us inside for refreshments.

"C'mon in," he said. "I asked my wife to make us some snacks. How about a chilled glass of Chardonnay, or do you fellows drink Margaritas?"

"I'll settle for a glass of iced tea," I said.

"What about you, Travis? I bet you'd like a Heineken."

"No, thank you," he said politely, "But I wouldn't mind a beer."

Mr. Cline laughed. "Everybody knows Heineken's a beer. It's just imported." He brought in a bottle of wine that was chilling in an ice bucket. A deeply tanned blonde with streaky hair came in from the kitchen, carrying a large silver tray filled with hors d'oeurves. At her heels were the two poodles. "I'm Deenie Cline," she said.

She wore silver bracelets inlaid with turquoise. Matched earrings dangled from pierced earlobes. Her western pants, which flared at the bottom, were so tight she had trouble walking. She had to stoop to put her tray on the table. I could see her panty line.

"How do you like living in the country?" I asked as I munched on a celery stuffed with cream cheese.

"I just adore it," she said. "Arnold's busy with his goats and I've started a garden." She gazed out the window. "We're so lucky. We're living out our dreams." Then she snapped, "Travis! You haven't touched a thing. Here!" She smeared a glistening black substance on a triangular-shaped piece of toast and stuck it in Travis's face. "Try one of my caviar spreads."

He looked at me. Then he looked at her. He nibbled at one edge. "It's very good," he said, unconvincingly.

"Maybe Travis doesn't know what caviar is," said Arnold.

Travis turned to me again.

"It's fish eggs," I said.

"I've never eaten fish eggs before," said Travis, quite embarrassed.

"These come from the Black Sea," said Arnold. "They're the world's finest."

As Travis searched for a place to dispose of his caviar the dogs started to growl, but Deenie took it from him and promptly dumped it in a garbage can. "You don't have to eat it," she said. Again she harped, "Here! Try one of these smoked oysters."

"Are they like mountain oysters?" asked Travis.

"I beg your pardon," said Deenie.

"I think Travis is just confused," I said.

Travis stood up. I knew he was feeling out of place. "I'm really not very hungry," he said. "I think I'll go outside."

As soon as Travis closed the door, Deenie said, "Your assistant...he's awfully provincial."

"Well, he's certainly not what you'd call worldly," I said, "but he's loyal. And he's damn good help."

"What's his background?" asked Arnold.

"He's one of the locals," I said. "Born here...lived here all his life."

"I can't imagine growing up here," Deenie said.

Arnold artfully poured two glasses of the Chardonnay into crystal goblets. He gave one to Deenie and took one for himself. Then he thoughtfully swirled his glass in a circle, inhaling the bouquet. "That young man needs help," said Arnold. He toasted Deenie with his glass. "After all, Doctor Goldman, I'm sure you're aware that education is the ticket to success."

"And it makes for a rounder person," said Deenie. She crossed her legs and toasted him in return.

"I think Travis is happy just the way he is," I said. Then I stood up to leave.

"But I haven't told you about my horse," said Arnold. He put his hand on my shoulder. "I got a hell of a deal." He made me sit down and Deenie served up another celery and cream cheese. I looked out the window. Travis was patting the palomino's neck and arranging its mane. Meanwhile, Arnold raved on, "They even threw in the trailer."

I took a second look. It was a tall horse, about sixteen hands and well muscled, but not anything extraordinary. "Where'd you buy him?" I asked.

"At the Wimberley flea market," said Arnold.

The first Saturday of the month, from April through October, was market day in Wimberley. You could buy or sell all sorts of goods, from old furniture and used clothing to artsy paintings and knicknacks. It was a countywide garage sale.

"You must have gotten a good deal," I said. "Travis seems to like him." I expressed my thanks for their hospitality and walked outside, followed by Deenie and Arnold, who, arm in arm appeared to be dancing the Cotton-Eyed Joe.

Travis took his place behind the wheel and I climbed in on the passenger side. The Clines leaned against the door. Arnold asked Travis, "What do you think of my horse?"

"Purty fair lookin'," drawled Travis. He reached in his pocket for a fresh plug. "I'd be interested in buying him if you'd ever want to sell."

"I'd never do that," said Arnold. "I'm going to put him out for stud."

"Won't do no good," said Travis as he loaded both cheeks with tobacco. He looked as if he were sucking on billiards.

"Why not?" asked Arnold.

"Cause he's a geldin'," said Travis.

"Is that serious?" asked Deenie.

Travis wiped his drool on his brown-stained sleeves before glibly explaining in the most basic of terms, "That means he ain't got any balls."

ROGER

B. J. Anderson was the foreman for the Fulton Ranch, a two-thousand-acre spread just north of town, owned by Joe Bob Fulton, a prominent Dallas oilman. B.J. tended to most of the ranch chores himself, repairing fences and looking after the stock, even to the point of doing his own "vettin," because, as he said, he knew more veterinary medicine than most veterinarians. If he had a cow or horse that was down, he might come by for medicine, but you didn't dare tell him how to use it. He supervised every operation in a brusque, business-like manner, a trait that mirrored his own rugged nature.

Town gossip rumored that once he'd been married but his wife got tired of living the life of a recluse and left him. He had few friends or visitors, except for Joe Bob Fulton, who arrived once a month, or the occasional wetback who'd work in exchange for food and lodging. As far as I knew, the man's interests were few: the Dallas Cowboys, whose fortunes he followed avidly, and his canine companion, a blue Australian Cattle Dog that he'd bought at the flea market in Wimberley.

Heelers, as everyone outside a show ring called them, were bred to drive livestock, usually sheep or cattle. If a wayward or stubborn steer would refuse to pass through a gate, the heelers would circle around the beast, nipping at his feet until he'd move on in the direction you wanted.

The dogs came in two colors, a frosty red and gray known as red heelers, or a silvery gray and white called blue heelers. Many a heeler had eyes of blue, brown and white, a feature that stamped them as wild or demonic, while their stubby docked tails made them seem almost comical. Still, they were highly prized by stockmen because heelers had all the ingredients a cow dog would need – agility, endurance and courage.

Every spring ranchers worked their cattle, castrating and dehorning the new calves and vaccinating them for blackleg and malignant edema, two common bovine diseases. B.J. had stopped by the clinic when I first saw his dog. They came in together.

"Nice looking dog you've got there, B.J. What's his name?"

"Roger Staubach," he said as he pored over his list.

"Why Roger Staubach?"

"Because when he was a pup, I started him off working sheep. He kept 'em busy all day running pass patterns." B.J. rolled his eyes upwards, checking my reaction.

I laughed. "I bet he gets treated well."

"No more than I do," he said. "I don't believe in spoiling dogs."

Many pets became mirror images of their owner's personalities but just because B.J. was tough as a boot was no reason to make Roger that way. I offered a suggestion. "The least you can do is feed him extra. He'll burn lots of calories working cattle. I can recommend a good quality ration."

"He'll make do on scraps," he said. "Makes him mean. Besides. Roger's my bodyguard. There ain't nobody that'll mess with him."

"Guess not," I said, as Roger's bland expression evolved into a snarl. "How many doses of vaccines did you say you wanted?"

"Order me a hundred doses of four-way vaccine and I

need twenty doses of horse wormer. I've got six new foals and I'm expecting more."

"Sure thing, B.J. Say, I hope you don't think I'm minding your business, but I'd fix Roger a harness to keep him from falling out of the truck. The worst fractures I've seen happened to dogs who've lost their balance and fallen from the back of pickups."

"Couldn't do that, Doc. Say he fell and I didn't notice. I'd be dragging him down the road. Now wouldn't that be just as bad?" From his expression, I could tell he regarded my suggestion as sheer lunacy but I was determined to champion my cause. I played my last card.

"You could let him ride up front with you."

"That's plain crazy," said B.J. "Mr. Fulton buys a new pickup for the ranch every year, and you're gonna put a dirty, smelly, slobberin' dog in the front seat? It'd screw up the carpet."

We walked outside.

"Here," he said. "Take a look inside."

B.J. drove a new Chevy Silverado complete with plush carpet, leather upholstery, crushed velvet up to the arm rests, together with air, automatic transmission, power brakes and windows, AM-FM radio, tape deck and two-way radio. A customized toolbox was fixed flush to the back of the cab. A gun rack with two rifles was mounted just inside the back window.

"I see your point," I said, "but I'd fix him a safety belt just in case. All you have to do is attach an I-bolt to the tool box, hitch a short leash on it, then snap it to Roger's collar. That way he couldn't fall out. There's even a state law that makes you buckle toddlers in car seats, and they ride up front."

Roger nimbly jumped into the bed of the pickup as B.J. leaned over the steering wheel and mulled over my proposal. "Now that's all we country folk need is for you vets to go out and get a law passed making it illegal to carry a dog loose in the back of a truck." He spit on the ground. "You may have gone to college and learned all those fancy medical terms, but I wonder if they teach you any common sense. See ya around." B.J. revved the motor and left the parking lot, peeling rubber. Roger, who'd been prancing on the toolbox, expressed his opinion as well, whirling around to bark at me as they drove away.

In spite of the reprimand, I felt B.J. meant no harm. It was just his way. He was as rough as this rocky Texas hill country with its thin veneer of soil and its limestone outcrops. Yet a man can't work in this country long before nature humbles him in one fashion or other, so I suspected that B.J. hid a sensitive, caring nature under that gruff exterior. Accordingly, I allowed the incident to escape my mind, and as it did, I forgot about B.J. and his running buddy Roger.

By summer, the activity at the clinic slowed to a lazy pace. The searing heat of the Texas sun in mid-afternoon kept most animals in search of shade, so I spent that time napping on the surgery table. But today, the sound of screeching brakes and the slamming of doors roused me from my daily siesta. A man carrying a full-grown Golden Retriever stumbled through the doorway and into the waiting room. He paused to catch his breath. "My dog's been in a fight," he said. "Where do you want me to put him?"

Patty quickly ushered him into the exam room and I followed right behind.

"Put him on the floor," I said. "I need to see if he can stand."

The man ever so carefully lowered his dog to the floor. The golden appeared bewildered, took three small steps, stopped and gradually sank to the floor, panting heavily.

"He's in shock," I said. I raised the dog's lip and pressed the gingival tissue with my thumb, blanching the color away. My imprint slowly disappeared, confirming my diagnosis.

"At least he doesn't have any major fractures," I said.

"How can you tell?" asked the man.

"He wouldn't be able to stand," I said. "Now lets get him on the table."

Patty, who had anticipated my directions, hung a bottle of lactated Ringers on the I.V. stand and had drawn up a syringe for the venepuncture. The needle threaded easily into the large cephalic vein and I connected the I.V. to the needle. I adjusted the flow to a hefty 200 drops per minute. The infusion of fluid rapidly improved the dog's vascular tone and I left Patty to oversee the drip while I searched for cuts and bruises.

"Say, look at these, Mr., uh...?"

"Reagan, Doc. J.W. Reagan. I've just moved from Houston and I'm building in San Marcos."

"Well, it appears as if someone tried to make swiss cheese out of your dog. Look at these punctures." I pointed to the dog's leg and neck. "Any idea who did it?"

"Not exactly, Doc. My Hector was riding in the back of my truck when I had to stop for a light. While I was waiting for the light to change, this red pickup with a dog in the back pulls along side, and before you know it that dog jumps into my truck and he and Hector are gettin' after it."

Patty's eyes met mine as we silently acknowledged the possible culprit. I could see her mime, "Roger?"

"I got out and tried to break it up," the man said, "but all I got are these bites on my hands." He raised his arms up to show me where he'd been bitten. I directed Mr. Reagan to a sink where he could wash. I had Patty bring towels and antiseptic."

"What about the guy in the other pickup?" I asked.

"He was yelling out his window trying to get his dog to let go, and dammit if the light didn't turn green just as that sonofabitch hound jumped back into his own truck. Then they hauled ass. Now whaddaya make of that?"

"Sounds like hit and run," murmured Patty as she handed him a towel. "What kind of dog was it?"

"I don't know the name," he said, "but it was a bob-tailed dog, about forty pounds, sort of blue color. And he had two different colored eyes. You know anybody around here with a dog like that?" Mr. Reagan's eyes darted first to Patty and then me.

Here it was. The moment of truth when your moral principles are tested. I hesitated and then easily slid into the sinner's corner. "There's lots of dogs like that," I said, "and everybody carries them in the back of their pickups. Maybe Hector got in a few licks of his own. Who knows, they might show up here for treatment."

Immediately I got the "you asshole" look from Patty, who'd started shaving the hair from around the wounds. To avoid further confrontation I continued with my standard puncture discourse.

"I have to leave these holes open, Mr. Reagan. If we suture them closed they'd just trap infection. They'll have to drain. You'll have to leave Hector with us until I'm certain these wounds won't fester."

"Whatever you say," he said. "I'll check back in the morning."

"And you'd better have a physician examine your hands," I added. "Dog bites can be serious."

After Mr. Reagan departed I rationalized my lying. First, both parties were at fault for not having their dogs under control. Second, if Mr. Reagan had wanted, he could have called the police. And last and most important of all, every time I got involved in someone else's business it would backfire. Self-cleansed, I finished treating Hector, climbed back on the surgery table and drifted back off into sleep.

Hector made a complete recovery and I sent him home

at the end of a busy week. I had the usual assortment of cases: animals hit by cars, snakebites, routine spays and neuters and a near fatal heatstroke. By Saturday's closing I was ready for a quiet weekend at home when the glare of headlights lit up the waiting room and a pickup rolled up to the entrance.

"It's B.J.," announced Patty. "Must be a problem at the ranch."

B.J. walked in quietly and stood before the counter, nervously fidgeting with his hat and shifting his weight from one leg to the other. He seemed subdued.

"Pardon me," he said. "Would you have time to see another patient?"

"Sure, B.J. Something wrong at Fulton's?"

"It's Roger. He got tangled in a dog fight 'bout a week ago and now he's feeling poorly. I've been doctorin' him with Combiotic shots and he just won't get well. I'd be appreciative if you'd check him out. He's in the pickup."

Roger had to be seriously ill before B.J. would opt for veterinary services, but I was miffed that he'd medicated the dog for a week with a feedstore penicillin before admitting he needed help. Arriving at closing doubled the offense. But I had sworn to treat animals, regardless how callous their owners might be, so I motioned for B.J. to bring Roger in while Patty flipped on the lights that I had just turned off.

It was evident that Roger was on the disabled list. After sniffing every inch of the jamb, he hobbled across the doorway, limping badly on his front feet. Gingerly, he placed each paw in front of the other, testing for proper footing before putting full weight on each limb.

"Looks like he's walking through a mine field," wisecracked Patty.

"Enough of the gags," I said. "Help me put him on the table." Roger struggled briefly, then relaxed as we hoisted him up. Patty held his head while I took his temperature.

"You can tell he's sick," said B.J. "Otherwise he'd eaten you alive. Do you think he's running a fever?"

By now the sight of this hurting animal and the benign neglect of his owner had pressed my patience to the limit.

I glanced at the thermometer. It read 104. "Hell, yes, he's running a fever." I was hacked. "And look at his feet. Look at them! They're puffed like balloons!"

Roger's front legs were so swollen I couldn't distinguish the outline of his carpal (wrist) and elbow joints. Crusts of matted hair and exudates ringed each perforation. I held the dog's leg so B.J. could see.

"There's infection trapped under these holes, B.J. When Roger got bit, hair, dirt and germs were driven deep into the underlying tissue, and since you didn't treat his wounds properly they sealed over, like this."

I could tell B.J. didn't like what I was saying and even less how I said it, but now I had the chance to show him how little he knew and I was making the most of it.

"We have to sedate your dog, clip the hair around all these holes and establish drainage. Antibiotics won't do any good unless there's drainage."

B.J. shuffled his feet and shifted his gaze from me to Roger. "It's my fault, Doc. I didn't have him under control, and I guess I messed around too long before bringing him in. Do whatever you have to do. I owe him at least that much."

Appeased with his admission I changed my tone to that of an interested bystander.

"That wouldn't have been a Golden Retriever he scrapped with, would it?" I asked.

"That's right," he said. "How'd you know?"

"The owners brought him here for treatment."

"Was he hurt bad?"

"About the same as Roger," I said. "The owner was bitten, too."

"Did you tell them Roger did it?"

"No. But there was enough blame to go around for everyone."

"That's not right," said B.J. "Give me the name of the Retriever's owner and I'll settle it up with him. And whatever Roger needs, go ahead and do it. I'll check with you in a couple of days."

B.J. left in his truck, leaving me to marvel at this wondrous transformation. "I can't believe that's the same man," I said. "He was apologetic, almost penitent. Maybe Roger means more to him than I thought."

"And Roger's not vicious," added Patty. "He's even letting me pet him." She was scratching Roger on his neck right below his muzzle and he was stretching forward, enjoying the attention. "He's just been neglected," she said. "His eyes make him look meaner than he is."

I reached in the refrigerator and drew up fifteen ccs of short-acting anesthetic. Roger almost seemed grateful to extend his leg so I could make the injection.

I made the venepuncture and began injecting the fluid. "Perhaps you're not as bad as you make out to be," I said as Roger first yawned and then fell asleep.

Roger stayed with us a week as the infections in his legs cleared with proper drainage and heavy doses of Keflex, a broad spectrum antibiotic. His wounds were flushed daily with a mild solution of hydrogen peroxide, which he stoically tolerated, and gradually his demeanor changed from a threatening guard dog to that of a familiar friend who'd happily wag his tail everytime he saw me. I was sad and a little reluctant when B.J. arrived to take him home.

"I've built him a dog house to get out of the weather," said B.J. "And, uh, order me a sack of that special food for working dogs."

"Sure thing," I said. "I believe you'll be pleased with this food and I'm certain a new home is just what Roger's been wanting. Patty's gone back to get him."

Roger came bounding from his run and scampered to the front. He barked at B.J. and me and licked us both, then ran to the door and scratched at it with his paw.

"Roger wants out," said B.J.

"If you wait a second," I said, "you two can go out together."

"Just open the door and let him go," said B.J. "I dropped the tailgate on the pickup. He'll jump right in."

"Surely you're not going to let him ride back there?" I cried. I stared at B.J. in disbelief.

"Now don't get ticked off," he said. "You gotta remember – he's a cowdog and cowdogs ride in back. Look at him. He's as happy as a hog in the sunshine." B.J. pointed to an animated Roger, who, after peeing on my doorstep, was pacing back and forth on the toolbox, eager to resume his duties.

"You did a good job of doctorin'," said B.J. "In fact, you're one of the better vets I've been around. Yep. Once you learn how we do things in these parts, you'll make out fine."

And for the second time in three months I watched this dynamic duo drive off. B.J., seated in his pickup like a man with a mission, and Roger, a passive passenger, content to follow his owner even to the gates of hell. I was crushed.

I had made a mistake. I assumed I could influence B.J. to change a custom that was an integral part of his personality. The western macho image prescribed the uniform: blue jeans, cowboy boots, western shirt and hat, and the transportation: a pickup equipped with rifle, toolbox and a dog in the back. Tradition and practicality determined where the dog would ride, and I might as well have tried to get Baptists to sanction gambling than get B.J. to put Roger in the front seat.

Nevertheless, loose dogs posed a danger not only to

themselves but to others as well. Why should an innocent driver have to swerve to miss an animal who's fallen on the highway or be resigned to run over the unfortunate victim? My logic seemed correct, but it flew in the face of long-standing practice.

As the summer wore on I caught occasional glimpses of B.J. and Roger as they traveled to and from town. B.J. out-fitted Roger with a bandanna and taught him to stand erect, resting his forepaws against the rear of the cab. His ears and neckerchief flapped in the wind as they flew down the road. It made a cute picture but I shuddered at the potential for disaster. As it was, I didn't see them again until fall.

Patty and I were in the pharmacy taking drug inventory when the sound of bawling cattle interrupted us.

"I'm not expecting anybody," I said, "are you?"

She shrugged her shoulders and proceeded to the front. "It's B.J.," she called. "He's got a load of calves."

Suddenly, B.J. burst through the door. He was frantic. This time there was no hemming and hawing. "I gotta real emergency!" he cried. "Roger's been hurt real bad."

Patty and I rushed outside. Roger was lying in the bed of B.J.'s truck. His face, which was bloody, seemed dull and lifeless. His right hind leg was twisted under his body in an impossible position. There was a black grease mark on his side.

"He was on the Seguin highway, dragging himself by his front legs," said B.J. excitedly. "He tried to bite me when I picked him up."

Apparently Roger had been hit by a car and would require special handling to prevent further harm. I sent Patty to get a roll of gauze, which I used as a noose and slipped it over Roger's muzzle, fastening it securely. Since dogs could bite from fear and pain, the restraint the gauze provided would quiet him as well as protect us. Roger initially resisted, trying to remove the muzzle with his paws, but he realized he was at a disadvantage and gave up. Together we slid Roger on the blanket and carried him inside. B.J. nervously paced back and forth.

"He ought to be familiar with that table by now, don'tcha think?" asked B.J.

I didn't have time for idle banter. I sidestepped his question and began feeling Roger's abdomen. "Have you seen him urinate?" I asked.

"What kind of question is that?" he said.

"If his bladder was full when he got hit, the impact could rip it open, and if his bladder's busted he can't pee, and right now Roger's too tense for me to tell by feeling his abdomen." Patty, sensing a rising tide of antagonism in my voice, diplomatically defused the situation by bringing in a urethral catheter. I greased it with KY Jelly and threaded it into Roger's bladder. A steady stream began dripping from the end.

"At least his bladder's okay," I said, "but I'm not sure about his spine." B.J. described Roger as dragging himself along by his front feet. That usually meant a broken back. For Roger's sake I was hoping for a fractured pelvis. I squeezed a toe on each of Roger's hind feet and both times he swung his head around and growled.

"He felt that, didn't he?" said B.J.

I nodded as I inserted my glove-protected finger into Roger's rectum and examined his pelvis. The normal oval outline of the pelvic canal was now triangular, with the apex pointing down.

"His pelvis is fractured," I said, "at the symphysis, the spot where the two sides join."

"And his leg, Doc?"

"It's fractured, too, but I won't know exactly how bad until we get him x-rayed."

I assisted Patty in getting Roger onto the x-ray table.

After we took our films, I returned to B.J. while she went to develop the pictures.

"How did it happen?" I asked, barely disguising my displeasure.

"You don't want to know," he said, avoiding my gaze.

"Quit dawdling, B.J. It's important I know how Roger got smashed."

I waited for an answer. The room was quiet except for the sounds of Roger's panting and the clanging of metal as Patty stirred the chemicals in the x-ray tanks.

"All right," he conceded. "I was hauling these calves down to Seguin for the Guadalupe County Fair and, well, I made this corner too fast and Roger slipped off the tool box."

"I can understand a broken leg, but he's pretty banged up just to have fallen from the truck."

"Yeah, well, what made it worse was after he landed on the road, the trailer hit him."

"God," gasped Patty, "it's a wonder he's alive." She handed me the wet films.

"Yeah, but he's a fighter," said B.J. in an unconvincing attempt to reassure me.

"I hope so," I said. "Look at these x-rays." I jammed the films under the holding clamps on the x-ray viewer. The radiographs documented the fractured pelvis and more. Roger's femur, the bone that extends from the hip to the knee, was broken in two places. It resembled a three-piece train with each car pointed in a different direction.

"The pelvis will heal itself," I said, "but this leg," I pointed to the x-ray, "will need surgery. Roger needs a bone plate."

Not one to accept an opinion without comment, B.J. answered, "Say, Doc, why don't you just splint it?"

"Because the fragments will rotate and we'll never get a union."

"Could you repeat that in plain English?"

"Sure! The damn leg won't heal right!"

Our sparring had reached the boiling point. We spent several awkward moments glaring at each other, neither of us willing to concede, until finally B.J. spoke. "Aw, hell, I'm sorry, Doc. I don't mean to be argumentive. I know I was stubborn and flat ignored everything you said. I was wrong. From now on he rides shotgun."

"We all make mistakes," I said. And the thought he'd made a whopper flashed through my mind.

"Call me when you operate," he said. "I want to be here when he wakes up."

"We'll hold him for observation overnight," I said, "and operate tomorrow. But you'd better get to Seguin. We'll take care of Roger." I put my arm around B.J.'s shoulder.

"Okay," he said, "but I'd like to say goodbye. I don't want him to think he's been deserted."

Patty had removed the muzzle and was cleaning the blood from Roger's mouth as B.J. put his arm around his faithful companion. "I really messed you up," he said. Then, as Patty and I excused ourselves I heard B.J. say, "Can you ever forgive me?" And Roger, believing as dogs do, that their owners can do no wrong, surely forgave him.

In the privacy of my office Patty reflected on what had just transpired. "I think B.J.'s feeling guilty," she said. "Do you think he's learned his lesson?"

"The man's not stupid," I said. "He won't make the same mistake twice."

The operation on Roger's leg was long and tedious. It was necessary to predrill two small holes into each bone fragment, align the pieces in their normal position and then overlay a pliable stainless steel plate onto the composite structure. The appliance was bent to match the natural curvature of the bone and then secured by special screws that fitted into the previously drilled holes. Since I possessed only an average amount of mechanical and artistic talent I was pleased that my repair seemed solid and permanent. I closed the incision and left Roger to wake in his cage. B.J. was waiting as I walked into my office.

"How'd it go?" he asked.

"Went well," I said. "He's still asleep, but you can go back and check on him."

"Thanks," he said, "but I want to apologize again for being such a horse's ass and I just want to say I appreciate everything you've done.

"Forget it," I said. "How about something to drink? We've got Cokes or coffee. What'll you have?"

"Coffee's fine," he said.

I found two mugs and we busied ourselves with pouring our cups and savoring those first few sips.

"You're not from around these parts are you, Doc."

"You're right," I said. "I grew up in Louisiana, northern Louisiana to be exact."

"That makes you a coon ass, doesn't it?"

"More of a redneck," I said. "You only qualify as a coon ass if you're raised south of Alexandria."

"I stand corrected," he said. He was enjoying poking fun at my suspect swampland upbringing. At least he didn't ask to see my webbed feet. B.J. pondered over his mug, then he took a long draught from his cup, smacking his lips as he finished. "Where'd you go to school?" he asked.

"I went to A&M."

"Over at College Station?"

"That's right. I'm an Aggie."

"A&M's a good school. One of my nephews went there. Studied agronomy."

Pleased that we had something in common, I responded enthusiastically. "Great," I said. "What's he doing now?"

B.J. walked to the sink and flipped the dregs of his drink

down the drain. "Got killed in Vietnam."

His sobering statement arrested our good-natured ribbing. I paused for what I hoped would be an appropriate few moments of respect. "I'm sorry," I said. I was genuinely saddened, yet the words seemed trite and barely sufficient, so I continued on a more hopeful note. "Do you have other family?"

"A sister," said B.J. "Lives in Kendall County, near Boerne." He dragged a chair over and sat down. "Her husband is an invalid." He reached in a shirt pocket, grabbed his cigarettes and put one in his mouth. I watched it oscillate up and down between his lips as he said, "Had a stroke. Paralyzed down one side." Then he fished in his pants' pocket, looking for a match, found one, lit the end of his smoke and silently sat there.

This conversation had gone from one depressing tale to another, but I hopefully ventured forth one more time and asked, "Was Boerne your home?"

"Born and raised there," he said with a flash. "I thought it was the greatest place this side of heaven. Plenty deer, turkey – lots of fishing holes on the Guadalupe. Course we froze in the winter and fried in the summer." He flicked his cigarette, catching the ashes in his hand while he studied the wall. "Dad made a piss-ant living raising goats," he said. "Mostly Angoras. But between the drought and synthetics he went bust. Wound up working in town selling dry goods." He took a long drag and leaned against the wall, his eyes momentarily vacant. Then he rose, walked to the sink, stuffed his cigarette out and said, "Don't let me bother you with my life's history. Let's go see Roger."

We went to Roger's cage and I released the latch. B.J. reached in and began petting his dog. His hand rhythmically stroked the quivering body. "How long will you have to keep him?" he asked.

"'Til he's able to get around by himself," I said. "But you're

to keep him confined. Don't let him run loose."
"Oh, I'm going to keep him in. Do you hear that Roger?
You're gonna stay inside. Whatever Doc says is what we're
gonna do. Right, boy? Look, Doc, he's saying yes."
Even though Roger's head was bobbing – I believed it
was due more to lingering anesthesia than a deliberate decision on the dog's part – I kept my opinion to myself and
left the two by themselves.

If Roger only had a broken leg he could have recovered
sooner, but the fractured pelvis made it difficult for him to
maintain his balance and it slowed his convalescence. His
hindquarters were wobbly and he needed additional support to aid in his eliminations. We slipped a towel under
his lower abdomen and helped him walk, wheelbarrow
fashion. Poor Roger was embarrassed. He was forced to
semi-squat while urinating because he couldn't lift his leg
in normal dog style. It was all he could do to keep from
peeing on his feet. But after three weeks, Roger's bones had
healed to the point where he could walk on three legs and
B.J. could take the dog home. I stood by to answer B.J.'s
questions.

"Do I need to do anything special, Doc?"
"Not really, B.J. Just let him out to go to the bathroom
and bring him by once a week for a checkup. In a few more
weeks he'll get around like nothing ever happened."
Roger was hobbling about the waiting room. I whistled
to get his attention and he limped over to me as fast as he
could. "C'mon, boy," I said. "It's time to go." Then I
picked him up and carried him outside.

The sight of his truck initiated a medley of howls and
yelps. Roger was on his turf again and he was letting me
know it. I put him in the front seat, rubbed him behind his
head and told him goodbye.

The weeks following Roger's surgery passed quickly. B.J.
brought Roger in for periodic checkups and everything was

going well. At the two month's post-op mark I was comparing a fresh set of pictures of Roger's leg with the initial set of films when B.J. said, "If we get your permission, Roger and I are going to Dallas to see the Cowboys play the Redskins. Mr. Fulton gave me tickets."

I scanned the films. The bone had healed nicely. there was no reason to say no. "You and Roger can do anything you want to," I said.

Appearing sheepish, B.J. made a confession. "He's been doing that already, Doc. Two weeks ago I thought he'd tear the doors down so I let him out. Just in the front yard. It's all fenced. He was moving real good, not limping or nothing." Roger sniffed his way to the exit door and pressed his nose flush with the jamb, sporadically snorting copious amounts of air.

"Knows the way out, doesn't he?" said B.J. as he strode to the door. He opened it wide, allowing Roger to bolt through. I became apprehensive.

"He's all right, Doc. He knows better than to get in the back." True to his owner's word, Roger was circling the truck, happily barking for B.J. to hurry and let him in.

I walked outside, where I propped my leg on the bumper of his truck and said, "As far as I'm concerned this is Roger's last visit."

"Didya hear that, Roger?" said B.J. "We're free to go."

Roger replied by barking excitedly. He knew he was well.

"There's no way I can adequately repay you," said B.J. "So how about going to the game? I got an extra ticket. We'll drive to Dallas Saturday, stay overnight in a motel and drive back Sunday late."

This time it was I who shuffled his feet while having to give an excuse.

"Wish I could," I said, "but the wife's got a ton of chores lined up. I'll have to watch it on T.V. If she'll let me."

"But I got good seats," he said. "And it's the biggest game of the year." B.J.'s expression was familiar. He gave me the same look when I advised him to put Roger in the front seat.

Again, I said no.

"You don't know what you're missing," he said. Then he told Roger, "I can't change this man's mind no way." B.J. opened the truck door and Roger leaped to the front seat. "See," said B.J. "I told you he's feeling great. Say, wanna bet on the game? I'll take Dallas and give you fourteen points. Five bucks. We'll settle up Monday."

"You got a deal," I said, slamming the door shut. B.J. pressed the door locks and rolled down the windows so Roger could hang over the sill. The dog's ears were erect and pointed, his tongue hanging down. His eyes followed me as I stepped away. I had to holler over the noise of the engine. "You two behave yourself, ya hear? And be careful." I was envious.

The weekend arrived and I spent half of Saturday afternoon and all Sunday morning mowing grass and cleaning the garage. Dallas spent all Sunday afternoon cleaning Washington's plow, 35-14. Staubach threw three touchdown passes, two to Drew Pearson and one to Tony Hill. Tony Dorsett rushed for more than a hundred yards, scoring twice.

As expected, B.J. arrived at the clinic late Monday. He looked haggard but I assumed he'd been celebrating.

"Hi, B.J. Did you enjoy the game? Boy, what a rout."

"Didn't see it," he said. He sort of stumbled and fell into a chair.

"Whaddaya mean you didn't see it?"

"I...uh..." B.J. choked on his words. He twisted away, pain branded on his face.

Immediately I thought about his sister's husband in Boerne. "Is somebody ill? Did you have an accident?"

"No," he said with a tremor. "We made it to Dallas just fine. Roger slept the whole way. He was great." B.J.'s voice was cracking. "We had to park next to the highway...had to...all the spots were taken." B.J.'s hands trembled. "I guess I wasn't thinkin'. I knew he'd jump out right behind me." He searched the ceiling for words. "I tried to grab him...but he landed in the street." B.J. hid his face in his hands and sobbed. "He never had a chance."

I felt the blood drain from my face as I imagined the horror of the moment. I tried to think of something reasonable to say, but my mind was confused and temporarily bewildered. Finally, I felt I had to make an attempt to utter some words of comfort and to let B.J. know that I was hurting, too, but just as I made a move to come near, B.J. stood up and erupted. "You and your damn advice!" he roared. "I did just like you said and look what happened!" He stopped to catch his breath. "So take a lesson, smart ass," and he pointed a castigating finger at me. "Next time keep your nose out of other people's business!" He turned around and stomped from the office, slamming the door with a reverberating "WHAM"!

After that, B.J. just dropped out of sight. I tried calling the ranch but no one answered. When I asked about him in town, folks said they hadn't seen him. Weeks went by and B.J. remained in seclusion. I thought the man would never get over losing his dog, until, finally, I saw his truck, parked in front of the post office. The cab was empty, but there, pacing about on the toolbox, was a young Australian Cattle Dog, a bob-tailed blue heeler with two different colored eyes.

DEEP SLEEP

The couple sat quietly in the waiting room. He had to be in his early twenties. She didn't look a day over seventeen. She braided her hair and wore it in a circle on top of her head. He wore a blue workman's shirt with a company name stitched on the front. Her cheeks were red from crying. He stoically held a silk pillow covered with a lace handkerchief. Periodically, they would lift the dainty cover and inspect what lay underneath. Then they would look at each other despondently and shake their heads. He'd take her hand and offer reassurance. Patty introduced them as Mr. and Mrs. Johnson.

"We don't have a lot of money," said Mr. Johnson, "but we can make payments."

"Don't worry about the money," I said. "Now what do we have?"

I drew back one end of the handkerchief.

"It's a mouse," gasped Patty.

"It's a hamster!" I said.

The patient was lying in state, flat on its back, moribund. I checked to see if it was breathing.

"I think it's dead," said Patty.

"He can't be," said Mr. Johnson. "He was alive when we left." Mrs. Johnson erupted in tears.

I held the tiny animal in the cup of my hand. It felt cold. I gently pinched a toe and it's whiskers twitched.

"He's in a coma," I said.

"Thank God," sobbed Mrs. Johnson.

I wouldn't recognize a hamster coma in a million years, but at least my diagnosis meant the animal was alive, without implying a cure.

"How long has he been unconscious?" I asked.

"Since this morning," said Mr. Johnson. "He was fine when we went to bed."

Mrs. Johnson sniffled and her husband put his arm around her waist. "You see, Doc," he said, "originally we had three."

"Where are the other two?" asked Patty.

"They died," said the couple.

"We buried them last week," said Mr. Johnson.

"Booger's the only one left," said a teary Mrs. Johnson, "and now he's actin' like they did."

Patty looked at me mournfully.

Suddenly, Mrs. Johnson's knees buckled and she reached for her husband. I opened the refrigerator and grabbed a cold pack, holding it to Mrs. Johnson's head as Mr. Johnson helped his wife to a chair. She was embarrassed.

"I'm sorry I'm such a bother," she said. "I didn't eat any breakfast."

"You know that's not the reason," said her husband. He kissed her on the cheek. They exchanged glances.

"It's all right to tell," he said.

"I'm six weeks pregnant," she said as she took her husband's hand.

I continued questioning. "How long did you have your hamsters?"

"Three weeks," he said. "We bought them at Wal-Mart."

"They were on special," chimed in Mrs. Johnson.

Discount store pets were notoriously bad risks. I suspected some form of contagion.

"First we bought Bobby," she said, "but we thought he might be lonely so we bought two more, Betty and Booger."

"We really wanted a dog," added Mr. Johnson, "but our apartment's too small."

Mrs. Johnson blushed. "We kept them in our bedroom. We were hoping they'd have babies."

I questioned Mr. Johnson about the hamsters' diet and whether they had exposure to paints, furniture polish, or floor waxes. Just the vapors from those products could prove fatal to an animal that small. His answers seemed to rule out disease by infection or poison. I was stymied.

I left Booger with Patty and walked the Johnsons to their car. After Mr. Johnson settled his wife in the front seat, he said, "My wife's real upset. Losing Booger would be like losing the baby."

I would never equate a human life with a hamster's, but these kids seemed sincere. I couldn't let them down. "We'll do our best," I said. But as the survival rate in comatose hamsters is marginal at best, I added the qualifier, "Don't get your hopes up," and the Johnsons, praying for a miracle, departed.

When I returned, Patty was stroking Booger lightly on his tummy. "If you were only awake," I heard her say.

That gave me an idea. Toy Poodle puppies can become unresponsive and drowsy after overexertion or excitement. We knew the cause to be low blood sugar. Perhaps Booger was hypoglycemic. If he were, he should respond to glucose. I filled a tuberculin syringe with a concentrated sugar solution and squeezed a drop on Booger's tongue. I waited, and waited and waited. He never moved a muscle.

"Hey, Doc. Whattaya doin' with the rat?" It was Travis. He had come to pick up his check.

"It's not a rat. It's a hamster," I said.

Travis bent over the slumbering rodent.

"What's his problem?"

"I wish I knew," I said.

"Maybe he's drunk," he said. Travis modeled a profile, pursing his lips and wrinkling his nose. "Looks like me after a party.

"Shoo!" scolded Patty. "Go back to your cows."

He headed for the door. "I wouldn't waste money on something that small," he hollered. "They ain't worth fifty cents."

I fashioned a hot water bottle from an empty olive jar and Patty made a bed from an old hand towel. She folded the towel over twice, slipped the hot water bottle inside and inserted Booger between the makeshift sheets. Then, bedding and all, we placed Booger in a birdcage and I went on to other things.

It wasn't an hour later that Patty reported, "Booger's moved!"

I dropped what I was doing and went to see for myself. Booger had crawled from underneath the covers and was sprawled on the cage floor. His respirations had increased and occasionally he blinked.

"At least that's a start," I said. I gave him another drop of sugar water, reheated his hot water bottle and repositioned him under the covers. "Let's check on him in another hour," I said.

By the end of the second sixty minutes, Booger had clearly awakened. Now he sleepily stumbled about, investigating every nook and cranny. This time I sprinkled bird seeds in a saucer and pushed it in the cage. Booger poked his nose in the air and sniffed. Within seconds he discovered the food and was eating. He was on his way to recovery.

I strutted to the office and pulled a veterinary book off the shelf. I reviewed the section that discussed mice. ger bils, guinea pigs and hamsters. I wanted to find a name for the disease I'd just cured.

That afternoon, when Mr. Johnson called, I urgently advised, "Booger's ready to go now," emphasizing the "now" as I wanted to discharge the patient before a relapse could occur. An hour later, the Johnsons arrived.

"Booger," squealed Mrs. Johnson. "I never thought I'd see you again." Booger was clinging upside down in his birdcage. He dropped to the cage floor and began excitedly racing back and forth. Mrs. Johnson opened the cage door and inserted her hand. Immediately, Booger hopped on. She held the squirmy fuzzball up to her nose and nuzzled him with her cheek. Then she put him in his regular hamster habitat and the couple cooed over him through the clear plastic.

"Did you ever determine what the problem was?" asked Mr. Johnson.

"I think so," I said, and I picked up my reference book. "You say you kept them in your bedroom?"

"That's right," he said. "At first they stayed in the living room, but when it got too hot, we moved them."

"We put them next to the window unit," said Mrs. Johnson. "Does that make a difference?"

"It can," I said. "Hamsters are extremely sensitive to changes in temperature. It affects their metabolism."

I opened the book to the section on laboratory animals and showed them the part that said, "A sudden drop in temperature can throw them into a stupor."

"What's that mean?" they said.

"It means that Booger was hibernating."

Mrs. Johnson broke into tears and ran outside, while her husband paid the bill and exited without fanfare. Patty was aghast.

I closed the book and replaced it on the shelf.

"Can you beat that?" said Patty. "They hardly seem grateful."

"Don't be so hard on them," I said sympathetically. "They just realized they buried the other two alive."

MONTEZUMA'S REVENGE

The porous limestone rocks that lie on the surface of the Texas hill country dive underground as they head to the coast. Twenty miles southeast of San Marcos they are buried a half a mile below ground. In the hills to the north the limestone is the source of fresh water, but to the south, trapped between geological faults, the rocks may contain oil. Such was the case at Luling, a small ranching community on the blackland prairie twenty-five miles from San Marcos.

The oil at Luling appeared to be easily recoverable, especially since it was shallow, but it was either dispersed in very restrictive strata or it was produced with an overabundance of water. Given either scenario, a Luling well declined rapidly and became a marginal undertaking. Luling became known as a petroleum backwater. But in the 1970s, with the surge in commodity prices in general and the oil price rise in particular, even a Luling well became profitable, and the town began to prosper as never before.

Luling's only veterinarian was Doc Goodson, a 1940 graduate of Kansas State University. As an officer in the Veterinary Corps he was assigned to Fort Sam Houston in San Antonio, and he'd liked Texas so much he decided to stay.

This morning he had left a message. "He wants to consult with you on a large animal case," said Patty. "He wants you to meet him in Luling. Can you make it?"

I immediately said yes. It was an easy decision. First, I was eager to escape the humdrum routine of a day in the office, Travis was keen to be excused from cleaning cages and stalls – and I knew the trip would be pleasant, graced with views of fertile fields and undulating pastures that extended from the southeastern limits of San Marcos all the way to Luling. The trip took thirty-five minutes.

Arriving in Luling, we met Doc Goodson who had parked in the shade of an overhang at Guerra's Exxon station. He turned onto a side street with us in pursuit, and before we had gone a block we had left Luling behind. This time the view was starkly different. On either side were oil wells and tanks and scar-like gravel roads that ran from one well to another. Stacks of rusty pipe rested on metal racks. The landscape resembled a junkyard. Even the air seemed bad.

"Stinks like rotten eggs," said Travis, pinching his nose closed.

I recognized the odor from organic chemistry. "Actually, it's hydrogen sulfide," I said.

We whizzed along for a mile or so until Doc's truck made an abrupt turn, crossing a cattleguard and continuing down a dirt road. We made the turn as well, but stopped at the entrance long enough to read a wooden sign posted on the fence: "Boyd Briscoe Lease, 85 Acres, Railroad Commission 275684, Sams Oil Co., Glenn Sams, Operator." Then Travis gunned the engine and we rocketed on through.

We passed tall round storage tanks coated with tar-like grime and large gaping pits filled with dirty black water. Off to one side and above the trees, a Texas flag whipped proudly from the masthead of a drilling rig. And there were oil wells. Scads of them. Neatly arranged in rows like soldiers, their horse-like heads rhythmically rose and fell, pumping oil with each stroke. I allowed myself a moment to dream. What a way to make money. It looked easy. I closed my eyes and floated, if only for an instant, before I landed on the floor.

"Dammit! Travis! Watch where you're going!" I grabbed the armrest and climbed back on the seat.

"Honestly, Doc. I didn't see that pipe until it was too late."

The pickup teetered over the crest of a hill and toppled down the opposite side, where the terrain flattened into a nearly level pasture. Directly ahead was a murky green stream marked by a line of shrubs and trees. A sign that read Plum Creek was tacked to an oak at the water's edge. We bridged the creek at a low water crossing and went on to higher ground. There, on the other side of the pasture were pipe corrals and loading pens. Doc Goodson had parked nearby and joined a gentleman who was studying the cattle that milled inside. We drove up and parked. Doc greeted us with a handshake, but the stranger completely ignored us while he leaned on the railing, resting his chin on his arms. Then he pivoted on his heels and faced us. The man was tall and rangy, narrow of face and sunburned, with dark brown hair that emerged in disarray from under a baseball cap that advertised a local feedstore.

I extended my hand as Doc Goodson introduced us.

"This is Mr. Briscoe," said Doc Goodson.

Brusquely avoiding my outstretched arm, Mr. Briscoe growled, "What took ya so long?"

"Doctor Goldman had to come from San Marcos," explained Doc Goodson.

Mr. Briscoe raised his hat and slicked down his hair. "Well I jes' hope you're as good as Doc Goodson says you are. Now look at them cows and tell me what's wrong," he jammed his hat on his head and faced the other way.

Travis fished his lariat from the truck and the four of us climbed over the railing and approached the herd. Two cows who had been lying down rose stiffly and stood there, watching us. The others ambled sluggishly away, though for only a short distance. Then they stopped and stared as well.

"They've done gone crazy scratchin' and rubbin' at their heads," said Mr. Briscoe. He pointed to a steer that was squinting. "And this one's gone blind."

At first glance they seemed normal, but when I looked closer I saw that their heads were swollen and their skin was oozing a brown syrupy fluid. Some of the cows teats were peeling. The sticky exudates attracted biting flies and the cattle were constantly swinging their heads or swishing their tails to keep the pests away. "Look at that one," said Travis. "He's rubbing his face on the bars."

"Are they all like this?" I asked.

"Just them okie calves," said Mr. Briscoe. "My angus-bremma crosses are fine."

Okie is a slang term for a whiteface calf and bremma is Texan for brahman.

Through the bars, Mr. Briscoe spied two scrawny black-and-brindle angus-brahma steers that grazed nearby, close to a well. "See," he said. "Those two are fine." Then he charged and hollered and waved his arms like a man beserk. "GIT OUTTA THERE," he cried, and the pair ran off. "Goddam wells." He took off his hat once more, ran his fingers through his hair and wiped his sweaty hands on his pants. "Last month my best calf got hung up in a walking beam," he said. "Busted a leg." Then he sauntered to the opposite side of the pens where he'd trapped an okie heifer in the loading ramp. She was nervous and kept rocking forward and then backward, banging against the steel pipes that Briscoe placed in front of her chest and behind her rump. Every time the pipe clanged it scared the poor beast even more, setting off a flurry of more banging and clanging. Briscoe ignored the noise and said, "Now look at this one. She's one of the worst."

The poor animal looked miserable. The skin on her ears was peeling, while a network of cracks in her hide seeped fluid along her chest and back.

"And, Doc," said Mr. Briscoe. "It's the damndest thing. If a cow's got any white on her, she's gonna be sick."

Travis took the animal's temperature while I conferred with Doctor Goodson. "What do you think?" I asked.

"You tell me," he said. He took a stick and playfully drew patterns in the dirt. Doc Goodson had a reputation as being an excellent large animal practitioner, and surely, after thirty years of practice, this man had to have seen it all.

"This one has 103," said Travis.

I nodded as I ran my hands over the animal. Then I checked the color of its gums. I turned to face Mr. Briscoe. "Where'd you get this bunch?"

"Bought them from a pepper belly in Cuero," he said.

I felt my face get red.

"Whatsamatter, Doc? Ya never heard anybody call a Mezzican a pepper belly?" Then, without warning, he stepped to one side, turned his back to us, zipped down his fly and began peeing between the rails."

I called, "Don't you mean Hispanic?" I waited for an answer while he relieved himself.

"Yeah, sure," he grumbled. He zipped his fly closed and turned back around. "Anyway, the poor bastard . . . I mean Hispanic," Briscoe fashioned a devilish smile, "ran out of feed." He chuckled. "These cows were nothin' but skin and bones, but we got some rain right after I bought 'em and they started pickin' right up. They were doin' real good."

Then he pointed to his animals and his expression turned sour. "Now look at 'em." He removed his hat and scratched his head. "So whatta they got, Doc? You're supposed to be the expert."

I knew I was being tested, but I wasn't sure by whom. I walked around the sick group once more, stalling for time. There were two or three possibilities. The cows could have scabies, a mange-like skin disease caused by a microscopic mite. But while cattle with scabies exhibit itching and hair loss, the skin usually flakes and doesn't show pronounced swelling. Or it could be ringworm or some other fungal disease, but that didn't explain why only light-skinned cows were affected. Only one disease could account for all the symptoms I saw, but it wasn't very common. I took an educated guess.

"I think your cattle have been photosensitized."

"Photo . . . sensi . . . aw, hell!" blared Mr. Briscoe. "That's what Goodson here told me yesterday." Mr. Briscoe spit a wad of phlegm on the ground. "If you ask me, I think they've been poisoned."

"Actually, they have," I said.

"Well, dammit, Goodson," stormed Mr. Briscoe. "Didn't I say they'd been poisoned?"

"But Mr. Briscoe," said Doc Goodson. "This is an entirely different situation."

"I don't know what you two are talking about," I said, "but these cattle are reacting to sunlight." I was feeling more confident. "You see, Mr. Briscoe, a certain toxin or poison caused your cows' livers to produce a light-sensitive chemical that circulated in the bloodstream. When the blood gets close to the surface of the skin, and when it's circulating in an unpigmented area, the chemical reacts with sunlight and sets up the reaction that you're seeing here."

Mr. Briscoe was incredulous. "First you tell me they can't drink the water and now you're telling me they're sunburned?"

"I didn't say a word about water," I said.

"That was another case," said Doctor Goodson.

Mr. Briscoe stormed around and muttered profanities, banged on the railing and dropkicked a tin can. "If it ain't the water, what is it?" he fumed.

"Are you feeding any hay?" I asked.

"No," said Mr. Briscoe. "What's on the ground is what they get."

We climbed back over the bars and started walking in the pasture. The weather had been dry from early June through late July, but the sporadic summer showers that floated up from the gulf had kept some patches of grass alive between desert-like dirt. Even those few areas of green consisted mainly of weeds. I stopped and stooped in front of a small flowering plant. It sprouted a single, white, trumpet-like bloom at the tip of a single stalk. Fleshy, slender green leaves formed a rosette around its base, I noticed the pasture seemed to be full of them.

"What about these rain lilies, Mr. Briscoe? Have you ever seen your cows eating these rain lilies?"

"On occasion," he said. "When it gets real dry and there's not much else to eat." He eyed me warily. "Now don't tell me it's them!"

"It's their leaves," said Doc Goodson. "When their leaves dry out, the plant becomes toxic."

"But I've always had rain lilies."

"But this year there's more of them," said Doc Goodson. "They can take over a pasture before you know it."

"So what do you want me to do? Dig 'em all up?"

"Just move your light-colored cattle to a different pasture," I said. "The black ones should be all right."

Mr. Briscoe griped to Doc Goodson about his bad luck and murmured he might haul his animals to his brother-in-law's. All I wanted was to treat the sick ones and return to the office, so Travis and I funneled each affected animal down a passageway and into a squeeze chute where we medicated it with antibiotics, antihistamine and steroids. Then we packed our gear and started to leave.

"Before you go, there's something I want you to see," said Mr. Briscoe. He jumped in his pickup and slammed the door closed. Then he made a motion with his hand like a cavalry sergeant and we fell in line with our pickups, charging back over the low water crossing, retracing the route we had just traveled. But just short of the entrance we veered away and drove to the drilling rig instead. Closeup it was awesome. We had to shout to be heard over the din of machinery.

Huge diesel engines roared and belched black fumes while massive pumps sucked and gurgled. Shiny drill pipe squealed and clanged as it grudgingly bored into the earth. Mr. Briscoe pointed to an acrobat near the rig's crown. I had to shade my eyes to see. The man was balancing on the derrick by one foot and arm while he positioned a length of pipe over the previous joint. It was dangerous work.

"Wetbacks," yelled Mr. Briscoe. "Nothing but wetbacks on this rig. The government ought to send 'em all back to Mexico."

We climbed an eroded slope and found ourselves at the edge of a moat. It was filled with a silvery brown, mud-like slurry. A large-mouthed pipe suctioned fluid from the pit and circulated it to the rig and back. Mr. Briscoe coned his hands around his mouth. "This is a drill pit," he hollered. "They keep it full of chemicals to make drilling mud. Everyone knows this stuff's poisonous." We walked along the edge. "Come over here," he said. "See these tracks." Cattle hoofprints were everywhere. "The cows come up here to see what's going on. I think when they come nosin' around they drink this stuff."

I reached down to feel the semi-dried goo and squished it between my fingers.

"It's possible," roared Doc Goodson, "but it's not

likely."

"But this ain't the only place," protested Mr. Briscoe. "There's three other locations where Sams has drilled and he hasn't filled in his pits."

"Then you need to get in touch with the Railroad Commission," bellowed Doc Goodson. "They're responsible for regulating that sort of thing."

"That won't do no good," said Mr. Briscoe. "Everybody knows they're controlled by the oil companies."

We skidded down the man-made hill and walked back to the trucks.

"This is gonna cost me some money," said Mr. Briscoe.

"But with all your wells, that shouldn't be a problem," said Travis.

"If I had wanted your advice, I'd've asked for it," snarled Mr. Briscoe.

Doc Goodson steered Travis and me away from Mr. Briscoe. "I'll finalize things with Briscoe," he said. "We can talk over lunch at the Luling City Meat Market."

The Luling City Meat Market occupied a turn-of-the-century building on Luling's single main street. All the parking spaces were full. Inside, the place was bustling. I marveled at the crowd.

"Is it always like this?"

"Just since the boom," said Doc. "At noon it's a madhouse."

Its patrons were a mixed lot, Anglos, Hispanics and blacks. About half were oil field hands. They wore uniforms from oil service companies like Dowell or Halliburton while the rest were local ranchers in dusty jeans and deeply scuffed boots. Off in a corner, two city types who Doc identified as oil promoters were engrossed in deep conversation with a leathery stockman. Doc explained that nowadays cattleman were more interested in how much oilmen would give for landowner royalty than what cattle on the hoof would bring at auction. We snaked our way around noisy crowded tables until we came to the rear of the building where large beef roasts and slabs of ribs cooked slowly over a smokey oak fire. The charbroiled cook wiped his hands on a dirty white apron and took our order.

"Give us some brisket, about two pounds, a couple of sausage rings and a half a side of ribs," said Doc Goodson.

The attendant tore three sheets of butcher paper, placed them on a scale and weighed out our meat. Then he threw in six slices of bread and advised we could get soft drinks and tableware at the front counter. While I bought soda pop, Travis and Doc carried our dinner to a table and spread out the food. The grease from the meat seeped through our makeshift plates, producing a stain. I handed everyone an opened soft drink bottle and we sat down on wooden benches.

"Just eat it with your fingers," said Doc Goodson as he pulled the ribs apart.

I sliced a piece of brisket and tasted it. It melted in my mouth.

"This is the best barbecue I've ever had," I said.

"They ship it all over the country," said Doc Goodson.

I ate a few more pieces and then started on the sausage. I was chewing and talking at the same time. "Tell me about Mr. Briscoe," I said. "He's certainly a strange bird."

Doc Goodson finished gnawing on a rib and started on another, waving it like a baton as he spoke. "To understand Briscoe, you have to go back twenty years, when oil was selling for two dollars a barrel. Briscoe was in a bind and needed money. Of course back then there weren't any wells on his place, so he sold his mineral rights to Salazar and Arredondo, independent oil producers out of Kingsville. Briscoe figured he'd made a good deal."

"Uurrpp. Excuse me," said Travis.

"Anyway," said Doc Goodson, "when the price of oil shot up, Salazar and Arredondo retained a royalty on Briscoe's place and subleased the minerals to Sams. Sams got investors to go in with him and they drilled all those wells. It was strictly business, but Briscoe feels he was cheated. He's been sour on Hispanics ever since and he can't stomach oil people."

"But it was his own fault," I said.

"Briscoe knows it. He just won't admit it. It eats on him like cancer." Doc Goodson did a quick postmortem on his second rib and discarded the naked bone. Then he speared a piece of brisket. "How would you feel watching a load of oil leave your property week after week, knowing you weren't going to get a dime?" He popped the meat in his mouth and chewed on it like a cow with her cud.

"How much is a load worth?" I asked.

Doc Goodson reached for his prescription pad and made some calculations. "Hmm. At two hundred barrels a load and thirty dollars a barrel, with a twenty percent royalty, that would be twelve hundred dollars, net, to Briscoe."

Travis swallowed hard.

"I guess I'd feel pretty sick," I said.

"And there's the matter of the other poisoning."

"What other poisoning?"

"Six weeks ago there was a fish kill on Plum Creek and some of Briscoe's cows got sick."

I picked up a rib and inspected it. "What were the symptoms?"

"Twitching, mild staggers. Some minor diarrhea."

"You could match those symptoms with a lot of things," I said.

"But I think it was due to salt water," he said.

"Where do you get salt water in the middle of Texas?"

"Comes with the oil," said Doc Goodson. "You skim off the oil and get rid of the water. Used to be you could dump the water in a pit and let it evaporate. Now you have to pump the brine in the ground so it doesn't contaminate drinking supplies."

"Where does the salt water on Briscoe's place go?"

"Back into the same formation that used to make oil," said Doc Goodson. "Sams turned a depleted producer into a disposal well. Instead of pumping oil out of the ground he pumps water back down the hole. He charges everybody fifty cents a barrel just to get rid of their water. He's making a killing."

Travis tooted as he breathed across the top of his empty soft drink bottle. "What if you can't afford it?" he asked.

"You dump the water anyplace you can," said Doc Goodson.

"Like Plum Creek," I said.

"Isn't that against the law?" asked Travis.

"You bet," said Doc Goodson. "When Briscoe discovered what happened, he got the big boys from the Railroad Commission to investigate. They went up and down that creek looking for tire tracks, but they never found any. Briscoe's threatened to sue if it happens again. And that's why I called you. I figure two opinions are better than one, especially if you're dealing with attorneys." Doc Goodson finished eating and wiped his hands and mouth with a paper towel, the kind you find in gas station restrooms. "Enough of the oil business," he said. "How's your practice?"

"I'm staying busy – mostly small animals. What about you?"

"I've been doing government work – testing cattle for brucellosis."

Brucellosis is a reportable disease that causes infertility in cattle and undulant fever in man. Cattle sold through regular markets undergo mandatory testing. Animals that test positive are sent to slaughter and the farm of origin is quarantined. Some ranchers were known to oppose the program so vehemently they went to court. Others attempted more forceful measures.

"Of course," he said, "not everyone wants you to test."

"You can't satisfy everyone," I said.

"Except Travis," said Doc Goodson as he observed my helper polish off the last few bites of sausage.

"You'll never fill him up," I said.

We got up to leave. "Thanks for lunch," I said.

"My pleasure," he said. "I told Briscoe I'd check his cows later in the week. I'll keep you posted."

It was early one Sunday, three weeks after my trip to Luling when Doc Goodson phoned me at home. He sounded urgent. "I need you at Briscoe's right away," he said fearfully. "His cattle are sick and the creek's full of salt water."

I phoned Travis, rousing him out of bed. He met me at the office. Again we sped off for Luling. Already it was getting hot and a thirsty animal would be willing to drink anything, so there was the potential for significant losses. As we drove, Travis asked what we could expect.

"The most severely affected will go down, overheat and severely scour. That's when you loose them. Some may act like they're blind, but the majority just lose muscle control and stagger."

I prayed that Briscoe would have another source of water.

When we arrived at Briscoe's gate there was no one waiting, so we drove straight in. Except for a brand new wellhead where the drilling rig had been, the lease appeared the same. Travis flew over the pipes and ruts and skidded through the curves. I held on to my black bag with both hands. We angled down the hillside and gunned for the flat as we headed for the creek.

"There's Doc's truck," said Travis. We swerved off the

gravel and drove directly across the pasture. Then I saw Doc Goodson. He was bending over a steer, giving it fluids. We drove alongside and I jumped from the truck before Travis could stop.

"Most of 'em have just got the staggers," said Doc. He pointed to some cows. They were wobbling and stumbling like drunks. Those would be all right. It was the lifeless mounds that loomed above the grass that caused me the most concern. "And there's one cow down in the creek," he said. "Briscoe's gone to see if he can find anymore."

Travis and I hurried to the first motionless lump. Its feet stuck out like antennas – it was beyond help. I yelled to Doc Goodson, "You can forget about this one." The next victim was a brahma heifer calf, one of the animals Briscoe purchased from the gentleman in Cuero. She was lying on her side, occasionally twitching her tail in a futile effort to rid herself of flies. Travis tried to help the heifer sit up. "Whoever did this ought to be horsewhipped," he said. The animal struggled to right herself. She labored and grunted, adding to a puddle of liquid feces that had dammed up behind her. Then she stuck out a fleshy gray tongue and plaintively bawled. With that she collapsed, rolling her eyeballs up and back in their sockets so that only the whites were left showing.

"Is she dying?" asked Travis.

"She just did," I said. "We'd better check the creek."

We slid down the embankment and almost landed on a black angus who was sprawled unconscious at the edge of the water. Globs of frothy saliva drooled from its mouth and floated downstream. Travis tied a rope around its neck so I could make a venepuncture, when somebody hollered, "They've done it again, Doc. The bastards. They've poisoned the creek." It was Briscoe. He scrambled down the slope like a wild man, babbling obscenities. "I'll get those son of a bitches if it's the last thing I do."

I was glad to see him, because we would need all the help we could muster. I inserted a needle into the cow's jugular and attached a bottle of fluids. "Give us a hand, Mr. Briscoe. Would you mind holding this bottle?"

"I'm gonna sue, Doc. I'm gonna take 'em for all they're worth, the no good, low down, son of a . . ."

"WILL YOU HOLD THIS BOTTLE, MR. BRISCOE!"

"I'M NOT DEAF," he yelled back.

"I'm sorry," I said. "I lost my temper."

Briscoe took the bottle from me and said, "If you'd only swaller some of this creek water you'll see what I'm so riled about."

Certainly I would have to eventually test the water, but I didn't want to do it under these conditions and under his orders. After all, who was the expert, he or I? Yet, for the sake of expediency I placed personalities aside and humored the man. But no sooner had I bent over than a dead fish floated by. As I turned away, Briscoe spat past my face. "That's what I'm mad about," he sputtered. "Even the turtles are gone."

I waited as the creek flushed his expectora away, then I dipped my fingers in the water and put them to my lips. "Phtooey." I wiped my tongue on my shirtsleeves. "It's saltier than the gulf. I hope you have a water well?"

"None close," he said. "I mean the creek's always been good and it's never gone dry."

"What did you do the last time?"

"Doc Goodson had a couple five-gallon jugs of fresh water and we used that. It was only one or two that needed drenchin'."

"I've got one five-gallon jug," I said, "but that won't be near enough. When you finish with those fluids I want you to round up all the cows that can walk, get them penned and let's get them fresh water."

"Why haulin' water'll take me all day," he replied.

I didn't have time to argue, for in the meantime the cow
had responded to the infusion and was trying to raise her
head. I grabbed her horns and straightened her head so she
wouldn't choke. Then we passed a stomach tube down her
throat and pumped two gallons of fresh water into her
stomach.

"Do you think that'll do her any good?" asked Briscoe.

"Get your cows penned and let me worry about the sick
ones," I said. "And one more thing. Have you notified the
Railroad Commission?"

"Hell, yes," he ranted. "And the Department of Water
Resources."

Briscoe started up the creek bank and disappeared over
the top of the embankment. I heard his pickup start. As he
drove away he began honking his horn, a common practice
of calling cows in this part of the country. I was glad he was
gone.

Meanwhile, Travis helped me position the black angus so
she wouldn't fall into the stream. Then we climbed the
bank to rejoin Doc Goodson. He was struggling with a steer
and was out of breath.

"If this critter was a little bit sicker," he grunted, "I could
do this by myself. Say, Travis," he said, "give me a
hand."

Travis hooked his thumb and middle finger into the
steer's nose, substituting his hand as a cattle tong, but the
steer began swinging its head to and fro, slinging Travis
around like a limp sock. I put a squeeze on the animal's
head in an attempt to steady it while Doc Goodson began
passing a flexible tube down the animal's throat. To ensure
that the tube was in the stomach and not the lungs,Doc
blew on the opposite end, but just as he exhaled the steer
sucked in his ribs and coughed, inflating Doc Goodson
instead. I thought the poor man would explode. Doc staggered for a second, then regrouped and implored, "Try

holding him steadier, if you don't mind."

I bulldogged the steer once more, like a cowboy in a rodeo, and this time we were successful in hooking a stomach pump onto the beast. After we treated four others in the same manner I noticed a strange pickup driving in the pasture. "Who's that?" I asked.

"Eloy Cisneros," said Doc Goodson. "Mr. Sams' pumper. He checks the wells to be sure they're all on."

We watched as Eloy stopped to talk to Briscoe and then drive over to us. "You fellows look as if you could stand some help."

"We're all right," I said, "but maybe you could assist Mr. Briscoe. He needs his cows corralled."

"I offered," he said, "but he told me he didn't need help from a Mexican."

"I wouldn't let somebody talk to me like that," said Travis.

"He's just upset," I said.

"More like crazy," said Eloy. "I've tried to be nice but that man's motor always runs hot. The first time I drove on the lease he ran me off with a shotgun. Said he didn't want chili choppers on his place. Mr. Sams had to call the sheriff. Life's too short to let stuff like that bother ya. I feel sorry for him. Are your sure I can't help?"

"You could call Dowell and have them send a water truck," said Doc Goodson. "We need a load of fresh water."

Eloy was pleased to be able to help and after I heard, "Roger and out" on his radio he advised the water was on its way. Eloy tagged along as we treated the only other cow that was down. He and Travis held the animal's head while Doc and I worked the stomach tube. I questioned Eloy about the lease.

"Where does Mr. Sams get rid of the salt water that comes from these wells?"

"He has a disposal well," he said. "It's at the front of the lease. You can't miss it. It's next to a cement holding tank."

By then a large orange tank truck had arrived. I stepped into the cab and directed the driver to the pens where Briscoe had corralled his animals. The driver parked his rig in front of a large trough, opened a valve at the rear of the truck and clear, potable water poured out. The animals staggered over and began drinking. Briscoe walked among them, clenching his fists until they turned white.

"I'm gonna nail their ass," he vowed. "I don't care what it takes, but by God, I'm gonna do it."

"That won't be easy," I said. "And it won't be cheap."

He turned on me like a cornered animal. "You don't understand. I don't care what it costs as long as we get who did it. Is that clear?"

"But we're veterinarians, Mr. Briscoe. Not criminal investigators. We'll need outside help."

"I don't care what it takes," he stormed. "You find out . . . understand?"

Evidently Briscoe figured he had made his point or that arguing with me was a lost cause. Either way his ranting tapered off. I suggested he go into town. "We'll need galvanized tubs and hay bales for the downer cows," I said. Briscoe assented and left in his truck. After he left I met with Travis, Doc Goodson and Eloy. We were almost through.

"Do you think it's safe to leave that cow down in the creek?" asked Travis.

In the excitement I had forgotten all about her.

"I'll pull her out," said Eloy. "Mr. Sams keeps a winch truck on the next lease."

When Eloy returned with the winch truck he backed it to the edge of the embankment and unwound a length of cable. Meanwhile, Travis had looped a lariat around the cow's rump and another around her horns. Eloy tied the loose ends to the cable and I got behind the animal so I could push.

The cow's head straightened as the slack disappeared. If we weren't careful we could break the cow's neck. "Take it up easy," I yelled. I grabbed the cow's tail as she struggled to stand. The animal bellowed and thrashed, then rising hind end first, she stuck her rear in the air until her back legs were firmly under her. Then she stood on her front feet as well and suddenly she was up and over the bank. She faced her tormentors and bawled but within moments her knees began to quiver and she fell to the ground.

"Is she gonna be all right?" asked Eloy.

"She's got her head up," said Doc Goodson. "She's just exhausted."

I left the cow in Travis's care while Doc and I began taking samples. Doc took blood specimens from the downer cows while I collected samples of creek water and tissues from the cows that died. When we finished we decided that I would ship the specimens to the lab and he would check the cattle in the morning.

I stuck the samples in a styrofoam container and drove into Luling, where I bought a bag of ice to keep the specimens cool. While leaving town I saw a sign on a building that read, "Sams Oil Company," so I decided to stop. Inside, a receptionist was typing on some forms.

"I'd like to see Mr. Sams," I said.

"He's on the phone," she said. "Long distance. But I'll be glad to tell him you're here."

She wrote my name on a memo pad and went into his office, returning after a very short stay. "He'll be right with you," she said.

After a couple of minutes the buzzer on her intercom rang and she advised," You can go in now."

I strode into the next room, where I saw a rather bulky

man with a protruding belly sitting behind a large mahogany desk. A large silver buckle rested on his abdomen. He was tilted backwards in an oversized leather chair with one arm folded behind his head and the other on his knee. His feet were propped on his desk. He sported rattlesnake skin boots and a tight silk western shirt that was under such tension it gaped between the buttons. Heavy gold chains hung from his neck and a Rolex was around his wrist. A working model of an oil well was prominently displayed on his desk with his name, Glen Sams, inscribed on a metal plate. He was reading my name from the secretary's memo.

"Doctor Goldman," he murmured. "From San Marcos." He scrutinized me, matching my face with the name on the pad. "I deal with plenty of doctors," he said. "Radiologists, internists, orthopedists. What kind are you?"

"I'm a veterinarian," I said.

"Never had a veterinarian as a client," he said. "Are you looking for a write-off?"

"I came to talk about Mr. Briscoe."

From his expression I just as soon said I was from the I.R.S.

"What about him?" he said tersely.

"Somebody dumped salt water in Plum Creek. Two of his cows are dead and a whole bunch more are sick. I'm trying to prevent it from happening again. Maybe your pumper, Mr. Cisneros could report anything suspicious."

Sams lowered his feet to the floor. "I'll be straight with you, Doctor Goldberg."

"Goldman," I said.

"Whatever," sighed Sams. "Listen. Me and Mr. Briscoe don't see eye to eye. In fact his problems don't interest me in the least." Sams turned on his toy oil well and the little pump began rudely jerking up and down, like a crazed chicken pecking at the ground.

"But it's not only Mr. Briscoe," I said. "This affects

everybody downstream. There's nothing living in that creek for half a mile."

As Sams aimlessly swiveled his chair left and right he pointed to an array of antlered deer heads that decorated the walls. "I'm just as big a nature lover as the next guy," he said. "But you tell me, who else besides your Mr. Briscoe is complaining? Name 'em."

Sams was right. I didn't have a single other name. I slumped in my chair.

"Of course you don't have any names," he said. "And you know why?" Sams stopped his rotating. "Because they're all getting a fat royalty check while your Mr. Briscoe doesn't get a dime." Sams seemed disgusted. "Ever since I leased his place he's bitched about my wells."

"Okay," I said. "I'll concede the man's hard to get along with, but this is the second time someone's dumped salt water in the creek. It's against the law."

"Don't talk to me about law," he said. "When I had every legal right to drill on his property he locked me out. I had to get a court injunction ordering him to give me access. And you know, attorneys aren't cheap. Then, after I gained access I 'dozed some roads to the drill sites. He said they tore up his pasture and he sued for damages. I paid through the nose for that. After that rip-off I replaced his cattle guard because he said my trucks wore his out, and last month I paid him seven hundred dollars because one of his calves got caught in a walking beam. He even complains about my wet-back laborers."

"I noticed he doesn't care for Hispanics," I said.

"I don't know why," said Sams. "His daughter ran off and married one." He turned off the pumpjack. Then he asked, "Do you know anything about the oil business?"

"Very little," I said.

"Do you know how much it costs to drill and equip one of those dinky little wells?"

"I don't have any idea."

He took a legal sized pad and began writing out a list. "After I pay for drilling, pipe, cement, frac job, flow lines, tanks, electric poles, motors and pumping units, I'm out a hundred thousand, minimum."

He underlined the final figure, tore off the sheet and handed it to me. "That may be small potatoes to you, buddy, but it's a hunk of change to me."

I checked his math as it was the only thing I was familiar with.

"You understand," he said, "we're talking about a well that in twelve months will make less than ten barrels of oil and more than a hundred barrels of water – per day. And you can't sell the water."

"And you can't bring a dead cow back to life."

I got up to leave.

"Look, Doc," he said. "You seem like a nice fellow. Why spin your wheels with a jerk like Briscoe. My advice to you is get yourself another client. Surely there's plenty of vet work in San Marcos." Sams manuevered himself out of his chair, put his arm around my shoulder and said, "But if you want to invest in oil, come see me."

Travis and I drove back to the office, where Patty prepared the specimens for shipment to the Texas Veterinary Medical Diagnostic Laboratory in College Station. We went down the admission sheet that specified the tests we wanted on each sample. Patty examined a vial full of clear fluid. "What do you want them to do with this?" she asked.

"Have it analyzed for oil field brine," I said. "And have them do a complete serum electrolyte analysis on the blood."

"Got it, she said. "Now what else do I check?"

"There's a special box to indicate if there's a possibility of a law suit."

Patty turned the form over and searched the page. "Here it is," she said.

"Good," I said. "Just be sure to mark it."

"What about this heading? 'Infectious Diseases.'"

"Check leptospirosis and anaplasmosis," I said.

"There's only a few more," she said. Patty fiddled with her pen. "If this winds up in court maybe we should check them all."

"Why not?" I said. "Briscoe said not to spare any expense. Besides. No need to leave a loophole for some smartass lawyer." Patty completed the form and put it in the package. The specimens left on the five-thirty bus.

On the following day a phone call from the lab confirmed the safe arrival of the samples. The chief diagnostician said a full report would be forthcoming as soon as possible, though it might be delayed, mainly because of the threat of legal action. It would be best, they said, if they double checked all their results. Meanwhile, Doc Goodson reported that Briscoe's cows were recovering. He also invited me to join him when he would make his final visit, which was scheduled the following week. This time I met Doc at his office and we drove to Briscoe's together.

Once more we crossed the now familiar entrance, but this time, just inside the lease, was a peculiar red and white truck with a slanted rear. It was approximately the size of a small moving van and it was parked next to the cement holding tank. "I wonder why Halliburton would log a disposal well," Doc Goodson said.

"I don't follow you," I said.

"Logging a well will tell you the condition of pipe downhole and whether the formations on the outside hold oil or water."

"Is it unusual to log a disposal well?"

"Yes," he said. "Unless there's a problem."

Suddenly Briscoe appeared at the logging truck door and

waved as we drove by. "Stop off here when you get through!" he hollered. "I've got somethin' to show you."

We signaled that we would and continued on towards the back of the pasture where a group of his cows were grazing. They were snipping at the grass, competitively jostling one another for a particularly tasty morsel before they moved to fresh vegetation.

"Nothing wrong with this bunch," I said.

Then we came across a single crossbred cow. A slick, glistening membrane hung down between her thighs. It was afterbirth.

"She's had a calf," said Doc Goodson.

"Doesn't have much of a bag," I said.

"Doesn't appear that she's even been nursed," said Doc.

The cow stood eyeing us, with grass sticking out both sides of her mouth. But just as we edged closer she spooked and ran away. We scoured the rest of the pasture for her little one, but it was nowhere to be found. However, a cow with a newborn calf would often hide its baby, so we weren't especially alarmed. As the rest of the herd appeared fine, we returned to the entrance and parked next to the Halliburton truck. A gray car emblazoned with the seal of the state of Texas and marked with the title, "Railroad Commission" was parked adjacent to the truck.

"YAHOO! YAHOO! I GOT THE MOTHERS! YAHOO!"

Briscoe had slid the door of the logging truck open and was yelling for all he was worth. When he saw us he jumped to the ground and ran over, waving a roll of paper over his head.

"I got proof," he screamed. He jammed the scroll in my face. "Right here," he said. Then Sams appeared in the truck's doorway and he and two men drove away in the Railroad Commission car.

"Lemmee show you, lemmee show you," said Briscoe excitedly. He grabbed us by our arms, marched us to the van and shoved us inside, where he unrolled his evidence. Then he collared a Halliburton technician to explain the findings.

The technician began his explanation by pointing to a line that ran down the margin of the paper lengthwise. Except for blips that came with heartbeat regularity the line was perfectly straight. "These blips come every thirty feet," he said, "It marks where one joint of pipe threads into the next. And these numbers," he pointed to a succession of increasingly higher integers that flanked the line, "tell how many feet down we're logging."

On the opposite side of the sheet was a second line that made its way lengthwise down the page, too, but the path it took was erratic and it made sharp shifts to the right and left, like the reading on a seismograph. "This line shows what's on the outside of the pipe," our interpreter said. "See where it shifts to the right. That indicates a water sand at one hundred and thirty-five feet."

The Halliburton man took a ruler and lined it perpendicular to the flow of the paper. "Now let's check the pipe," he said.

Midway between the blip at one hundred and twenty feet and the blip at one hundred and fifty feet were three extra blips. "Those marks indicate perforations," he said.

"Sams has been pumping his stinkin' salt water into that freshwater sand and it's been drainin" into my part of Plum Creek," roared Briscoe.

Briscoe appeared transfixed. His eyes narrowed menacingly and his breathing accelerated. He rewound his evidence into a tight roll and whapped it on the side of the truck. "I got him dead to rights," he said.

His claim went unchallenged.

"It ain't enough that a man steals your oil, but when he

poisons your stock, too, you know he's some kinda low life. Whooeee," he crowed. "I'm flat gonna put him outta business."

Briscoe's crude and irrational manner had always made me uncomfortable, but now he spoke the truth. His perseverance had paid off. He deserved compensation. His future never looked brighter, and in that vein I suggested a happier theme. "Your cattle seem to have recovered well from the salt water."

"But you got a cow with a retained placenta," said Doc.

"And we didn't see her calf," I said.

"I saw it yesterday," said Briscoe. "Born dead. Came too early."

"We ought to examine the mother," I said.

"Do it tomorrow," he said gleefully. "I'm fixin' to celebrate."

Doc and I stepped from the van and left Briscoe to gloat. As we stood there chatting, two more men arrived in an official state car, stopping at the entrance. The man in the passenger seat exited and began nailing a sign to a fencepost while the driver watched.

"Must be the Railroad Commission, posting the severance order," surmised Doc Goodson. "Now Sams won't be able to sell any oil."

Meanwhile, the driver, satisfied his partner was managing well, got out and shouted, "We're looking for Mr. Briscoe. We were told he was here."

"He's in the logging truck," I said.

"What do you need him for?" asked Doc.

"We understand his cows were poisoned."

"That's right," I said.

Doc and I walked across the cattle guard toward the strangers' car. Instead of the insignia of the Railroad Commission it was marked with the emblem of the Texas Animal Health Commission.

"Some veterinarian from San Marcos submitted blood samples from Briscoe's herd," said the man who acted as spokesman.

"That was me," I said. I showed him my card.

He looked it over to his satisfaction and said, "In that case you'd be interested in this." The man reached toward the rear of the car and grabbed a briefcase that sat on the seat. After searching through the files he found the document he wanted. While the other man hammered home the final nails, I listened to his partner tell me the news. "We ran all the tests you requested," he said. "Six out of seven cows tested positive for brucellosis. Effective immediately, this place is quarantined."

From that point on federal inspectors swarmed over Luling like a plague of locusts, screening livestock for signs of the disease and interrupting normal commerce. They traced Briscoe's cattle to Cuero, but the Hispanic gentleman who sold him the stock had gone out of business, a result of the dry spell Cuero suffered that year.

When the Railroad Commission shut down Sams' operation, his investors no longer received checks and they squealed against the severance like stuck hogs, but the Railroad Commission stuck to its guns and prevailed. Doc said most of the investors were slick northerners who were only interested in avoiding taxes and therefore deserved a good skinning.

Sams was fined a whopping sum by the State of Texas and had to sell his lease to pay off what he owed, but the new operator just drilled another disposal well and was able to resume production.

Unfortunately, most of Briscoe's herd were brucellosis reactors and were consigned for immediate slaughter. Briscoe had to be forcibly restrained when the authorities arrived to ship his cattle, and in the process he suffered a paralyzing stroke that left him hospitalized. Eventually his family placed him in a rest home in San Marcos.

I felt guilty about all that had transpired and went to pay him a visit, but he didn't recognize who I was, so I left his room and walked to the nurses' station, where I told the attendant that Mr. Briscoe didn't know me.

"That's about par," said the attendant. Then he pointed to a young woman who was just entering Briscoe's room. "That's Mr. Briscoe's daughter," the attendant informed me. "She said her father didn't know her either."

BETH

A scattering of light to the east filtered through the overcast, marking the start of a new day. I was in the pickup, driving home from a call. Nine months ago one of my clients' best heifers was bred by a neighbor's bull and this morning the heifer was having difficulty calving. The heifer had needed a section, and I delivered the calf without incident, but on the way home, alone with my thoughts, I began to have doubts. Not doubts about the operation, but about people and whether they really cared about their animals. I could forgive a mistake made in ignorance, but carelessness was another matter. After all, it was only for the lack of a few strands of barbed wire and checking the fence line that this operation could've been avoided. Still, why should I complain? Early morning calls are part of the territory. This was my job, my chosen profession. Nevertheless, an emergency like this made me question whether I had made the right decision.

Three weeks ago two mares and a gelding were found slowly starving to death in a back lot on the city's south side. The owners had skipped town, leaving the horses to fend for themselves. And only last week, I had to dispose of an unwanted litter of puppies for an irresponsible breeder, yet when I suggested spaying the mother, I was told it was too expensive. Uncaring attitudes made me mad. I parked in my driveway and walked into the house, slamming the door behind me. From the bedroom Kay hollered, "We're going to be late!"

I yelled back, "That's what happens when you're married to a veterinarian." I sat on the kitchen floor, pulled off my boots and walked back to join her.

Kay sighed. "Sometimes I wished you had chosen another profession."

Me too, I thought. Then I spoke up. "It wasn't my fault that Mr. Neuberg's heifer needed a section."

"Why didn't Mr. Neuberg wait 'til that heifer grew up before he bred her?"

"He would've," I said, "but the Schneider's bull had other plans." I grinned mischievously while I unbuttoned my shirt and headed for the shower.

Kay handed me a towel. "Don't take all day," she said. "The children are dressed and waiting."

Of all the days to have an emergency this wasn't one of them. Today was Rosh HaShanah, the Jewish New Year, one of the two most important days in the Jewish calendar, and we were due in San Antonio at Temple Beth-El. It would be a one hour drive.

I slammed the door on the shower stall shut and turned on the faucet. The water hissed and spurted from the showerhead. It felt good.

Kay raised her voice. "What did the cow have?"

"A bull calf," I said. "A real beauty."

The mother was a short blocky angus and the daddy was a tall rangy brahma. The calf's shoulders were too wide to pass the pelvic canal, making the operation necessary. Mother and son were doing well, but the doctor was pooped. Hoisting a ninety-pound newborn through the side of its half-ton mother was physically demanding. That alone was incentive enough to make me rethink my life's avocation. Especially since it all could have been avoided. I turned off the water and wrapped myself in a towel.

"Maybe I should try something else," I said as I dried off.

"What would you do?" asked Kay.

She threw me a shirt and picked out a tie.

"I don't know. Maybe I'll become an accountant."

"Fat chance," she said. "You can't even balance the checkbook."

A blonde-haired pixie burst into the room.

"Daddy! Why are you always late?" It was Rachelle, my six-year-old daughter. She took after her mother, holding me accountable for my tardiness.

"Because I was taking care of a sick cow," I said. "She was trying to have her baby and couldn't."

Kay placed Rachelle in her lap and asked, "Remember the owl? We kept it in the bathroom until it was strong enough to fly."

Rachelle nodded yes.

"And do you remember we decided to stay home and feed it instead of going to the movies? We gave up something to care for an animal that couldn't take care of itself. Sometimes that's what your father has to do."

Rachelle hopped down from her mother's lap. "Okay, Daddy. You're forgiven," and she busied herself with trying on some of her mother's jewelry.

Then there was a rap on the door. "Are you decent?"

It was my older daughter, Dorie. She was almost twelve.

"Come in," said Kay. "Your father's almost dressed."

"Do I have to go to services?" whined Dorie.

"Indeed you do," I said, "and no excuses."

"But I have a test on Monday and I'm going to miss the review."

"Religious holidays qualify for an excused absence. I'll write you a note."

"Never mind," she said. "I'll call Loretta and get her notes." Dorie stood in front of the mirror and helped herself to Kay's rouge, turning her head this way and that to gauge the effect. Then she pouted, "But do I have to stay for the sermon?"

I straightened up from tying my shoes and sternly replied, "If you can wear makeup you can sit through the service."

"If Dorie gets to stay, why can't I?" whined Rachelle.

"Because you're too young," said her sister. "You'll get bored."

"Dorie!" snapped Kay. "You're not the mother."

Rachelle momentarily triumphed in the aftermath of her sister's parental putdown – then she pressed on with her case. "I promise I won't," she said. "Just give me a chance."

"All right," Kay said. "But if you can't stay quiet, off to the babysitter you'll go."

Kay smoothed down Rachelle's dress and tucked in Dorie's blouse, and the three of them got in line for inspection. After a cursory once-over I kissed each one of them. "Everyone looks lovely," I said. "But remember! No fighting."

I herded my brood into the car and off we went to San Antonio.

We had just passed New Braunfels when Kay asked, "I wonder what the Rabbi's sermon will be about?"

I yawned. "If it's about Israel or if it's the standard pitch for the United Jewish Appeal, I'll probably fall asleep."

"Don't you dare," she warned. "You'll embarrass the family."

"Daddy."

"Yes, Rachelle."

"I won't mind if you fall asleep."

I smiled at my youngest. "I'm glad someone cares about my health," I said.

"I understand the new social hall is almost complete,"

Kay said.

"Then I guess we'll get dunned to pay off our building pledge."

"Boring," said my oldest.

I choked back another yawn.

"Daddy. Why do we celebrate Rosh HaShanah?"

"Because it's New Years," I said.

Kay turned to face Rachelle. "What you father really meant to say is that according to Jewish tradition, it's the birthday of the world."

"But why does it come in the fall and not the winter?" asked Rachelle.

"Because fall marked the end of the growing season," chimed in Dorie, "and the people thanked God for providing them with food and asked for his blessings for the coming year."

"You're also supposed to take stock of yourself," said Kay, "and reflect on the kind of person you have been over the past year."

"She's too young to understand that," I said.

Kay scowled and continued, "And you're to ask forgiveness of anyone you have hurt."

"Have I hurt anyone?" asked Rachelle, innocently.

I spoke to her reflection in the rearview mirror. "Did you apologize to your sister when you stole her lipstick?"

"I didn't steal it."

"Yes you did," said Dorie.

"I did not."

Kay faced forward in a huff and looked at me accusingly. "Now see what you started."

"But I was only trying to explain Rosh HaShanah."

"Let's change the subject," suggested Dorie.

"Daddy."

"Yes, Rachelle."

"Why did you become a veterinarian?"

"Now that's a very good question. Sometimes I don't even know myself."

"Honestly!" said Kay. "What kind of answer is that for a child?"

"Let me start over," I said. "It's something I always wanted to do."

"Your father has always loved animals," said Kay.

"But I heard Daddy say he was going to be an accountant."

Kay's eyes shot me a piercing look. "Your father just gets upset when people neglect their pets."

Rachelle had no more questions and the rest of the trip was peaceful. When we arrived at the Temple, the regular parking lot was full and we had to park a block away. We got out and started walking to the temple, passing the reception hall still under construction. I urged my party to move on, especially Rachelle, whose dawdling drove me crazy. She could always find something that would interest her. Even today, she was lagging behind.

"Hurry up," I urged.

"But Daddy, Mommy – look!"

Kay and I kept walking, without looking back.

"But . . ."

"Whatever it is," Kay said, "put it down."

"Let's move it, girls. We're already late."

"Go easy," said Kay. "They're not in the army."

"But Mother," said Dorie. "Rachelle has a kitten."

We stopped in our tracks and turned around. Ten yards behind us, Rachelle had mysteriously procured a calico kitten and was holding it in her arms.

We ran back to hear her explain, "It was lying in the gutter, all curled up." She handed the cat to Kay.

I estimated the cat's age as less than four weeks. It was so weak it couldn't raise it's head.

"Poor thing," said Kay. "It's emaciated."

"There used to be three of 'em," said an Hispanic gentleman who stood nearby. I recognized him as one of the janitorial assistants who worked for the temple. On holidays he assisted with parking.

"The momma cat hid her kittens in that hole in the wall. Haven't seen her now...been three or four days."

"But what about her babies?" asked Kay.

"Dunno." He shrugged his shoulders. "I guess they died."

A collective wail of horror emanated from my entourage, who looked to me for guidance.

"What are we going to do?"

"Don't get any ideas," I said. "We have seven cats already."

"But Dad," protested Dorie. "You can't just leave it. It'll die."

What was I to do? Fate had presented me with a kitten that already had two paws in the grave. But I'm a veterinarian. Animals are my responsibility. I swore to take care of them. Still, I felt used. If pet owners were more responsible, this wouldn't have happened. But I couldn't leave this kitten to face an inevitable, cruel demise, so I left it in God's hands.

"Put it in the car," I said, "and be sure the windows are open. If it makes it through services, we'll take it home."

With a whoop the girls ran off to stash the kitten in the car. When they returned they smothered me with kisses and murmured endearments like, "what a nice daddy you are" and "you're the best daddy in the whole world." Nevertheless, I felt like a patsy. I reassembled my clan and we entered the temple together. Since we were late and the service had begun, the ushers made us wait in the foyer so our entrance wouldn't disturb the worshippers.

I peered through the small foyer window while Kay fussed over the girls, making sure they were presentable. At an appropriate point the Rabbi signaled and the doors swung open. As we entered the sanctuary a multitude of heads slowly faced backward. I knew what they were thinking. We were tardy and they had been on time. I steered my gang to a partially empty pew and headed out across the row, trampling on toes and generally causing a disruption. I enjoyed the notoriety and acted as if nothing were amiss.

"It just galls me to be late," Kay spat as we finally reached our seats.

"They didn't have to deliver a calf before breakfast," I said. I felt smug and leaned back in the pew.

In front of me was the speaker's platform and beyond the platform, the ark, which held the scrolls of the first five books of Hebrew scripture. The inscription, "Thou Shall Love Thy Neighbor as Thyself" encircled the ark in a marble facade. From both sides of the sanctuary, stained glass windows rose from the walls. Above my head towered a domed ceiling. The main hall seated over eight hundred. On major holidays, the place was packed. We were lucky to find seats.

Kay and Dorie helped Rachelle get settled while I thumbed through the prayerbook, half-heartedly searching for the correct page, but soon I found myself earnestly skipping past the present readings until I reached the section entitled "Ethics of the Fathers," a collection of homilies and pithy sayings written more than two thousand years ago. In spite of their age, I often found them quite valid and usually more interesting than the current prayers. I was reading them when Kay poked me in the side.

"Do you think she's all right?"

"Who?" I said.

"The cat?" she said.

"I don't know," I said. "I hope so." I tried to become reabsorbed in my readings.

"Daddy."

"Hssssss." Snake-like sounds were radiating from the people who were sitting in front. I answered in a whisper, "Yes, Rachelle."

Now she was whispering, too. "Will the kitty be all right?"

"I think so," I said.

"Shhhhhh." A congregant turned around and silently demonstrated his disapproval – first to Rachelle and then to me.

I put my finger to my lips and motioned for Rachelle to be quiet.

"Are you sure he'll be okay?" she mimed.

"I mimed back. "No, I'm not sure. Now be quiet."

I replaced the prayer book in its slot on the pew and chose a Bible instead, casually thumbing through the pages, oblivious to the service. I was looking for stories about animals and the regulations concerning them. The average person would be familiar with Noah and the ark or Balaam and the talking ass, but how many people knew that animals were protected by law, as the sabbath ordinance illustrated, "...you shall not do any work...nor your ox, your ass, nor any of your cattle."

I examined the pages until I came to the passage where the Israelites were commanded not to destroy trees when they took an enemy city, "...for the trees of the field are not men that you should besiege them." Truly an ecological message. I turned to Kay and stuck the Bible under her nose and whispered, "I know an attorney who won a case using this as a defense."

His clients were hired to unload a liquor truck. However, they also availed themselves of some of the cargo and were arrested for theft and intoxication. The judge let them off after the scriptural defense, "Thou shall not muzzle the ox while it is treading out the corn."

"Joel!" she snipped. "Can't you pay attention to the service? Set an example for the children."

I recoiled as Kay chided, "How can you expect us to keep our minds on the prayers if you don't?"

"Daddy."

"Yes, Rachelle."

"I have to go to the bathroom."

"Dorie," ordered Kay. "Go with your sister."

"Do I have to?"

"Don't look at me," I said.

"Never mind," said Kay, "I'll go myself."

"Save our places," was Kay's last command as she inched her way by.

"If mother's going, I'm going too," said Dorie. Then she, too, stood up and shuffled behind her mother and sister.

"Check on the cat while you're gone," I suggested.

They repeated the hustle and bustle over the same toes and knees they had previously crushed. I hunkered down in my seat.

While my family made their escape, the rabbi finished the traditional New Year's reading of the sacrifice of Isaac from the Book of Genesis and was preparing to give the sermon, so I prepared for it as well, leaning my head on my shoulders and closing my eyes.

The rabbi's voice was resonant and reassuring, easy to fall asleep to. "Today," he said, "marks the beginning of the New Year. In keeping with the holiday theme of starting anew, I have chosen a topic from the prophets – a theme derived from the Book of Jeremiah that you will find on page nine hundred and twenty."

This was something unexpected. I opened one eye as the rabbi, resplendent in white robe and prayer shawl, opened his Bible and read, "Lo, the stork in the heaven knoweth her appointed times; and the turtle and the crane and the swallow observe the time of their coming, but my people know not the justice of the Lord."

An animal story. Right up my alley.

Finished with the reading, he closed the Bible and let his eyes wander over the congregation. I squirmed in my seat. He was focusing on me. Maybe he noticed my presermon warmup or perhaps he was wondering about the vacant seats I was guarding. He gave me a fleeting look and passed his gaze to someone else. Then he explained, "Jeremiah is describing a mystery. The mystery of migration."

"Excuse me. Are these seats taken?" I was so engrossed I didn't notice that the usher had come down the aisle.

"Yes, they are," I said. "My wife had to leave. One of the family took . . . uh . . . sick. They're coming right back."

The usher shared his disappointment with the couple he was escorting and relegated them to folding chairs on the far side of the sanctuary. I was uncomfortable in reserving our seats, but I expected Kay and the girls to return momentarily.

"My dear friends," continued the rabbi. "Jeremiah interprets the periodic migrations of animals as willful obedience to certain laws. God ordained natural laws. We in the modern age, of course, call this, instinct."

A murmur arose from the listeners as they recognized a natural phenomenon and acknowledged that fact one to another.

The rabbi went on. "But Jeremiah, in an age of unsophisticated science, understands the seasonal movement of animals as part of a divine blueprint, a heavenly plan."

The rabbi paused as his message carried to the furthermost parts of the temple. I hung on every word.

"Excuse me, sir." It was the usher again. "Will these seats be occupied soon?"

"I'm expecting my family any minute," I said. "They're checking on a cat. It's seriously ill."

The usher furrowed his brow. Then his demeanor

changed again as he sympathetically replied, "Maybe they ought to take it to a veterinarian."

"I'm sure they will," I said.

I turned in my seat in time to hear the rabbi say, "Jeremiah is amazed how animals are consistently faithful in following the path God sets for them . . . and yet . . . and yet . . ." His voice lanquidly echoed from the walls while we held our breath, waiting for the reproof that was bound to come. "And yet man," the rabbi's voice grew stronger, "despite his superior intellect . . ." – I swore he was looking straight at me – " strays from the course God sets for him and disrupts the harmony of creation." The rabbi encircled his prayer shawl about him like an eagle folding his wings and said, "We, who are free to move independently from nature, are directed by the Creator to use our skills for the betterment of His world. That is your task. That is your mission."

I politely excused myself to the congregants that shared my pew and edged toward the aisle where I buttonholed the usher, "You can have those seats," I said.

"Thank you very much," he said, somewhat annoyed. Then he took me aside and whispered, "I do hope your kitty is feeling better."

I left by the front door. The clouds had cleared and the sun was brillant.

"Joel!" waved Kay. "Here we are." She and the girls were sprawled on the grass, trying to feed our newly found orphan.

"I felt guilty about saving our seats," I said, "so I gave them up and went looking for you."

"I'm sorry I took so long," Kay said. "The girls and I drove to the Seven-Eleven and bought a jar of baby food. We've been trying to get the cat to eat."

Kay bit her lip and I thought she might cry. Dorie and Rachelle were just as distraught. All I needed were three sobbing females. I raised the kitten's lips and inspected its gums.

"Isn't she pathetic?" they said.

"She's terribly anemic," I said. "She's going to need some blood."

"But services aren't over," they said.

"We'll catch up next week on Yom Kippur," I said.

"Does that mean we're going home?" asked Dorie.

When I acknowledged in the affirmative, they all cheered.

We returned to San Marcos where our kitten had a date with Mazel, our fourteen-pound, orange, feline, candy striper.

Mazel was one of two orphan kittens that had been abandoned on the clinic's doorstep over two years ago. His sibling quickly found a home, but Mazel wasn't so fortunate. After months of trying to place him, I gave up, and allowed him to live in a cage in one of the wards. Patty soon began leaving his cage door ajar, and Mazel, assuming he was free to go wherever he pleased, quickly took over. He positioned himself on the checkout counter where my clients spoke to him before they spoke to me. He commiserated with the patients and amused their owners. At night he guarded against intruders. He was featured in the local newspaper. He made himself indispensable. His name comes from the Yiddish word meaning luck. He was waiting at the door when we arrived.

"Look, Mazel," said Rachelle. "We have another Jewish cat."

"How do you know Mazel's Jewish?" asked Dorie.

"Because Daddy fixed him."

"I think you mean circumcised," said Dorie.

"Mommy," questioned Rachelle. "What's circumcised?"

"Dorie!" barked Kay. "Stop baiting your sister and give us a hand."

I weighed the kitten on a postage scale. It weighed ten ounces.

Kay restrained Mazel while Dorie offered moral support. I withdrew four ccs of blood from Mazel's leg vein and gave Dorie the blood-laden syringe. Then, I put Mazel on the floor and took the kitten from Rachelle's arms.

The kitten's jugular was no wider than the lead in a pencil. I prayed for success as I slipped a new needle under the skin of the neck and jabbed for the vein. A bleb mushroomed up around the site.

"Damn!"

"What happened?"

"It went right through. It's swelling."

"Try the other side," said Kay, "and take your time."

She tilted the cat's head in the opposite direction and I took a fresh needle and syringe. Again, I slipped the needle through the skin and attempted to enter the vein. A wisp of blood entered the syringe.

"You got it," whooped Kay.

I swapped hypodermics for the one with Mazel's blood and slowly pushed on the plunger.

"Don't go into shock," I said, "please . . ." I squeezed the plunger ever so slowly. It was taking forever. "Almost finished now . . . one more cc . . . there." The kitten's chest heaved up and down as her tiny heart struggled to adapt to the increased load placed upon it. Then for the first time, the cat meowed.

"Oh, Joel!" beamed Kay. "Maybe she'll be all right."

Rachelle grabbed Mazel and kissed him on the nose, "You're a good boy," she said, but he jumped from her arms and ran, stopping a safe distance away to lick the spot where I had drawn his blood.

The girls bundled the kitten in a towel and we took it home, where they hovered over it like mother hens. They placed it in a shoebox and kept it next to them while we had dinner. After the meal, we gathered in the den, where Kay asked, "Don't you think it was strange how Rachelle found that cat?"

"Knowing Rachelle as I do we should've expected it," I said.

"But, honey," said Kay. "Half the congregation passed that cat by and no one ever noticed."

"And if we'd been on time, we'd never found her," said Dorie.

"That's the way the world is," I said. "Most folks don't know what's going on beyond their own noses. And what's worse, they don't even care." I rummaged through the paper, looking for the sports.

"Dorie," said Kay. "Don't listen to your father. He's become a cynic." Then Kay pulled the newspaper away from my face. "By the way," she said. "You didn't tell us about the rabbi's sermon."

"He didn't say anything we didn't already know."

"Like what?"

"Like birds fly north in the spring and south in the winter."

"Daddy!" Rachelle bounded in and jumped in my lap. "Will our new kitty live?"

"We did all we could," I said. "We'll know in the morning."

Rachelle folded her hands as if she were saying grace. "I'm going to say a prayer for her."

"Me, too," said Dorie.

The girls kissed me and Kay goodnight and went off to bed. I fell asleep in the chair and Kay had to wake me to get me to bed. I slept like a man drugged.

When I awoke the next morning, Kay was already up and about. It was unusually quiet.

"Where are the girls?" I asked.

"They're still asleep. They stayed up all night watching

over the kitten."

I stretched my arms over my head.

"Don't turn over," she said.

"Why not?"

"Because there's a cat in the bed."

I sat straight up. The kitten was sitting on top of my pillow, her feet curled underneath her tummy. Her tail was displayed fan-like in a royal train. Her sides pulsed in and out as she purred.

Kay was ecstatic. "Beth ate by herself and she even washed her face."

"Who's Beth?"

"The kitty," Kay said. "The girls decided to name the cat, Beth. After Temple Beth-El." Then Kay drew the curtains back and asked, "Have you decided what you're going to do if you quit practicing?"

I reached for Beth and put her on my stomach. She was pleased to be in this new position and began kneading her paws.

Kay expectantly sat down beside me. "I'm waiting for your answer," she said.

The kitten was warm and soft. It was purring so hard it shook.

Kay murmured, "Isn't Beth an angel?"

I rubbed Beth under her chin and her purring became louder. I thought about the circumstances that saved her life.

"Well?" asked Kay. "What are you thinking?"

I held Beth in my hands and put her alongside my face. Her purring tickled my ear as I replied, "Do you know that angel in Hebrew can also mean messenger?"

Kay took my hand and held it to her cheek. "And what's her message?"

Beth's purring had reached a crescendo.

"She says I'm not supposed to quit."

That Rosh HaShanah, the message for me was sent straight from heaven when Beth, the messenger cat, completed her mission when I fulfilled mine.